Nature's Super Medicines 7

The Seven Essential Ingredients for Optimal Health

DR. JOHN HEINERMAN

PRENTICE HALL PRESS
Paramus, New Jersey 07652

Library of Congress Cataloging-in-Publication Data

Heinerman, John.
   Nature's super seven medicines / by John Heinerman.
      p. cm.
   Includes index.
   ISBN 0-13-271636-4 (PPC) — ISBN 0-13-857731-5 (C/J)
   ISBN 0-7352-0011-4 (P)
     1. Herbs—Therapeutic use. 2. Spices—Therapeutic use.
   3. Dietary supplements. I. Title.
   RM666.H33H446   1997
   615'.321—dc21   97-7727
                                      CIP

Printed in the United States of America

10 9 8 7 6 5 4 3 2 1   10 9 8 7 6 5 4 3 4 2 1

10 9 8 7 6 5 4 3 2 1

ISBN 0-13-857731-5 (C/J)   ISBN 0-13-271636-4 (PPC)

ISBN 0-7352-0011-4 (P)

PRENTICE HALL PRESS
Paramus, NJ 07652

A Simon & Schuster Company

On the World Wide Web at http://www.phdirect.com

Prentice Hall International (UK) Limited, *London*
Prentice Hall of Australia Pty. Limited, *Sydney*
Prentice Hall Canada, Inc., *Toronto*
Prentice Hall Hispanoamericana, S.A., *Mexico*
Prentice Hall of India Private Limited, *New Delhi*
Prentice Hall of Japan, Inc., *Tokyo*
Simon & Schuster Asia Pte. Ltd., *Singapore*
Editora Prentice Hall do Brasil, Ltda., *Rio de Janeiro*

To
Nathaniel Gee, a young man of great promise;
and
Douglas Corcoran of Prentice Hall,
who gave me the inspiration for this book.

Introduction

In the world of alternative health care, there is a wide array of many natural substances from which to choose. Some of them are very popular while others are not so well known. Quite often those things which enjoy widespread use are also more readily obtainable and affordable than items which may be somewhat scarce and in less circulation. Garlic, ginseng, and cayenne pepper have been with us for a very long time and are within the economic reach of most people on the planet. On the other hand, ginkgo, melatonin, and DHEA are in shorter supply and generally cost a lot more.

But beyond this, there are other problems inherent in the remedial solutions offered up by alternative care. One of these has to do with a disturbing trend of late to incorporate modalities that may have an exotic side to them, rather than sticking with those things that have a proven track record of success but may not be so glitzy. That which is glamorous in the beginning becomes appealing to us because it stirs our imagination and fires up excitement within. The trouble, though, is that such "fashionable" supplements quite often lose their charm after awhile, as public interest in them soon wanes. Just look what happened to the New Zealand green-lipped mussel of the early 1980s. And does anyone still remember the phenomenal sales success of devil's claw from the mid-70s? The point is well made, I'm sure—"hot today, but old tomorrow."

These are some of the criteria that guided me as I gave serious consideration to what things I should include within this particular work. All of the items herein included not only are pretty standard for natural health care, but some of them hearken back to the very beginning of time. Take garlic, for instance. The Egyptian pharaohs were feeding tons of it every month to their Hebrew slaves at the time that Moses made plans with God to lead them out of their captivity and into freedom. Or, how about ginseng, as another great medicine? Why, Chinese emperors were drinking cups of this tea much as many of us do coffee every day, while the Great Wall was being constructed. And in far-off India, turmeric was being utilized on a fairly regular basis by Ayurvedic doctors practicing some of the world's first known medical techniques, such as suturing up wounds, for example.

Still, other items surround us in great abundance. The hundreds of millions of bees that exist worldwide assure us that there will always be plenty of bee pollen and beeswax, honey, propolis, and royal jelly. Chlorophyll, quite literally, exists everywhere you look and your eyes see green, be it in lawns, leafy vegetables, or cereal grasses. And a pungent spice like cayenne pepper is used by so many different cultures, it can honestly be said to have global appeal no matter which points of the compass you may travel to.

Vitamins A, C, and E have always existed in the foods and herbs that mankind uses to satisfy its hunger and stay well by. But only within this century have they been discovered and discussed by numerous men and women of science. Their extreme popularity, in part, may be attributed to the massive advertising efforts put forth by the huge health food supplement industry. And consumers have reacted favorably to them because they know just how effectively they work for the body's immune and nervous systems.

In looking over a vast array of good things to write about, I chose each of these previously mentioned items for the reasons already given. They are truly "Nature's Super Seven Medicines," because they also happen to be some of the finest *foods* around. And, as such, they can make us feel good, look great, and live long, because at the same time they are also nourishing our bodies with those revitalizing elements we seem to be needing so desperately these days.

John Heinerman, Ph.D., Spring 1997

Table of Contents

CHAPTER FOUR
Eternal Ginseng 143

The Revealed Health Mysteries of the Orient's Greatest
Medicinal Treasure

CHAPTER FIVE
Wheat Grass 181

The Food of Kings and Common People

Chapter One

Gifts From the Hive
The Magic of Beeswax, Bee Pollen, Honey, Propolis, and Royal Jelly

Altered Shakespeare: "To Bee or Not to Bee"— That Is the Question

The following is a "true" story based on geological evidence of the past. A long time ago, actually about 80 million years back, in the Cretaceous Period, there lived a certain bee, who along with a countless number of cousins helped to pollinate an explosion of many flowering plants. It was a time when the hickories, magnolias, oaks, china firs, giant sequoias, and swamp cypresses were also making their presence well known.

Our little winged friend probably buzzed over marshes where duckbilled dinosaurs were chewing on new tough-leaved kinds of vegetation with their powerful batteries of grinding teeth. As it flew over a horned dinosaur munching on ferns and cycads, it turned its eyes to again "remember" this familiar scene. At the same time, it swung its abdomen around to face in the direction of magnetic south. The image stored in a specific part of the insect's retina from a previous flyover now matched up with the same scene below, while the magnetite in its tiny abdomen gave it an innate compass direction.

As it flew on toward higher, drier land, a herd of bone-headed dinosaurs were running in all directions, trying hard to escape from the mad pursuit of a savage and very hungry gigantic Tyrannosaurus rex.

Suddenly, an unexplained, dark "cloud" came out of nowhere and hovered dangerously overhead. Our cavorting buddy turned part of its eyes upward and instantly "recalled" the danger from another time before. A large pterosaur, leisurely soaring farther up, spotted this tasty morsel and began cruising downward after it like a big, winged missile. Fortunately for our little friend, though, hundreds of feet separated the two, and the bee was able to fly low enough into the leafy branches of a nearby tree and thereby rid itself of the momentary danger.

But one of life's little ironies was about to be played out here in the next few moments. The bee had landed on a leaf bud of an ancient birch tree covered with sticky sap. After all that it had just been through to avoid becoming some huge creature's midday snack, it was now stuck fast in this resin and couldn't get away.

3

There it stayed permanently entombed until sometime in the late 1980s, when David Grimaldi, an assistant curator of the American Museum of Natural History in New York City, discovered it, still perfectly preserved in a walnut-sized piece of translucent amber. Entomologists who carefully studied Grimaldi's fossilized bee discovered that its wings and legs were remarkably modern in design.

In fact, *little* about it had changed in all that time, which doesn't really support the theory of evolution that well. And then, as now, science once again established that it is aerodynamically impossible for those fragile gossamer wings to lift that heavy, ungainly body off the ground and carry it through the air in sustained flight. But, fortunately for those of us who prize gifts from the hive, bees have never known that. Otherwise, they might have felt inclined to crawl rather than do the unimaginable and actually attempt to fly—which just goes to prove that the more we learn about something, the less we find it has really changed.

Just how *smart* are bees, anyway? Well, what I'm about to share will probably surprise, if not outright astonish you! Evidently, common honeybees are far more clever than any of today's most powerful supercomputers. And besides this, they are a marvel of miniaturization. One of the world's most powerful computers can attain the incredible processing speed of 16 gigaflops. In layman's terms, such a machine can perform 16 billion simple arithmetic operations, such as adding two numbers, each second. In contrast, a *conservative* count of all the electrical and chemical events taking place in a bee's brain shows that a single, lowly honeybee performs the equivalent of 10 trillion operations per second. Amazing, isn't it?

And bees are extremely energy-efficient—more so than a computer is. According to *Byte,* a computer magazine, "a honeybee's brain dissipates less than 10 microwatts. . . . It is superior by about seven orders of magnitude to the most efficient of today's manufactured computers." Hence, over ten million bee brains can operate on the power needed for a single 100-watt light bulb. The most efficient of today's computers uses hundreds of millions of times more energy to perform an equivalent number of operations.

But if you think this comparison is amazing, consider something else even more remarkable. In a history-making research article, "Learning and Memory in Bees," published in the July 1978 issue of *Scientific American,* German researchers Randolf Menzel and Jochen Erber presented compelling evidence to show that bees have *reasoning* capabilities much like those of higher creatures possessing spinal columns (called vertebrates). Their conclusions were as follows:

> It is apparent from the work that we and others have done with bees that associative learning in the bee follows all the major learning steps that have been established for vertebrate animals. Moreover, bees have sensory, short-term and long-term memories quite similar to those found in vertebrate species. The neural [nerve] strategies underlying learning and memory storage in the bee also do not differ basically from what is known about vertebrates.

Honeybees not only are smarter than computers, they can outperform them in other functions, too. They can see in color, smell, fly, walk, maintain their balance, navigate, do chemical engineering, manufacture, repair, protect, take out the garbage, control indoor climate, and even relocate when necessary. They do all of this and more without any outside assistance or direction. They function independently. But the same cannot be said

for big, expensive supercomputers, which require teams of programmers, engineers, and technicians to keep them functioning properly.

Bees also have some other characteristics about them that—do I dare say it?—seem almost to be decidedly *human* in some ways. But these things are more negative in scope. At times bees, like ourselves, can become their own worst enemy. If honey is exposed to them when no flowers are in bloom and the weather is mild, the bees from different colonies will fight over it. Sometimes this fighting, or robbing, becomes intense and spreads from hive to hive in *moblike* action. If all the bees in one colony are killed, the honey is quickly stolen and carried to other hives. This further intensifies the robbing so that a cluster that was carrying honey into its hive a few minutes earlier is attacked, all of its occupants killed, the honey again stolen, and the process repeated. Usually, once robbing becomes intense, only darkness or foul weather will stop it.

And bees, like us, are just as susceptible to bacterial and viral invasions. American foulbrood, caused by the spore-forming bacterium *Bacillus larvae,* is the most serious brood disease. It occurs throughout the world wherever bees are kept. The spores are highly resistant to heat and antibiotics. This disease can be rapidly spread in healthy colonies by transferring equipment or allowing healthy bees to feed on honey from infected colonies. Isn't influenza a lot like this? It is spread worldwide, is highly resistant to conventional drugs, and is easily spread from person to person through the air or by physical contact.

Bees are also susceptible to intestinal parasites much as humans are, who eat food or drink water in places where hygienic conditions may be questionable. Acarine disease is the most common one among them. It is caused by a tiny mite, *Acarapis woodli,* that burrows itself into the tracheae of the bee through the bee's breathing holes or spiracles in its thorax or midsection. Bees affected by this mite are unable to fly and have disjointed wings and distended abdomens. Humans suffering from parasitic infections also often experience fatigue, unusual thinness, frequent diarrhea, digestive disturbances, and distended abdomens.

In fact, the more we examine bees the more we're astonished to find how similar they are to us in many ways. But, even with all this, they are still one of nature's greatest creative marvels to behold and contemplate.

The Prehistoric Use of Bee Products

Just how important are honeybees? Well, *without* them fully one third of *all* food consumed in the United States would disappear tomorrow. This great amount of food is directly or indirectly dependent on bees as the chief instrument in the vegetative cycle of pollination. Back in the mid-1980s, this was amply demonstrated by a four-year experiment on crimson clover in Alabama. The study showed that by using two honeybee colonies per acre, the seed yield was increased from 280 pounds per acre to a whopping 510 pounds. Their role in agriculture is enormous and can never be underestimated.

Ancient cultures, both primitive as well as sophisticated, understood the impact of bees on human existence better than many of us do at present. Bees have been deified in holy writ since time immemorial. The Talmud and Torah of the Jews, the Christians' Bible, the Koran of Islam, and the Book of Mormon have all praised the efforts of the industrious bee and given it holy status. In fact, that section in the Book of Mormon written by an ancient Jaredite prophet known as Ether (2:3) some three millennia ago in the Americas is quite explicit with regard to these useful creatures. In speaking about what their ancient ancestors brought with them to the New World from the Tower of Babel in central Iraq somewhere, Ether noted this:

> And they did also carry with them deseret, which, by interpretation, is a honey bee; and thus they did carry with them swarms of bees . . .

Bees were important in a lot of different ways. Egyptian priests and physicians regarded them as small, winged messengers from the gods, sent to earth to create wonderful food and medicine for man. The Chinese extolled the virtues of these insects and equated them with their own emperors in terms of importance. In the Ayurveda ("science of life" in Sanskrit) of ancient India, bees were the physical composites of invisible forces that imparted life and health through the substances they willingly manufactured for the good of all.

The Chaldeans and Babylonians attached immortal significance to things bees made. This belief carried over into later civilizations that followed, such as the early Greeks and Romans. Wicked King Herod of New Testament infamy got into an argument with his wife, Marianne. In a fit of rage, he strangled her; then realizing just how far his spousal abuse had gone, he sought to bring her back to life again. According to Cunningham Geikie in *The Life and Words of Christ* (London: Strahan & Co. Ltd., 1880; I:48, 54) "he . . . preserved the body . . . for seven years in honey" in the hopes that she might become herself once more. A parallel belief to this existed in modern time and was mentioned in the September 1943 issue (p. 501) of the *National Geographic* magazine. In what was then Burma (now Myanmar), "honey [was] used to preserve the bodies of dead Buddhist monks until suitable funerals [could] be arranged. . . ." The intention here was to keep everything in perfect order just in case the departed spirits chose to return to their abandoned tabernacles for reanimation purposes.

A lengthy article in the April 1976 issue of *Archaeology* [29(2):80–81] explored in depth the beekeeping practices in ancient Greece and briefly touched upon some of the religious significance attached to this early form of apiary.

The Codex Tro-Cortesianus from Central America depicts in great detail the bee industry among the ancient Maya and shows that it was wrapped up in religious rituals. The Maya gods were believed to be heavily involved in everything that bees did, hence the considerable reverence given to the winged creatures.

Illustrations of the prehistoric use of certain bee products in the Stone Age can be found in some of the cave artwork of Europe and South Africa. The first substantial evidence for honey gathering and the use of beeswax or honeycomb appear in the rock paintings of eastern Spain. They are dated from 18,000 to 11,000 B.C. The cave of Altamira near Santander on the Spanish north coast is especially famous for a ceiling painting of polychrome bison and other Ice Age fauna in one of its side chambers, which has been called "the Sistine Chapel of prehistoric art." On the ceiling of this side chamber may be seen quite clearly four scutiforms, executed in brown lines and intended to represent bees' combs. Painted next to these "combs" are several small ladders, indicating honey-hunting activities at a very early period of time. What this also tells us is that bees actually existed during major glacier periods of the last Ice Age, along with Neanderthal people. Apparently, bees were able to survive the cold without much problem.

Over 4,000 rock-art sites containing either rock paintings or petroglyphs have been discovered in South Africa and Zimbabwe (formerly Rhodesia). It appears that most of these rock paintings were executed during the last four millennia. It is known that many of the paintings were drawn by the ancient ancestors of the Bushmen, a race of yellow-skinned pygmies believed to be the aborigines of Southern Africa. They were hunters and food gatherers who practiced a Stone Age culture right into modern times.

Intensive research in a small area of the Natal Drakensberg of South Africa brought to light some 76 rock paintings showing various aspects of Bushman honey-gathering activities. There are several paintings of swarms of bees, others of honeycomb, bees' nests, and human honey gatherers with variously constructed ladders. Still other rock drawings in the immediate vicinity seem to illustrate the chewing of honeycomb by humans and the gulping down of honey scooped up by hand. An even more intriguing find was another painting that has astonishing similarities to the well-known honey-gathering scene found in one of the caves of eastern Spain.

Scientists who have studied such findings don't seem to think that these ancient ancestors of the Bushmen were regular bee-keepers as such. It isn't logical for these seminomadic Stone Age people to go to the trouble of fabricating hives. More than likely they would rob honey and honeycomb from wild beehives they encountered in their wanderings.

Bee Products: Up Close and Personal

The gifts that bees give to mankind include beeswax, bee pollen, honey, propolis, and royal jelly. A brief discussion of each follows, but be advised in advance that you may find several of these descriptions somewhat nauseating if you are one of those with a delicate digestive system.

Beeswax. A bee consumes between 6 and 10 pounds of honey for each pound of wax that is secreted in small flakes from glands on the underside of the abdomen. The beeswax is used in the construction of honeycomb, which serves as a nursery to contain the brood and to store honey. Honeycomb is considered a delicacy by some and preferred to chewing regular gum; I am one of those who has always delighted in chewing on a piece of honeycomb instead of on a strip of spearmint gum.

After beekeepers recover as much honey from the combs as possible by drainage or extraction, they then place the material in water heated to slightly over 145°F. This melts the wax, which rises to the surface. After it cools a bit, the wax is poured into molds to solidify.

Some of the beeswax is reused by the beekeeper for new comb foundations. But the majority of it is used in making quality candles (especially those used for religious ceremonial functions), or for giving artificial fruit and flowers a shine, as well as for modeling wax. Beeswax is also a key ingredient in the manufacture of furniture and floor waxes, leather dressings, waxed paper, lithographic inks, cosmetics, and ointments.

Bee Pollen. Before we discuss what bee pollen is, you need to know a thing or two about pollen in general. There are two basic kinds. One is anemophile pollen, which is the wind-carried type. As gentle breezes waft over landscapes decorated by trees, plants, flowers, and grasses, the anemophile pollens are blown up into the air at random. Such wind-driven pollens assist some plants in their own fertilization. But most of the other pollens cause considerable distress to individuals who have a hypersensitivity to them. The "achoo" factor comes into play here, and the person allergic to them starts sneezing like crazy and experiences runny eyes and a ticklish nose and throat.

But the more breather-friendly type of pollen is the entomophile kind. These pollens are regular hitchhikers, picking up rides on honeybees, bumblebees, wasps, hornets, and other winged insects who forage for nectar among many colorful plant blossoms. Entomophile pollens are more solid and substantial

than the wind-driven kinds. Plants producing these types of pollens require the assistance of bees to guarantee their fertilization. Occasionally, some entomophile pollens get airborne but doesn't trigger allergic reactions in people as the anemophile variety does.

Bee pollen is essentially entomophile pollen that has been specially "processed" by a honeybee while out on numerous excursions to gather nectar and pollen. The insect settles itself on a flower and nimbly scrapes away the loose dustlike male element from the plant's anthers with its jaws and forelegs. Each time this is done, a little spit drooled from the bee's mouth helps to moisten the powder. On the expanded tarsal portions of the bee's legs are many fine hairs all bunched together to form pollen combs. These combs are utilized by the insect to brush the powder from its coat and legs during flight. With artful dexterity, the bee uses its auricle like a small rammer to push the gathered flower dust into each of its pollen baskets. These are nothing more than concave depressions surrounded by a fringe of long hairs located on the exterior surface of its tibias. When fully loaded, this golden dust has been tamped down into a single compact granule, which forms one grain of bee pollen.

What's even more interesting is that scientists, for all of their technological wizardry and educated cunning, have never been able to duplicate bee pollen in the laboratory. Back in 1989, German scientists in Würzburg were able to construct a tiny robotic honeybee that, by dancing a figure 8, giving out nectar samples, and broadcasting the correct wing sound in a beehive, was able to send out real worker bees to a specific field location previously selected by the researchers (see *National Geographic,* January 1990, pp. 135–140). While man-made pollen has been created with every known nutrient present that is in the real stuff, bees will die when fed this lab-produced synthesized food. What is missing, of course, is the actual bee spit itself, with its many wonderful enzymes, that is dabbed onto the loose flower dust. Equally absent is the necessary oxygen that is absorbed into these dust particles as the bee presses them into its side saddles while in midflight.

Honey.   The great Roman scholar Pliny the Elder (A.D. 23–79) described honey as "a perspiration of the sky or a sort of saliva of the stars: in his massive 37-volume *Historia Naturalis,* an encyclopedia of natural sciences for the time in which he lived. Today, though, few of us would ever think of delicious honey in such unflattering terms as "bee barf," but that comes about as close to describing what this sticky substance *really* is!

Put in plain language, foraging worker bees suck nectar from flowers and store it in honey sacs (average nectar payload is a bit more than one thousandth of an ounce). At the hive, foraging bees regurgitate nectar into six-sided cells. Then worker bees take over, ingesting and regurgitating the nectar for about 20 minutes. This isn't some crazy stunt from a college fraternity house either; it turns nectar into honey by concentrating sugars and eliminating the water.

The bees' buzzing keeps the hive in constant motion, which further evaporates and concentrates the honey. Wax-making worker bees then seal each cell until the honey is needed to feed the bees.

In order to make just one pound of honey, bees must go out and fly the mileage equivalent of five times the earth's circumference to harvest 75,000 loads of nectar and must then process as previously mentioned. A busy beehive can produce up to 300 pounds of honey in a single season under ideal weather conditions.

Propolis. Another name for propolis is bee glue. When out on numerous foraging expeditions for nectar and plant pollen, bees will gather this stuff from certain trees and transfer it back to the hive in their pollen sacs. They usually obtain the sticky resin from the buds of some trees and the oozing exudations from the bark of others, most notably the conifers.

Back home, this stuff is blended together with a tiny bit of wax flakes secreted from special glands on the abdomens of wax worker bees. They then use the propolis as a sort of caulking compound to plaster any unwanted holes, cracks, or crevices leading to the outside. Mostly considered a nuisance substance by bee-keepers, it is sometimes appreciated by those who move their hives around a lot for crop pollinations. This unique caulking compound helps hold all parts of the hives intact as they're being bounced around when trucked to distant locations.

Propolis is employed in a nifty way to line the interior of brood cells in preparation for the queen bee's laying of many eggs. Since propolis has such wonderful antiseptic properties about it, this sticky lining ensures a virtually hospital-clean environment for the rearing of bee brood.

It also comes in very handy as a highly efficient packaging material for unwanted debris. And, in the event an outside intruder such as an ant or wasp penetrates the interior of the hive, it is quickly stung to death; if it is too large for removal, its remains are immediately covered with a thick layer of bee glue, entirely sealing it off so that the hive stays immaculately clean.

Royal Jelly. Of all the gifts to emerge from the beehive, probably the least understood is royal jelly. This substance has about it almost an aura of mystery. It is probably one of Mother Nature's best-kept secrets. In fact, beekeepers seldom get to see or even taste this stuff, since it is transferred directly from worker bees to the queen bee herself.

Royal jelly is a thick, creamy, milk-white fluid. It is produced inside the tiny bodies of nurse bees while they are digesting bee pollen. This helps to explain its hormone- and protein-rich make-up. It emits a somewhat pungent odor.

To the queen bee, this regurgitated fluid from the stomachs of nurse bees is a delightful and delicious eating experience, something probably akin to ambrosia for all of us. But to the delicate senses of many people, this rich bee vomit comes across not only as mentally nauseating, but also physically quite tart and bitter when applied on the tongue.

For the duration of her life, the queen bee subsists on nothing else but royal jelly. This royal milk is vital in the *making* (not birthing) of new queens. Eggs intended to become queens are pampered from day one onward: They are carefully laid in specially prepared, extra-large brood cells that resemble peanut shells. These eggs, however, are identical to many others destined to become worker bees. But the latter are given royal jelly for only three days during the short larval period and then none thereafter, making them the sexless laborers in the beehive.

Beeswax, the Vanishing Cosmetic Raw Material

There are three major types of beeswax: a yellow kind, a white variety (bleached beeswax), and beeswax absolute (absolute cire d'abeille). Yellow beeswax is the crude beeswax first obtained from the honeycombs themselves. White beeswax and beeswax absolute are derived from yellow beeswax, the former by bleaching with the combined action of air, sunlight, and moisture (or with peroxides) and the latter by extraction with alcohol.

Beeswax is produced worldwide. At one time, it was pretty well known by millions of school kids everywhere. In the British Isles, school children would tell some of their nosy classmates to "keep to your own beeswax"; in Canada and America it was slightly varied to say, "Mind your own beeswax"; and in parts of Latin America, it wasn't uncommon to hear some kids say, "Stick to your beeswax and leave mine alone."

Yellow beeswax is a yellow to brownish-yellow or grayish brown solid with an agreeable honeylike aroma and faint but characteristic taste. White beeswax is a yellowish-white solid with a faint, characteristic odor that is less pronounced than that of yellow beeswax. It is nearly tasteless and translucent in thin layers. Beeswax absolute is a pale-yellow solid with a mild, sweet, and oily odor reminiscent of good linseed oil with a hint of honey to it, depending on its sources, of course.

Beeswax (the yellow and white varieties) contains about 71 percent esters of fatty acids (mostly palmitic and 15-hydroxy-palmitic acid) and 12 percent free acids (cerolein). Up to 23 percent of the monoesters is myricyl palmitate, which together with myricyl alcohol has been referred to as myricin. Myricyl alcohol, also known as triacontanol, has been used as a plant-growth regulator by some farmers to increase their field crop yields of tomato, cucumber, and lettuce. Interestingly, alfalfa herb is very high in triacontanol, too. Since bees love this herb's mostly bluish-purple flowers and frequent them a lot, this may help to account for the high amount of myricyl alcohol or triacontanol in beeswax from hives that sit near extensive alfalfa fields.

Beeswax absolute contains mostly cerolein, as well as some volatile aromatic compounds. When isolated, cerolein resembles a fat in appearance.

Beeswax has some medicinal applications, but it isn't as popular anymore as it once was. It was formerly employed by some doctors as a protective and soothing agent in the mucous membranes in the treatment of diarrhea and dysentery. It also found favor in the preparation of some elegant pharmaceuticals and compound ointments for surgical dressings. The beeswax would be melted in a metal container over boiling water (something like a double-boiler), permitted to slightly cool (but not enough to thicken), flavored with a little sugar, mixed in with some warm milk or coffee, and then given to the patient to slowly sip. About one-half teaspoon of melted wax per 1-1/2 cups of warm liquid was used for diarrhea and typhoid dysentery. A Confederate surgeon by the name of Francis Peyre Porcher, M.D., gave this remedy to many sick soldiers under his care during the Civil War. As he noted in his book, *Resources of the Southern Fields and Forests* (Charleston: Evans & Cogswell, 1863), every one of them recovered to go out and "fight them damn Yankees some more." Porcher frequently made an herbal salve from goldenseal root and beeswax to apply to gunshot wounds and powder burns suffered by men during heavy combat. He would dig up some of the roots, clean them off, pound them into a pulp, and then put one handful of them into 1-1/2 pints of hog lard (olive or sesame oils will do just as nicely) and boil them on medium to low heat for 1-1/2 hours before straining. Then he would return the oil to another kettle and add to it some hot, melted beeswax. (The amount used depended on just how thick a consistency he desired his salve to be.) After this, he would pour the contexts into short, round, empty tins and allow everything to set. He would put the lids over the containers and store them in a cool place until they were needed.

Historically, first written mention of beeswax occurred with the ancient Egyptians; references were sometimes made to beeswax in connection with Queen Cleopatra's cold creams, lotions, lipsticks, hair dressings, and favorite nail polishes. It is also said that her attendants used a little fragrant beeswax in her bath soap. During the Middle Ages, this material became valuable enough to be exchanged as a form of currency. Today, natural beeswax still is specified for church candles in the religious rites of Roman Catholicism and the Greek and Russian Orthodox faiths. Beeswax candles also figure quite prominently in some of the black-magic rites of Jamaican voodooism.

Natural beeswax once had a multitude of cosmetic and pharmaceutical applications, but now has pretty much become obsolete since being replaced with synthetic substitutes. They provide lubrication emolliency and gloss and film-forming properties for a broad spectrum of cosmetic and toiletry formulations. These synthetic substitutes also contribute important features in achieving essentially equivalent emulsification attributes to those provided by the natural material.

Both natural as well as synthetic beeswax have been used in the preparation of different cold creams, lip pomades, lip glosses, nonalcoholic stick colognes, suspension-type antiperspirant sticks, and protective skin ointments for the elderly. When used in such anhydrous systems (the stick-type products), the natural and synthetic beeswax provides rigidity and strength. Furthermore, they impart desirable gloss, skin-feel, and mold-release characteristics.

Utilization of natural and synthetic beeswax go well beyond cosmetics and toiletries, however. They are useful in shoe polish, furniture polish, car wax, waterproofing compounds, antimetal corrosion coatings, auto lubricants, and so forth.

Many Medicinal Applications for Bee Pollen, Honey, Propolis, and Royal Jelly

There are numerous applications for the remaining gifts of the beehive. But instead of covering each one individually, I've decided to include them together in one section. The particular health situations for which they can be useful are listed alphabetically.

Alcoholism. A psychiatrist practicing in Madrid used bee pollen regularly on many of his patients. Dr. R. Loomis Paret discovered it to be "a wonderful therapeutic agent in general psychiatry and the treatment of alcoholism."

"Pollen alone cannot cure most cases of serious depressive syndromes," he said. "But, when it is combined with the usual antidepressive drugs, it makes patients recover in a shorter length of the time after being given smaller doses."

But alcoholism was where he found it worked the best. Dr. Paret explained his findings this way: "Bee pollen is most efficient in the abstinence-syndrome [delirium tremens or D.T.'s] which appears whenever the alcoholic ceases drinking. The chronic alcoholic lacks many vitamins and proteins. But pollen is very efficient at supplying him with these."

Allergies. A doctor in Great Britain by the name of Gordon Latto, M.D., has been treating his hayfever patients with a special type of unfiltered honey that is rich in bee pollen. He has reported in several medical journals that attacks were reduced during the first year of treatment and that in the second year, there was a total remission of hayfever symptoms.

Leo Conway, M.D., of Denver, Colorado, has gone one step further with this treatment. He treated his patients directly with pollen itself. He stated in one article that just about all of his patients (95 percent) who faithfully took 3 to 5 capsules of bee pollen every day for one year "remained free from all allergy symptoms, no matter where they lived and regardless of diet." He claimed that the remaining small number, who took the capsules infrequently, still managed to experience "partial relief."

Athlete's Foot.   Christine Williams of St. Clair Shores, Michigan, informed me back in the fall of 1986 that if you spread honey between your toes twice or thrice a day, it will clear up athlete's foot in a hurry. In 13 years of using this, "it has never failed to work."

Bedsores.   These lesions begin as redness over certain pressure points in bedridden patients. In time they will commence ulcerating unless they are promptly treated at this stage.

The first thing that needs to be done is to cleanse the sores and thoroughly dry them. Then there should be a relief of pressure by frequent changing of body position every 2 to 3 hours. A foam-rubber doughnut device may be of some assistance here.

The second phase of this treatment involves the external application of a little honey on each bedsore. A sterile wooden tongue depressor or the flat edge of a new plastic knife may be used for this purpose. The amount of honey to be put on each lesion should be no more than what would cover the surface of your own little fingernail.

The final action to take is crushing a few zinc tablets with a heavy object of some kind. Then sprinkle a pinch of this mineral powder over each honey-covered sore. The ideal thing would be to have the patient lie on his or her stomach during the night to allow the oxygen in the air to work in conjunction with the honey and powdered zinc. If this isn't possible, then a tiny circular piece of gauze may need to be placed over each of them and taped in place. This will prevent any of the honey from sticking to the bedsheet and causing a mess.

Where honey has been judiciously used by careful staff workers in some nursing homes, the elderly patients there have nicely recovered from their bedsores and have shown healthy new skin in their place.

Burns.   Honey has been used since ancient times to treat an assortment of burns, be they induced by accidental contact with fire or lengthy exposure to the sun's rays. *La Presse Médicale,* a popular French health magazine reported in one of its issues a while back that modern medical science is just now beginning to discover honey's healing powers. The magazine cited a recent study in which some doctors in Paris experimented with the use of pure natural honey for treating burns and various types of flesh wounds.

Honey was applied directly to the wounds and covered with dry sterile bandages. This dressing was changed every 24 hours. The results showed honey to be an outstanding and highly effective agent for cleansing and healing injured skin surfaces. The honey killed most germs on contact and stimulated new tissue growth over burns and wounds. *La Presse Médicale* concluded: "As it is simple and inexpensive, honey should be better known and added to the list of commonly used antiseptic products."

A friend of mine from Johannesburg, South Africa, told me that his relatives helped to pioneer the Northern Transvaal country over 100 years ago. He said that his grandmother had to rely on a number of folk remedies she learned from the native Bantu tribe during the Boer War of the last century.

He said that most of her folk remedies weren't handed down to his generation, save for only a few. One of the more notable ones was the use of cold water and honey for burns. "We found it infallible," he stated. "And if immediately applied, it is almost a cure. My son put his foot in a pot of boiling water. Immediately we washed down the whole leg with cold water, smothered it with honey, and wrapped it in a towel. The next morning we removed the towel, and there wasn't a mark evident anywhere."

I recall another misfortune that happened to me a number of years ago. Both the cause and cure of it was, believe it or not, *honey*! It happened this way. We were then residing on a small farm in the south-central Utah community of Manti. I had set a large square tin can of granulated honey on our coal-and-wood stove, which had a roaring fire going in it at the time, in the hopes of melting it down. I didn't realize that pressure from beneath would eventually build up, pushing much of the still solid honey upwards, which is precisely what happened. I saw this pillar of honey slowly rise out of the can and quickly reached for two padded pot holders in an attempt to grab the can and move it away from the heat.

In doing so, however, a miniature geyser of boiling honey spewed forth from the side and stuck to the skin of my right inner forearm. Instinctively, I ran outdoors and threw myself into a big pile of recently shoveled snow. The coldness of the snow instantly numbed my arm and took all pain away. When I could tolerate the chilliness no longer, I came back inside and my father treated the injury. He applied some room-temperature liquid honey mixed with a little olive oil and baking soda before the cold-induced numbness wore off. He then dressed the wound with a loose-fitting strip of gauze, so as to allow air to circulate over the area. The dressing remained on for about 36 hours; when it was removed we were both surprised to find out just how much the burn had healed. Once again, this testifies to the remarkable healing power of honey.

Asian doctors have been very savvy in using honey for first- and second-degree burns. Both in China and Japan, doctors have employed this type of treatment with great success. Honey was spread on a piece of clean cloth, which was then directly spread on the cleansed site of injury. This was done a few times each day until a scab was formed; the honey application was then reduced to one or two times daily. Of the 85 patients treated by this method, most generally formed a transparent scab two to three days after treatment started. This scab peeled off by itself, usually on the sixth to tenth day, leaving completely newly formed skin. This treatment was reported to be effective even with patients who were admitted to the hospital late and whose wounds had already been infected.

In 1990, both *Time* (December 3rd issue) and *Newsweek* (May 7th issue) reported a fantastic burn cure from mainland China. They reported that some 50,000 Chinese patients had been treated with a special honey-herb salve in China's national burn center. As *Newsweek* recounted: "Photographs document the progress of patients who have come with deep second-degree and superficial third-degree burns covering up to 94 percent of their bodies. Within months, the same patients appear not only healed but virtually unscarred."

An American surgeon, Dr. Anthony Barbara from the Hackensack Medical Center Burn Unit in New Jersey, traveled to China to meet with a number of these patients. There he saw with his own eyes and was able to compare, on the same patients, parts of the body treated with conventional care versus those parts treated exclusively with the miracle honey salve. By his report, the conventional treatment left the skin "rough, scarred, and marked with patches of excessive or reduced pigmentation." This was in sharp contrast to the honey-treated skin that, though just as charred in the original photographs, appeared "supple and unblemished." Seven months later the American Burn Association and other medical establishment groups reluctantly admitted that "a few patients have healed surprisingly well under these circumstances"; but then they turned right around and dismissed the ointment without giving satisfactory reasons for doing so. Some of the media reported that their obvious prejudice may have been due to jealousy for the Chinese doctor who developed it in the first place. The media correctly assumed that had an American doctor come up with the same formula, these same organizations would have been singing praises of his discovery and extolling its wonderful virtues all over the place.

Besides honey, however, propolis or bee glue is extremely advantageous for relieving the terrible suffering and healing the excruciating wounds produced by scalding water on the skin. The following is a true account as related by Jim Devlin and shared here for the first time in a book with his kind permission.

"My name is Jim Devlin. I would like to tell you about what a miracle product called honeybee propolis did for me. I was working on a water distiller when the top blew off and my face, hands, and arms were burned very badly with scalding hot steam and water.

"DAY 1. I never bandaged the burns with the exception of my forehead on the first night. I continually used bee propolis, though. Every morning for 4 or 5 days my eyes were swollen shut. The steam removed the paint from the kitchen cabinet and took the skin off my forehead. I immediately cleansed my face, neck, arms, and hands with aloe vera from an aloe plant and then covered everything in liquid propolis.

"My next-door neighbor, who is a registered nurse, wanted me to go to the burn unit at the local hospital. But I refused to do so. I faithfully continued to cover everything with the propolis. In just two hours, the intense pain ceased and never returned. All through the worst days of the ordeal I was alone and took complete responsibility for my treatment program.

"DAY 3. This is the morning of the third day after the accident. This was before the swelling in my eyes had gone down for the day. I dressed very carefully; I wore dark glasses, a hat, and long sleeves and drove myself to Prescott Valley [in Arizona]. I noticed in the bathroom cabinet mirror that my blisters were going down quite a bit.

"DAY 5. At this point my right eye is still sore, although the swelling has gone down a lot. The skin has peeled back to expose the new skin except around the eyes and nose.

"DAY 6. The skin around the eyes and nose is now peeled back. The blisters on my arm are starting to heal over.

"DAY 7. The skin on my face is now completely restored. I am still applying large amounts of propolis to both my face and my arm with good success.

"DAY 10. I went to a flea market. But before doing so looked myself in the mirror again and noticed that my face is completely healed by now. My arm is also healing very nicely. I am continuing to apply propolis as the arm progresses.

"DAY 14. My arm is almost completely healed at this point. I am still applying the propolis continually, but now more sparingly."

Cancer. Way back in 1945, Dr. William Robinson, who was with the United States Department of Agriculture (USDA), reported in the *Journal of the National Cancer Institute* that he had found feeding bee pollen to laboratory mice delayed the growth of implanted breast-cancer tumors.

"Results indicate that under suitable conditions the development of mammary tumors in the mice can be influenced by pollenized food," he wrote. He theorized that "pollen contains an anticarcinogenic (anticancer) food." No follow-up work to his research was ever reported after that.

But some years later in Europe, research doctors there produced a substantial amount of work on bee pollen. Dr. Peter Hernuss, an oncologist with the University of Vienna, reported in 1975 that he had discovered "a noticeable decrease in the side effects of radiation" in female cancer patients put on bee pollen. Their nausea, bladder inflammation, appetite loss, and rectal swelling all disappeared.

And in the late 1950s, two Swedish doctors from Uppsala—Erik Ask-Upmark and Gosta Leander—stumbled onto a beneficial effect for prostatitis and prostate cancer. Doing independent research and reporting, they separately observed that bee pollen in prostatitis and prostate cancer patients' diets remarkably improved the men's conditions, reversing almost 79 percent of their cases.

Bee glue or propolis has also exhibited some amazing activity against cancer. Mitja Vosnjak was once the deputy minister of foreign affairs of the old Yugoslavia and later an ambassador to the former East Germany and then, after that, to Austria. In the book, *The Miracle of Propolis,* he told about a friend of his, Rudy, who was wasting away from terminal cancer.

The attending physician prescribed that Rudy take about 10 or 15 drops of propolis in a little water, 30 minutes before a meal, 3 times a day. That was all his friend took, and nothing else. Within a few days, as Vosnjak told it, Rudy informed him in a conversation that he felt "no pains, no cramps, and no blood." Rudy paused a moment, then added with some reluctance, "If this continues to hold, then it will be a real medical miracle for me!"

After one and a half months, Rudy started gaining weight, as a result of significant appetite improvement and better eating habits. Vosnjak noted that, by now, his friend had "healthy pink cheeks, the same enthusiastic, self-confident look in his eyes, decisive movements and quick, firm footsteps. Above all, he overflowed with plans and ideas, had great hopes that he would be able to work again, to catch up on the past seven years and wipe them from his life as if they had never existed."

It was this unpleasant gift from the hive that helped turn the tide in Rudy's favor and bring his cancer under control.

Common Cold. Nothing is quite as catching these days as the common cold. Tens of millions of Americans will spend an estimated $7 billion a year on hundreds of decongestants, syrups, drops, tablets, and pills in an attempt to cure the two or three colds they seem to keep getting every year. Most of these medications are ineffective, if not downright useless; some, in fact, could be quite dangerous.

Why take your cold to Contac® or let Dr. Mom treat it, when a few simple gifts from the beehive can help you more than anything else you've tried? Two things you should be taking to recuperate more quickly are bee pollen (2 capsules twice daily) and propolis (7–15 drops in the back of the throat once or twice each day).

But the best and most versatile of the bee products to use for getting over a bad cold is honey. It works great for relieving hoarseness and sore throats. Combine 4 teaspoons of powdered slippery elm, 2 cups of boiling water, the juice of a lemon, and 2-1/2 tablespoons of honey in the following way. Pour the boiling water over the slippery elm. When cool, strain it. Then sweeten with honey and flavor with the lemon juice. Take 1 tablespoon at a time every hour on the hour.

To expel mucus from the back of the throat, the following honey-fruit gargle is quite helpful. Simmer 2 tablespoons of dried pomegranate rinds in 3 cups of water for 20 minutes. Then strain. Next, stir in 3 tablespoons of honey. Gargle as often as needed.

This particular remedy is outstanding for getting rid of hoarseness or relieving the pain of a sore throat. Stir 1 tablespoon of honey, 1 teaspoon bee pollen, and 1 teaspoon of fresh lemon juice into 1 cup of hot water. Stir the contents vigorously and sip slowly.

To break up congestion in the lungs, a tea can be made from any of the following herbs and sweetened with some honey to allay their bitterness. Boil one pint of water. Add 2 tablespoons of catnip *or* peppermint *or* coltsfoot *or* horehound *or* sage *or* hyssop. Stir thoroughly, cover with a lid, and set aside to steep for 20 minutes. For a double-decongestant tea, uncover after 10 minutes and add 2 teaspoons of bee pollen or 5 drops of propolis tincture; replace the lid and steep another 10 minutes. Then strain and slowly sip 1-1/2 cups of the *warm* tea.

Corns and Warts.   Getting rid of an irritating corn or unwanted wart is fairly simple with propolis. Just put a few drops (3–5) directly on the corn or wart in order to thoroughly penetrate it. Then cover it with a small bandage. Remove it the next morning and repeat the same procedure before starting your day's activities.

Coughing.   Chew some honey cappings or small pieces of honey-dipped dried fruit or licorice root instead of commercial cough drops that are high in sugar. Or just suck on a cough lozenge that has had a few drops of liquid propolis squirted onto it first.

Here is a nifty way to make what I like to call "Nature's Own Contac®" for clearing up head colds. All you need are some garlic cloves and a little honey. Peel the garlic cloves and put them in a jar. Then add the honey a little bit at a time over a couple of days until the jar is full. Set in a sunlit window until the garlic has turned somewhat opaque and all the garlic flavor has been transferred into the honey.

This garlic honey makes an ideal cough syrup. Take a teaspoon every few hours or whenever necessary. Keep in mind, however, that this honey has a lot of concentrated garlic power in it: *one teaspoonful* can pack the powerful wallop of several cloves of garlic; so be careful how much you use at one time. Garlic honey also soothes a sore throat. It also makes a wonderful application for acne or herpes lesions.

Crippled Sexuality. As men and women age, their sexual performances often slow down; this can be the result of shrinking reproductive glands and diminishing sex hormones. But bee pollen has been taken by a number of older people throughout Europe who have claimed that it has put new life and vigor into them, rekindling their sexual interests.

It is a chemical fact that the predigested sugars in bee pollen rapidly convert in the bloodstream to the glycogen so vital for the active production of male semen. In turn, this soon leads to a growing inclination toward more amorous feelings and sensual gratification.

On top of this, bee pollen is high in aspartic acid. This is an amino acid important to bodily rejuvenation processes, particularly those of the sex glands. (It should be mentioned here that aspartic acid salts have been used to treat chronic fatigue and sexual lethargy in older people.)

Still other potent components of bee pollen include sterines, steroid hormone substances, and gonadotropic hormone (a plant hormone similar to the gonadotropin secreted by the pituitary gland to stimulate reproductive organs).

The last known link to human sexual functions is found in the fact that men with acute or chronic prostate inflammation have been successfully treated with a preparation made from one of bee pollen's many hormones.

Another wonderful gift from the beehive for assisting sexual dysfunction is royal jelly. With just one queen bee in a hive producing less than a gram of this precious liquid, it takes a *lot* of beehives to generate this important health product.

Once royal jelly is extracted by beekeepers using sophisticated equipment, it is maintained in its fresh state by freezing. It is then thawed as needed to produce finished products. In order to be sold as a health-food product, the liquid is usually either freeze-dried or pasteurized and sealed in small bottles (the contents used all at once, so that it is not kept after opening). The protein content of royal jelly is about 13 percent, making it susceptible to deterioration if exposed to heat or air for any prolonged period.

In an issue of the *Journal of the Egyptian Medical Association* (56:381–390, 1973) there appeared a preliminary report some time ago on the spermatogenic effect of royal jelly. A group of 15 men suffering from a deficiency in the number of spermatozoa in their semen (below 20,000 cubic millimeters) took royal jelly for 4-1/2 months straight. The result was that 10 of them experienced high sperm counts in their semen well beyond 20,000 cmm. In six months, 13 out of the 15 had achieved high counts above this figure. And because of royal jelly, their sperm acquired a greater ability to move about spontaneously, which is good for increasing the chances of fertilization in a woman.

Cuts, Nicks, and Scrapes.   Propolis tincture is especially valuable in treating minor cuts, nicks, and scrapes. Anywhere from 5 to 10 drops may be required, depending on the size of the area to be covered. Propolis tincture can also be utilized to expedite the healing of acne and nonspecific skin rashes.

Diarrhea and Dysentery.   The following data appeared in Julian H. Seward's (ed.) *Handbook of South American Indians* (Washington, DC: United States Government Printing Office, 1948; 4:325). Among the sub-Andean tribes of the Cauca Valley in the northwest part of South America, male and female shamans are frequently consulted to treat a wide variety of illnesses with magic and natural remedies. Those afflicted with diarrhea and dysentery are given a large quantity (unspecified) of bee honey to drink. Some archaeologists who have conducted scientific research in his huge area in past years and who themselves contracted both maladies have resorted to this native remedy with good results. CAUTION: Those suffering from diabetes or hypoglycemia should *not* attempt this.

Endocrine Problems. Remy Chauvin, M.D., and his associates at the Institute of Bee Culture in Bures Sur Yvete, Paris, have conducted double-blind studies and research into the benefits to be gained from bee pollen. The following is a short summary of their interesting findings.

The antibiotic principle in bee pollen was extracted and found to be extremely active. Certain cultures of microbes were killed almost instantly with bee pollen extract, especially those agents responsible in the hard-to-control diseases such as salmonella (the typhoid types). The scientists believe pollen's capacity for regulating intestinal functions may rest in its ability to destroy harmful intestinal flora.

These scientists have found bee pollen to be helpful in treating problems such as fatigue, allergies, and other respiratory disorders (i.e., bronchitis, sinusitis, and colds). The nutrients in bee pollen stimulate glands and strengthen the immune system to create more energy and resistance to infection.

Equally impressive is the fact that bee pollen helps to balance the endocrine system, showing especially beneficial results in menstrual and prostate problems. Chauvin and his collaborators hypothesize that problems in endocrine gland functions may lead to an extensive range of health problems. They could be as closely related as colitis, constipation, and colibacillosis, or as diverse and separate as poor circulation, neurasthenia, depression, and baldness. They summed up their findings by noting that adequate amounts of bee pollen every day would help to restore normal endocrine functions.

Gray Hair. Former U.S. president Ronald Reagan has been a big fan of bee pollen since 1961. During his two-term presidency, a supply of bee pollen was always on hand, not only in the White

House but also aboard *Air Force One,* the President's aircraft, and *Executive One,* the jet that his wife Nancy frequently used.

The bee pollen he frequently consumed was in the form of a 153-calorie snack bar supplied by an Arizona company. This firm shipped to the White House 5-pound boxes of the granules as well. A White House spokesman acknowledged to a Capitol Hill reporter one time that "the President attributed his lack of gray hair to his consumption of bee pollen."

Infection.   Probably next to garlic, honey is one of the strongest antibacterial agents found in nature. To show you just how effective honey can be against infection, I'm going to take a slightly different approach from one the reader might expect.

To start with, bees are clean little creatures. If they are killed and dipped in a culture medium of any kind, bacteria seldom grow in it. Some years ago a scientist, W. G. Sackett, anxiously noticed that honeybees were crawling "over the human excrement of the family privy" in Tennessee somewhere. He tested the maximum survival time of bacteria in honey, using bacteria of the typhoid-colon group. Much to his relief, he found that all the bacteria were killed within hours or days. He published the demise times of the various intestinal bacteria in an article that appeared in *The Agricultural Experiment Station of the Colorado Agricultural College Bulletin 252* (Fort Collins, CO: 1919; pp. 3–18):

B.	*dysenteriae*	10 hours
B.	*paratyphosus* A	10 hours
B.	*paratyphosus* B	10 hours—1 day
B.	*typhosus*	10 hours—2 days
B.	*proteus vulgaris*	3–4 days
B.	*coli communis*	4–5 days

The honey was heat-sterilized, inoculated with the bacteria, and then kept at room temperature (under these conditions the bactericidal activity is due mainly to the osmotic effect). The addition of 10 percent saline solution to the honey often increased its effect.

This somewhat off-the-wall evidence plainly demonstrates that honey doesn't support bacterial growth; if this were not so, the bees would have a hard time of it, and many housewives too. Honey is antibacterial for several reasons. The most obvious is a simple concentration effect: being extremely hypertonic, honey draws water from the bacterial cells, causing them to shrivel and die. This mechanism works so well that an offering of honey, piously buried in the ancient city of Paestum in Southern Italy in a sacred chamber 2,500 years ago, never decayed and is still recognizable to this day.

Obesity. When bee pollen is taken by itself, without food, it seems to work unhindered in correcting errors of metabolism that may be involved in unhealthy weight gain. A short explanation of how this works may help the reader to understand.

Sugars and fats are both energy-providing and carbon-containing foods; when they combine with oxygen, they burn up to produce energy. Sugars are higher in carbon elements; they are flammable and produce energy rapidly. But fats are lower in carbon and oxygen elements than sugars are. Therefore, fats are metabolized slower because their function is to supply reserve energy. Fats need more oxygen to be set afire and put into reserve for future use.

When bee pollen inverted sugars are taken into the human digestive tract, there is a hasty combustion. The fats will burn with the assistance of oxygen produced by their "fire." This induces a speedy increase in the rate of calorie burning and subsequent weight loss. It is bee pollen that promotes this internal reaction. It appears to help "reset" our individual "fat thermostats" a few degrees higher; this tends to keep the body thinner most of the time.

Honey is an effective substitute for sugar for those who are dieting. The natural sugars in honey are almost totally predigested, which makes them easily absorbed into the bloodstream; this provides an "instant" energy boost. Dieters can especially benefit from this property of honey. Its double-action sugars quickly satisfy a craving for sweets and tend to maintain that sense of satisfaction for a number of hours.

Peptic Ulcer.   Each year, roughly 1 percent of Americans develop peptic ulcers, and overall, up to 10 percent of the population will have an ulcer at some point during their lives. At least 80 percent of these types of stomach ulcers are now known to be caused by infection of the digestive tract with *H. pylori* bacteria. This bacteria infects about 60 percent of Americans by the time they reach age 60, but most of those infected don't develop ulcers. Rather, the bacteria merely seems to increase the chances of an ulcer by weakening the stomach's protective mechanisms and making the lining of the digestive tract susceptible to corrosion by stomach acids.

Rather than taking Pepcid AC® or Maalox® to relieve the symptoms of pain, heartburn, indigestion, and nausea, it would be more helpful to take some honey instead. At least that's what Dr. Basil J.S. Grogono claims in an article he wrote sometime in 1995 in Canada's *Medical Post.* He said that the lowly honeybee made a substance that was better than all the drugs or surgeries employed by gastroenterologists in the last several decades.

Citing a recently published report in the *Journal of the Royal Society of Medicine* in which the antibacterial properties of honey were well tested, he argued for the use of honey instead of potent synthetic antibiotics that can exhibit unpleasant side effects. He used one variety of honey imported from New Zealand that was made by bees feeding on a plant called the manuka. All of his patients recovered from their peptic ulcers when given this particular honey internally.

Sore Throat.   Studies conducted some years ago in the former Iron Curtain countries of the Soviet Union and Yugoslavia demonstrated the effectiveness of propolis or bee glue in the treatment of a sore throat that usually accompanies a bad case of the flu.

A Dr. P. A. Kravcuk from the old USSR tested propolis among 260 patients who had different forms of throat inflammation. All the patients had throat pains, especially when eating something or swallowing their own saliva; many of them also developed a dry, raw cough with it. Dr. Kravcuk reported that bee propolis helped in 90 percent of the cases. He felt that propolis was "a valuable therapeutic agent" in helping to clear up a raw, sore throat.

I personally know this to be a fact. The few times that I've contracted the flu, it has always evolved into a very sore throat. So I used some bee propolis (65 percent strength) from Montana's Naturals to help clear up the problem. I tilted my head all the way back and inserted a full eyedropper of the sticky substance, squirting all around those areas that seemed to be inflamed. There was a momentary burning sensation, followed by a slight numbness of the whole area. Within a few minutes, nearly all the soreness had ceased. My throat tissue felt as if candle wax had been dripped over it. But by the next morning, I was able to talk and swallow without any difficulties.

Propolis has also been used successfully against influenza. In the former beautiful city of Sarajevo, Yugoslavia, a Professor Izet Osmanagic conducted a test among a group of students from a nursing college who had been previously exposed to patients with influenza. Eighty students took bee propolis, and 182 did not. Of those who didn't take propolis, 63 percent became ill. Of those who took propolis, a mere handful—just 7 percent—became sick.

In his book, *The Miracle of Propolis,* a former Yugoslavian politician, Mitja Vosnjak, was quick to point out that propolis isn't a medicine in the typical sense of the word. "It isn't your normal everyday drug," he wrote. Rather, "it is a natural supplement." Then, in something of a poetic fashion, he queried: "Would you call the sun a medicine? Is forest air or fresh clear water a medicine? Is an apple or apricot such?" Then propolis isn't either, but something wonderful which nature has provided us with through the earnest efforts of the humble honeybee.

Wounds. Back in 1982, an Israeli newspaper, *Yedioth Ahronoth,* reported that some scientists working at the Nes Ziona Biological Institute in Tel Aviv had "prove[d] conclusively that treatment of open wounds with honey help[ed] prevent infection and speeds healing." The newspaper also stated that doctors in Tel Aviv's Serlin Maternity Hospital used honey successfully to accelerate the healing process after gynecological surgery for removal of cancerous growths in female organs.

Dr. Avashalom Mizrahi, a microbiologist and the leader of the research team, noted that "honey contains, aside from sugars, ingredients with properties similar to those of antibiotics." He said honey is a natural absorbent and is also easily absorbed into the bloodstream.

"Instead of using various pharmaceutical creams," the newspaper quoted Mizrahi as saying, "it is preferable to treat an open wound with honey." He began his own research on the healing powers of honey after reading of its successful medical application in the former Soviet Union. He said, "Honey lubricates the digestive tract, absorbs acids and helps dry up a [skin] ulcer."

A couple of years after this there was featured an article on the same subject, "The antibacterial action of honey," in the *South African Medical Journal* (67:257–258, Feb. 16, 1985). According to this scientific publication: "Organisms such as *Staphylococcus aureus, Proteus mirabilis, Escherichia coli* and *Candida albicans* failed to grow in undiluted honey in in vitro tests." Because of this, honey has been used in some South African hospitals for accelerating wound healing in "patients undergoing radical vulvectomy for vulval carcinoma." Furthermore, "honey also speeds up the healing of infected surgical wounds and bedsores."

Confirmation of this was done with an in vitro study at King Edward VIII Hospital in the city of Durban. Honey was evaluated in varying dilutions of common gram-positive and gram-negative pathogenic bacteria. The results showed that "all intestinal bacteria pathogens tested failed to grow in honey at a concentration of 40 percent and above. The growth of V. cholerae (as well as Strept. pyogenes and H. influenzae) was in fact inhibited in honey at as low a concentration as 20 percent. Honey also inhibited the growth of other pathogenic bacteria at concentrations of 50 percent."

Another study that appeared a few months later in the same year but in a different publication proved the value of honey in the treatment of infantile gastroenteritis. According to the *British Medical Journal* (290:1866–1867, June 22, 1985), when 169 infants and children were given an oral electrolyte solution with honey instead of glucose, their recovery times from bacterial diarrhea were substantially reduced.

Honey is a very effective wound healer as the foregoing data has shown. It is also one of the simplest wound dressings around. Consider the case of a busy St. Paul housewife who not too long ago gave herself a nasty gash in a kitchen accident with a French knife. Her injured hand looked as though it needed a dozen or more stitches at the emergency ward of the local hospital. But she never went there because her husband, Bob, couldn't get their car started. And since they lived on an isolated farm many miles from the nearest city, she decided on emergency treatment that her grandmother had used in her day. Betty (her real name) covered the wound generously with *raw* honey and bandaged it with gauze and adhesive tape. The next morning, she unwrapped and cut the bandages away and noticed that the torn flesh was already beginning to knit together. The lady's hand was never stitched. It mended, almost without any trace of a scar, with the help of honey alone.

Consider also that a simple formula compounded only with honey and petroleum jelly or hog's lard was widely utilized by doctors throughout mainland China during the Second World War for treating skin erythema, chronic leg ulcers, and small wounds, with good success. According to *The Chinese Medical Journal* (62:55–60) for 1944 there was a severe shortage of drugs regularly used for such wounds, so it became necessary to improvise and turn to more natural materials instead. Prior to the outbreak of war in that nation, cod liver oil and Vaseline had been used. But with an obvious shortage of them as the fighting progressed and intensified, a number of doctors soon turned to the use of honey and hog's lard. According to the report: "In a period of four months, more than 50 cases of chilblains, chilblain ulcers and small wounds were treated with honey ointment" resulting in "extraordinarily good results." The ointment was made with 80 percent liquid honey and 20 percent melted lard and applied with a wooden tongue depressor directly onto the leg ulcer or wound, after which it was wrapped with gauze and held in place with adhesive tape.

Wrinkled Skin. Bee pollen is a marvelous toner for the skin, providing it with increased elasticity. Those consuming bee pollen on a regular basis seem to have skin that is much younger, smoother, and healthier, with far fewer wrinkles, than those who don't. These observations were made by Lars Eric Essen, M.D., of Halsingborg, Sweden. When he prescribed bee pollen every day to over a hundred seniors for two months straight, they "seemed to show new skin growth, a fading away of wrinkles, and appear to move about more lively."

In addition to this, honey can add softness and fresh beauty to the skin. The wife of a beekeeper noticed that her husband's hands were always wonderfully soft and smooth during the honey-collection seasons. She began to use it herself as a beauty aid and also found that her own complexion improved and wrinkles didn't appear.

A middle-aged woman with some wrinkles to whom this was mentioned a few years later tried the honey application for herself and reported what took place as follows. Her name is June Bohanna Brown. "Each day, before my bath, I tuck my hair inside a shower cap, splash warm water on my face and neck to open the pores, then apply some honey directly to my skin. While soaking in the tub, the honey softens and benefits as I attempt to uncrease and smooth away my wrinkles. I then wash it off and finish with a dash of cold water. Because of the composition of honey it causes the skin tissue to hold moisture. Dry skin cells plump up and wrinkles tend to smooth away. This sweet substance when applied to the skin seems to bring a glow of pink, where only paleness was there before. I found that any skin inflammation is also benefited with the use of honey."

Yeast Infection. Candidiasis is caused by a yeastlike fungus called Candida albicans. This infection is manifested by vaginal discharge and irritation or burning sensation in the female reproductive organs. Several antifungal preparations commercially available have been prescribed by doctors for treating this problem. They include miconazole nitrate (Gyno-Daktarin), clotrimazole (Canesten), and nystatin (Mycostatin). According to the August 22, 1983, issue of the *Journal of Pharmacy and Pharmacology* (36:283–284), however, "treatment failures have been reported . . . when using the cream or pessary formulation of some of these antimycotic agents." This usually results then "in the use of several antifungal preparations before [a] complete cure is obtained."

But a "preliminary study of the antimicrobial activity of honey" demonstrated that it "had a broad spectrum [of] antibac-

terial and antifungal activity, and excellent activity against . . .
Candida albicans [when] compared with [the same amount of]
nystatin." Women who have been troubled for some time with
yeast infections and have tried a few of the standard antifungal
medications without much results might find better satisfaction
with using honey instead.

Some Thoughts on the Possible Therapeutic Benefits of Bee Venom

On April 23, 1978, world-famous golfer Jack "The Golden Bear"
Nicklaus was finishing the eighteenth hole of the Tournament of
Champions in Carlsbad, California, when he was suddenly stung by
a wasp. Nicklaus, who has always been allergic to such a sting,
requested and received emergency first-aid treatment. Without it,
he could have had an attack so severe that it could have turned into
anaphylaxis—an acute allergic reaction involving the entire body
that threatens breathing, heart action, and circulation and can
result in death within 10 to 15 minutes if not promptly treated.

An estimated 1.75 million Americans—about 1 in 235—are
allergic to the stings of bees, yellow jackets, wasps, hornets, and
fire ants. It is believed that almost 100 deaths yearly are directly
attributable to insect stings. But some allergists think this figure
should be ten times higher, believing that many cases that pass for
"heart attacks" or "strokes" may actually involve life-threatening
reactions to insect stings of various types.

Prior to 1975, the older and more established method of
treating such problems was to inject the patient with whole-
insect-body extract (WBE). In quite a few cases, patients who
were treated with WBE immunotherapy suffered less intense reactions later on when accidentally restung. But many other patients
with stinging-insect hypersensitivity met with very unpleasant if
not outright violent reactions when subjected to this routine
method of WBE treatment. One of those happened to be the wife
of a Wisconsin beekeeper, who had had two anaphylactic reactions following honeybee stings. And when WBE therapy was
administered to her, it almost proved to be her complete undoing
due to the near-fatal reaction she experienced with it.

It was then that her doctors at University of Wisconsin Hospitals in Madison decided to try a rather more radical approach: They extracted venom from honeybee venom sacs, mixed it with a coca solution, and gave it to her intravenously "in increasing daily doses until the equivalent of one venom sac was given per day." As the report in the *Journal of the American Medical Association (JAMA)* (231: 1154–1156, March 17, 1975) noted: "This maintenance dosage was continued for a month," the result being that "anaphylaxis did not occur after another bee-sting challenge" later on. This single report in a major medical journal inspired Dr. Martin Valentine and his colleagues at Johns Hopkins Medical School in Baltimore to begin their own investigative work into bee venom as a possible replacement for WBE therapy a couple of years later. The result was that by early 1979 the Food and Drug Administration (FDA) had approved the injections of insect venoms over WBE as being a lot safer and more effective to patients experiencing insect stings. It may be of some additional interest here to note that the venom from a certain type of ant (the pseudomyrmex) was being tested in humans as a possible treatment for rheumatoid arthritis, according to the May 1993 issue of *The Johns Hopkins Medical Letter "Health After 50"* (5(3):8). All of which just goes to show that at least for *some* medical procedures honeybee venom has become medically acceptable within the last couple of decades.

Nearly concurrent with these developments in the regular medical literature there arose similar interest in bee venom in the popular press as well. A freelance writer by the name of Patrick Frazier wrote one of the earliest and most insightful, evenhanded articles on the subject for the May 19, 1974, edition of *The Washington Post.* Appropriately entitled "Arthritis and Bees: Venom Research Overcoming Old Prejudices," he began by telling the incredible story of one Vermont beekeeper, Charles Mraz, who in May 1934, at the age of 29, still suffered acute arthritic pain in his knees from an attack of rheumatic fever the previous winter. Just to stand and walk made him appear as an elderly person three or four times his age. But it was spring and he had to get out and work in his apiary as usual.

Charles knew about the old wives' tale of bee stings being used as a remedy for arthritis, but like most others believed it was a bunch of nonsense. Figuring he had nothing to lose, however, he decided to experiment for himself to see if such a thing really worked or not. He caught two of his own honeybees and made them sting the inside of his knees where the pain was the most severe. Two welts raised from the stings but nothing else happened. He soon forgot about it and continued working with his hives the rest of the day.

By the next morning, however, he realized something wonderful had happened overnight. As he eased himself out of bed, it dawned on him that the arthritic pain in both of his knees was *completely gone.* His first reaction was, "My God, am I imagining that I had arthritis yesterday, or is it my imagination that I haven't got it today? To this day [May 1974] I cannot believe what happened," he told reporter Frazier. And that was the start of Marz's lifelong interest in bee-venom therapy for one of mankind's most crippling diseases.

Over the next five decades, Charles became an active proponent of this therapy for the treatment of arthritis. He worked closely with a few open-minded medical doctors such as rheumatologists in helping to treat thousands of patients suffering from excruciating joint pain. He usually worked through their clinics to do this, but wasn't adverse to helping those who came to seek out his services at his large bee farm (Champlain Valley Apiaries) in Middlebury, Vermont.

I was fortunate enough in the latter part of the 1970s to become personally acquainted with this wonderful man. At that time, he was entering his early seventies. I watched in amazement as he treated different individuals with *live* honeybee venom and saw individuals get up and move around without *any* pain whatsoever in just a matter of a few hours. I interviewed him at length, took copious notes on everything I saw and heard, and filed it away for future reference.

Mr. Marz eventually passed on, but the extensive materials I had gleaned in my brief association with him remained intact. Eventually, I found a use for them in this book. The following data came from Mr. Marz *firsthand* and is given in his own words. Now, just because this information is presented here in no way suggests or encourages readers to attempt this therapy for themselves. Bear in mind that it is still medically controversial and that nothing so radical should ever be attempted *without* strict medical supervision. Marz believed in working closely with doctors; the same pattern should continue for those who may wish to explore this matter further for themselves. But, neither I nor my publisher recommend bee-venom therapy as a substitute for more conventional arthritis treatments. The material given here is for informational purposes *only* and *not*—repeat *not*—intended for actual self-treatment of arthritis.

And now Charles Marz in his own words. "If one considers seriously trying bee venom therapy (BVT), a source of bees is necessary. There is no better source than [from] local beekeepers. They can be very helpful with instructions on how to handle the bees. The simplest method to carry bees is in a glass jar, with holes in the metal cover for air. In the jar some honey must be supplied for food and a piece of cardboard inside the jar for the bees to cling to. A half-pint jar will hold 50 or more bees for about a week. When more are needed, it is only necessary to clean the jar, put in more fresh honey and cardboard, and take it to the beekeeper to be replenished.

"When picking up bees to use, they must be picked up by the head or thorax (where wings and legs are attached) and crushed with the tweezers. The sting is at the tail end of the bees and it is only necessary to touch the skin with it. The sting will immediately stick to the skin and come out of the bee and remain in the skin. The sting gland of the honeybee is a very complex mechanism. The two shafts of the sting are barbed and slide alongside of each other and are activated by a bunch of muscles. This will cause the sting to bury itself into the skin even after it leaves the body of the bee and at the same time, pump the venom into the wound. The longer the sting is left in the skin, the more venom will be introduced, up to about 5 minutes or so that the muscles are active.

"The next step after one has the bees available and knows how to handle them [just ask a beekeeper for this information] is where and how much bee venom to use. As a rule, the patient needs someone to help them apply the stings. It is difficult to do alone especially in the spine area. Also, the person assisting can help determine where the stings should be applied. The most effective areas seem to be the 'trigger points' [in Oriental medicine, they would be the acupuncture or acupressure points]. These can be found by pressing different places in the area where the arthritis is located. When a 'trigger point' is pressed, it will produce a very sharp pain and the patient will jump. These are the areas where the stings should then be applied, and they can be marked with a ball-point pen. (He noted here that in some respects this does closely correspond with the acupuncture points of Chinese medicine.)

"Before stings are applied, it is well to first apply ice or a frozen 'Scotch ice can' to make the skin cold. This will greatly reduce the pain produced by the sting when it is first applied. Before any therapy is started, the person must first be tested for any possible allergic reaction. This is done by applying a sting and then removing it instantly, after being assured that there is *no* history of allergy. Wait for 15 minutes or a half hour and if there is no allergic reaction in this time, there is no allergic problem. In half an hour another sting can be applied and this also removed quickly. This is usually enough for the first treatment.

"After this the serious business of therapy can be started. If the arthritis is of an acute type, or short duration, no damage to the joints and only a few local points involved, the treatment is usually only of short duration and only a few stings are necessary. Sometimes a local condition will clear up with only one sting, but normally, the therapy requires a series of treatments. The first day, start out with just the two test stings and continue every day for about a week with two to four stings each day, depending on the severity of the arthritis.

"While bee venom has a systemic as well as a local reaction, the best results are found by treating the 'trigger points' over the body where the arthritis is involved. Basically, arthritis of the upper part of the body stems from the upper spine and the lower part of the body from the lower spine. For this reason, it is a good idea to use the spine areas as a base of operations. Treat the spine first. Then work down from the spine toward the extremities: the shoulders, neck, elbows, wrists, hands, and so forth. From the lower spine, work toward the hips, knees, and ankles, where 'trigger points' are found.

"With experience, one can soon find out how many stings they can take without too much discomfort. At first, the stings may produce very little pain, but as the treatment is continued, the body will again be more sensitive to pain as the arthritic symptoms leave the areas. This is a good sign that there is improvement in the condition. If the arthritic condition is severe, after the first week of two to four stings each day, treat every other day using more stings as needed. It may be necessary to give 10 to 20 stings with each treatment for bad cases. It must be remembered, in serious cases of joint damage, no type of treatment can make new joints or tissue. In such cases, one can only expect to get relief of pain and to stop the progress of the disease.

"A full course of treatment generally will last from four to eight weeks, with treatments every other day. The stings should be applied to different areas each time so as not to treat an area that is still swollen.

"Usually when treatments are first started, there is very little or no swelling. Then as the treatment is continued, the areas will begin to swell much more, with redness and itching of the areas treated. Sometimes during this stage, the patient will feel worse, with more pain and pain in areas never before affected. There may even be nausea and a general feeling of discouragement. It is important to remember this is a good sign that the treatment is working, and treatment must be continued in order to be effective. The number of stings can be reduced, if desired. It appears that the cause for this reaction is the purging of toxins from the body by the stimulation of the biotic processes of the system. It follows the classic Hans Selye, M.D., [a renowned epidemiologist, since deceased] syndrome of the stages of reaction and then the stage of resistance. Soon after this, the stings will no longer swell and a person becomes 'immune,' just as a beekeeper might become immune after working with bees for a long time. When one reaches this 'immune stage,' the first course of treatment can be terminated.

"At this point a person will usually find their condition much improved. No more treatment is necessary for another month or two, and if there is no return of the arthritic symptoms, there is no longer need of any further treatments for a period of perhaps several years or as long as 20 years or more. However, if after a 'rest period' of a month or two, there are still arthritic symptoms, another course of treatments can be followed, starting with one sting and gradually building up as with the first course. However, with subsequent courses, the treatments are usually more effective and with quicker results so that a shorter course of treatments usually suffices. In very bad cases, three or more courses of treatments may be necessary covering a period of two years or more. However, for the usual cases where there is little or no joint damage, a few weeks of treatment will suffice.

"There is often the question for which types of arthritis BVT is effective. It appears to be effective in most kinds of true arthritis. Gout and other acute forms respond quickly. Spondylitis and rheumatoid arthritis forms where serious joint damage is involved will find limited results, unless treatment can be started before serious damage develops. It is interesting to relate that with children, BVT seems to be of special benefit as they seem to respond quicker than adults.

"The final thing which seems to worry most people who are thinking about starting something like this is, 'Is BVT safe for us to use?' My answer to that question is an emphatic 'yes'! Conventional drugs such as cortisone, which are routinely used to treat arthritis, can do the body far more harm than a little bee venom could. There are thousands of beekeepers all over the world to demonstrate that this substance has no adverse side effects even when taken over a long period of time. Just look at me as an example of that. I personally have taken a thousand stings or more per year for the past 50 years, as have many other beekeepers. Many beekeepers live to be 80 years of age or more. Your chances of dying from a bad reaction to a potent drug is 1,000 times more likely than it is from a honeybee sting!"

This concludes the information that the late Charles Mraz kindly provided me with back in the spring of 1978. The reader should keep in mind, however, that some individuals are extremely hypersensitive to insect venom. And if stung, such persons could suffer anapylaxis, which certainly is life-threatening. *Before BVT is attempted, individuals should check with their allergists to make sure that they are not hypersensitive to bee venom.* It may also be worthwhile to keep on hand a hypodermic needle filled with adrenalin in the event that anaphylaxis occurs during an administration of BVT. The adrenalin can then be immediately injected intramuscularly and bring the person out of such an acute allergic reaction before it becomes too severe.

Sweeten Up Your Honey with These Recipes

"Honey, chances are you'll love me once you get to know me." So begins the title of a little booklet distributed free of charge some years ago by the National Honey Board (390 Lashley Street, Longmont, CO 80501-6010). For those desiring to bake with honey, the following facts and tips should be kept in mind, as excerpted from the uncopyrighted booklet:

- For best results, use recipes that specify honey.
- When you substitute honey for granulated sugar in recipes for baked goods, remember these few things:
  - Substitute honey for up to half the sugar. With some experimentation, honey can be substituted for all the sugar in some recipes.
  - Reduce the amount of liquid in the recipe by 1/4 cup for each cup of honey used.
  - Add 1/2 teaspoon baking soda for every cup of honey used.
  - Reduce oven temperature by 25° F. to prevent over-browning.
- Because of its high fructose content, honey has a higher sweetening power than sugar.
- One 12-ounce jar of honey equals a standard measuring cup.
- For easy removal, coat the measuring cup with vegetable oil or vegetable oil spray before measuring out the honey.

CAUTION: Honey should not be fed to infants under one year of age. Nor should those suffering from diabetes or hypoglycemia use very much honey either in their diets.

Honey Nut Spread

1/2 cup honey
1/2 cup butter
1/2 cup walnuts or pecans, roasted and ground

To roast the nuts, place 1/2 cup of nuts on a baking sheet in a 325° F. oven for 20 minutes or until the shells blister and the nuts are lightly browned. Cool slightly afterwards.

Then rub the nuts between the palms of both hands or else between gloved hands or even with a clean towel in order to remove their shells or skins. Process in a Vita-Mix whole food machine for one minute until evenly ground (be sure to use the plastic container with the blade unit intended for grinding wheat and not the one used for juicing).

Stir together the honey and butter in a medium bowl. Next, add the nuts and stir until smooth. Serve at room temperature; store in the refrigerator. Yields about 1-1/4 cups.

Honey Raisin Scones

2-1/2 cups all-purpose flour
2 tsps. finely shredded orange peel
1 tsp. baking powder
1/2 tsp. baking soda
1/2 tsp. salt
1/2 cup butter
1/2 cup raisins
1/2 cup dairy sour cream
1/3 cup honey
1 egg, slightly beaten

In a bowl, combine flower, orange peel, baking powder, baking soda, and salt. Cut in butter until the mixture resembles coarse crumbs. Stir in the raisins.

Combine the sour cream, honey, and egg in a medium bowl and mix thoroughly. Then stir the honey mixture into the dry mixture just long enough for it to be moistened.

Knead the dough on a lightly floured surface ten times. Pat the dough into an 8-inch square. Cut into 4 squares; cut each square diagonally into 2 triangles.

Place triangles on a greased baking sheet. Then sprinkle with a little brown sugar, if desired. Bake in a 375° F. oven for 15 to 20 minutes until golden brown. Serve them warm with some Honey Nut Spread. Yields 8 scones.

Honey Mustard Dressing

3/4 cup mayonnaise

1/3 cup cooking oil

1/4 cup honey

1/3 cup lemon juice

1 tbsp. prepared mustard

1 tsp. pepper

1/2 tsp. minced dried onion

In a medium mixing bowl, whisk together the mayonnaise, cooking oil, honey, lemon juice, mustard, pepper, and onion. Cover and chill until ready to use. Serve as a dressing for spinach salad, chicken salad, seafood salad, or mixed greens. Makes 1-1/2 cups dressing.

Ribs with Zesty Honey Sauce

3 lbs. pork loin back ribs or pork spareribs

1 cup chili sauce

1/2 to 3/4 cup honey

1/4 cup finely chopped onion

1 tbsp. Worcestershire sauce

1 tsp. Dijon-style mustard

Cut the ribs into serving-size pieces. Place the ribs, bone side down, on a rack in a shallow roasting pan. Roast, uncovered, in a 350° F. oven for an hour; then drain and return them to their pan.

To make the sauce, combine the chili sauce, honey, onion, Worcestershire sauce, and mustard in a small saucepan. Bring to a rolling boil before reducing the heat to low setting. Then simmer, uncovered, for 5 minutes, stirring periodically.

Next, brush the ribs with some of this sauce. Roast, uncovered, for about 40 minutes more or until the ribs are ten-

der, brushing them with sauce every 12 minutes. Brush them with the remaining sauce before serving. Yields 4 servings.

Easy Honey Muffins

1/2 cup milk
1/4 cup honey
1 egg, beaten
2-1/2 cups buttermilk baking mix

Combine the milk, honey, and egg and mix well. Add the baking mix and stir only until moistened. Portion into greased muffin tins. Bake at 400° F. for 20 minutes or until a toothpick inserted near the center comes out clean. Yields 12 muffins.

Honey Garlic Dressing

1 package (3/4 to 1 oz.) Italian Salad Dressing Mix
2 tbsps. water
1/4 cup honey
1/3 cup apple cider vinegar
1/3 cup vegetable oil

Combine the ingredients together except for the oil. Mix well. Then gradually whisk in the oil. Use this on a salad of mixed greens with strips of sweet red and yellow peppers. Yields 1 cup.

All-Purpose Honey Teriyaki Sauce

This sauce and its variations can be stored in the refrigerator for ready use anytime.

1 cup honey
1 cup each soy sauce and sake (Japanese rice wine)
1 large clove garlic, minced
1-1/2 tsps. grated fresh ginger root
1 tsp. sesame oil

Combine all the ingredients and blend well. Makes about 3 cups.

Beef, chicken, pork, or fish can be marinated 1 to 3 hours in this type of sauce. One recipe is enough for about 4 pounds of meat.

Here are a couple of interesting variations. For a sesame marinade, add 1 tsp. of roasted sesame seeds to 1 cup of this sauce and mix thoroughly. For a stir-fry seasoning, just dissolve 1 tbsp. cornstarch in 1/2 cup of this honey teriyaki sauce to season 4 cups of stir-fry ingredients. Serve the stir-fry with sauce over rice, noodles, or baked potato.

According to the National Honey Board, there are more than 300 types of honey available. The light-colored honeys are generally milder; the dark-colored varieties are stronger. Here is a short list of some of the more interesting flavored or popular honeys available in the United States.

ACACIA HONEY, from California and China, is a pale yellow with a delicate taste.

ALFALFA HONEY, produced in the United States and Canada, is light in color and has a pleasingly mild flavor and aroma.

BASSWOOD HONEY, often water-white in color, has a distinctive "biting" flavor.

BUCKWHEAT HONEY, from the buckwheat-growing area of the country, is dark and full-bodied.

CLOVER HONEY often varies in color from water-white to amber, depending on its source, such as white clover and the white and yellow sweet clovers.

EUCALYPTUS HONEY, derived from more than 500 distinct species and hybrids of plants, varies in color and flavor but usually has a strong flavor.

FIREWEED HONEY, from a perennial herb, is light in color.

ORANGE BLOSSOM HONEY, often a combination of citrus nectars, generally has a mild taste and a light color.

POISON IVY HONEY, according to a 60-year-old Allen, Texas, beekeeper by the name of Wyvonne Robertson, is "the clearest, sweetest honey you've ever tasted."

SOURWOOD HONEY, produced from the blossoms of a tree common to the Appalachian region of America, is light in color with a mild flavor.

TULIP POPLAR or TULIP TREE HONEY is dark amber with a mild flavor.

TUPELO HONEY, from the southeastern United States, is often light in color with a mild, distinctive taste. It is heavy bodied and high in levulose.

One tablespoon (20 grams) of honey can be nutritious. It contains 61 calories, 0.10 grams of protein, 16.5 grams of carbohydrates, slightly over 1 milligram each of calcium, phosphorus, and sodium, along with 10 milligrams of potassium, 0.60 milligrams of magnesium, as well as trace amounts of iron, zinc, copper, vitamin C, vitamin B-2, vitamin B-3, vitamin B-6, panthothenic acid, and folic acid.

Honey is composed of two simple sugars, levulose and dextrose. The amount of each can vary considerably. Levulose varies from 40 percent to 50 percent and dextrose from 32 percent to 37 percent. The ratio of levulose is important in that it affects the tendency toward granulation or crystallization. Higher levels of levulose have the least tendency to crystallize. However, crystallized honey can be reclaimed by heating.

The moisture content of honey ranges from 14 percent to 23 percent, and the average is 17.2 percent. Small amounts of maltose and sucrose are also found in honey, with the maltose level at 7 percent and sucrose at 1.5 percent. Diastase enzyme is also present and is a carryover from the honey-making process. The bee provides this enzyme, which converts the nectar to honey.

It is interesting to note that honey doesn't freeze at any temperature that it is normally exposed to. One source reports that a mixture of one part honey to one part water can be used in automobile radiators as an antifreeze. But this is something I wouldn't personally recommend your trying, unless you're prepared to pay a big repair bill.

Honey should be stored at temperatures below 52° F., or in the 70° F. to 80° F. range, in airtight containers. Honey should never be stored in copper, zinc, or aluminum containers because of its acid content.

The moisture-retaining property of honey carries over into the finished product, especially in cakes where high levels are used. The main advantage is in the flavor and aroma that can be imparted to the finished product whenever honey is used in place of sugar.

Chapter Two

Cayenne Pepper
The New-World Drug
and Food Fascination
That Columbus Gave to Europe

Terminology

Cayenne pepper, the subject of this particular monograph, is a special kind of ground red chile pepper believed to have come from Cayenne, the capitol of French Guiana. This city is located on the island of Cayenne at the mouth of the Cayenne River. Cayenne was founded by the French in 1643, but it was wiped out by a Native American massacre and wasn't resettled until 1664. Several other European nations, besides France, contested for possession of the island, these being Great Britain, the Netherlands, and Portugal. Between 1808 and 1816, the British and the Portuguese occupied the island.

It is believed that the Portuguese first brought a particular species of capsicum to the island. The combination of stifling humidity and intense heat made this pepper grow like mad and gave the spice its very sharp, distinctive flavor.

The name cayenne itself, however, is believed to have come from *Tupi,* the *lingua franca* of the Amazon basin and the South American coast. The chief difference, if any, between cayenne and chile powder is that the latter is much coarser.

Capsicum, or red peppers, hail from the potato-tomato family (which are indigenous to South America). The capsicum species gives us chile peppers, red peppers, sweet or bell peppers, paprika and, of course, cayenne pepper. Many plant scientists are of the opinion that all of the domesticated peppers are really cultivated varieties of just one original species.

Finally, when we speak of chile peppers per se, we are referring to pungent varieties of capsicum. They can vary greatly in size and shape. There are the tiny, round chiles the size of your pinkie all the way up to the humongous types measuring nearly a foot long. And their pungency ranges all the way from mildly nipping the tongue to the volcanic strength capable of blowing your lips right off your face. When ripe, they're red as a rule, but can also be yellow, cream, or even purple-black. They are rich in vitamin C and the bioflavinoids (vitamin P).

In this study, all three terms will be used wherever appropriate. The first few parts, which deal exclusively with the history, domestication, and possible origins of red peppers will refer to them collectively as capsicums. In the section covering many of the world's most popular pepper plants, the term chiles (also spelled chillies) will be used instead. Actual references to cayenne pepper per se don't appear until the medicinal applications portion of this treatise. Finally, in the recipes given at the end, references to chiles and cayenne pepper both appear.

Background History

One of the most frequently asked questions I get with regard to cayenne pepper and garlic is this: Are they spices or medicinal herbs? People all over the country whom I meet quite frequently at health conventions, book signings, or over the radio have wondered about this matter for some years.

In giving it considerable thought, I came to the following conclusions. Plants such as cayenne and garlic are spices when incorporated into the preparation of a wide variety of dishes and drinks to satisfy the appetite and quench the thirst. But they also become medicinal agents when applied by doctors or herbalists to specific health problems. In this way then, at least some of our food also becomes our medicine as well.

Or, put another way: Spices are plants with a lot of romance, intrigue, and adventure connected with them; on the other hand, medicinal herbs don't have quite as much flair surrounding them and are more practical agents utilized for the mundane and routine purposes of healing.

The introduction of the capsicum, especially cayenne, to the world in general really began with Christopher Columbus. In a sense, it was spices that provoked a serious interest in the man to find an alternate route to the East Indies. It was for this reason primarily that the rulers of Spain, King Ferdinand and Queen Isabella, gave an audience to this Genoese mapmaker and navigator.

They patiently listened as he explained to them that there was a shorter, more direct route to the Orient than always having to sail around the Cape of Good Hope below the tip of Africa. Isabella, as the familiar story goes, hocked the "Crown Jewels," figuratively speaking, in order to help finance Columbus's trip. The cost in terms of *maravedis* (a fifteenth-century Spanish copper coin worth about 13 cents at 1995 prices) was roughly 1,167,542, which translated into $151,780. The riches that Spain eventually hauled out of the Americas amounted to something like 1,733,000 maravedis for every single maravedi that Isabella spent on that first voyage; this translates into a return of *200 million* percent for the Spanish monarchy.

On the morning of October 12, 1492, Columbus and his men finally set foot on land, after having been on water since the beginning of August. In his log, the "Admiral of the Ocean Sea" wrote, "we saw naked people" on shore. He promptly erected a large wooden cross "as a token of Jesus Christ our Lord" and concluded his simple ceremony of taking possession of this island by naming it "San Salvador" or Holy Savior. Thus he claimed his discovery not just for Ferdinand and Isabella, but for the Catholic faith of which he and his men were devout subjects.

He quickly named the strange natives "Indios," truly believing they had reached the "Indies" at last. He described them as being "friendly and well-dispositioned," but definitely being in the Stone Age so far as tools and weapons went. When he showed one curious "Indian" his Toledo steel sword, the man unwittingly grasped the blade and cut himself badly.

Now, such a serious wound required prompt medical attention. Imagine the astonishment of the admiral and his men when the tribal witch doctor came forward with a pungent red powder and liberally sprinkled it over the injured man's wound. To their utter amazement, within minutes, nearly all bleeding had ceased. This, then, was the first introduction of New World capsicum to Old World Europeans.

His native informants gave him enough reason to believe that these capsicums were a new kind of pepper, yet it wasn't the genuine article he had been looking for. Thus, his hopes of finding valuable black pepper came to no avail.

In addition to the capsicums, there were several other important plant discoveries made by Columbus and his crew, which would have impact on the rest of the world in the course of time. His ship's log entry for November 6 reads: "On the way inland, my two men found many people who were going to different villages, men and women, carrying firebrands in their hands and herbs to smoke, which they are in a habit of doing." Long before there was

Joe Camel, there was Native American tobacco, some of which was carried back to Spain. Little could Columbus know that this important plant would one day be worth more than any gold ever wrested from the New World.

In his eager search for revenue-producing plants, Columbus always had the bad habit of misidentifying herbs and trees found throughout the Caribbean islands as being identical, or nearly identical, to species valued in Europe. He knew he had to economically justify his expedition when he returned to Spain and, in his haste, made the many taxonomic mistakes he did.

For instance, one plant he believed he spotted was the Old World's aloe vera, whose sap was used in his time as a potent laxative. Several times he reported in his log of sending crewmen out to cut specimens. Unfortunately, he was wrong; he was having his men harvest the agave plant, a reasonably close relative whose leaves are similar to those of the aloe. Nor did he come anywhere close to the mark in being able to identify the New World's gumbo-limbo tree for his familiar Old World mastic.

Actually, the admiral's quest wasn't an entire failure. Granted that he hadn't discovered a shorter route to the Indies as he fancifully imagined was the case. Nor did he and his men find the particular spices they had been seeking. But the "gold" they brought back with them to Spain was in the form of two new aromatic herbs that would soon enrich the world's repertory of seasonings. Those two were the capsicums and allspice, both of which the Europeans incorrectly labeled *pimiento*. Later, a third spice would be added, namely the orchid that produces vanilla.

King Ferdinand and Queen Isabella really went all out to give the admiral the kind of royal reception befitting a visiting head of state. He was invited to sit with them and their son, the Infante Don Juan. Everyone gathered in Barcelona's Alcázar marveled greatly at the semi-naked, dusky-colored savages, at the brilliantly colored parrots, and at the assortment of golden baubles and bangles that Columbus had bought with trinkets and temporary goodwill. Following this extravagant coming-home celebration, there followed more honors and more pageantry in the weeks to come.

Truly, the capsicums, allspice, Native Americans, talkative birds, decorated ornaments, and everything else brought back from the Americas had done an immense amount of good toward bolstering the credibility of the man who opened the entire Western Hemisphere for the rest of the world. Not bad for someone who had been ridiculed, jeered, and laughed at by many skeptics and disbelievers earlier that same year.

Domestication in the Ancient Americas

Well before the advent of Columbus—in fact, by several thousand years—the ancient inhabitants of Central and South America were using the chiles on a regular basis for food as well as medicine. For example, archaeologists have uncovered evidence of red pepper dating back to 7,000 B.C. in the digs in Tamaulipas and Tehuacán, Mexico. And in South America, the capsicums have been found in archaeological sites all along the coast of Peru.

The origin of a domesticated crop, such as the capsicum species, is a process and not an event. Multiple origins are now believed to be responsible for their coming into being. An old adage such as "Which came first, the chicken or the egg?" can no longer apply to the simple theory of weed to cultivated plant. Granted there once may have been a single weed (or even several of them, for that matter) that bore some close resemblance to the later capsicums. But this weed is believed to have interacted with another or several plants of an entirely different species through the accidental or deliberate intervention of man himself. Ancient farmers in the Americas are believed to have crossed two or more different species of plants in order to come up with those capsicums, such as cayenne pepper, which are strongly pungent and terribly aromatic.

Whatever the relationship was between wild plants and domesticated crops, rest assured that it wasn't long before early Aztec, Maya, and Inca farmers discovered the wonderfully potent properties of red peppers, which they fully utilized for flavoring food and beverages and curing different illnesses.

The ways of gardening differed considerably between those of the New World and the forms used throughout Europe. The capsicums, squash, beans, avocadoes, corn, pigweed or amaranth, and zapotes were planted by nonsedentary people who still

roamed around a lot for hunting and gathering. These early peoples were quite dependent for better than 50 percent of their sub-
sistence on the harvesting of wild plants. Most of the western
hemisphere's domesticated native plants (with the single exception of the potato) like a warm start, summer rains, and a dry fall
with lowered temperatures. They start and mature late, and most
are planted at the beginning of summer and harvested at the end
of the fall. New World domesticates such as the capsicums don't
have the deeply developed root systems common to dry-land vegetation and some types of Old World crops.

When the Americas' three greatest civilizations (Aztec, Maya,
and Inca) finally developed agriculture, it was basically gardening
by planting individual seeds as opposed to Old World broadcasting
of seed in tilled fields. The typical house garden still in existence
in Peru after several thousand years represents the ancestral type
of cultivation in the New World, according to archaeologist Donald
W. Lathrap in *Origins of Agriculture,* edited by C. A. Reed (The
Hague: Mouton, 1977, pp. 713–752). In the Old World, field crops
were not harvested until the fruit matured, and green vegetables
were grown in separate plots. But, in the New World, various parts
of the plants were consumed at different stages of development.

The two most commonly domesticated capsicums in the New
World have been *Capsicum annuum* by the Aztecs in Mexico and
C. chinense by the Incas in South America. Both are similar and
afforded each of these great civilizations much flavor in their
meals and considerable healing power in their respective medical
systems. Although some of these uses were identical, others were
not. Having traversed much of Central and South America in past
years when my time then allowed for greater field work than it
does now, I discovered that the descendants of both groups
employed their own species of capsicums to help stay *cool.*
Admittedly, this is a little strange at first glance, considering just
how hot these red peppers are. But once I started incorporating
tiny smidgens of the stuff in my own meals each day, I was pleas-
antly surprised to see how cool I really felt. The pungent principal
ingredient in them, called capsaicin, makes the body sweat more;
this, in turn, induces a cooling sensation over the whole system. I
found that by using small amounts of each of these capsicums on
a regular basis while down there enabled me to cope with the
intense heat and humidity a lot better.

The peoples of Mexico sometimes employed their own *C. annuum* in ways that the less cruel Incas would never have thought of. The following rather bizarre narrative was provided by Fray Diego Durán, a sixteenth-century Dominican friar, who was born in Spain but raised in Mexico. His firsthand experience of Mexican culture and fluency in Nahuatl (the ancient language spoken by the Aztecs of old) made him one of the most knowledgeable of the missionary-ethnographers of his time. He based his original *History of the Indies of New Spain* on a now-lost Nahuatl chronicle as well as on interviews with living Aztec informants.

The setting for the following historical quote went something like this. At an unspecified time in the distant past, the people of Cuetlaxtla were ruled by the Aztecs from Mexico City. They were artfully persuaded by their neighbors the Tlaxcalans to stop sending any more tribute to the Aztec capital. And, just in case the Aztecs retaliated against them for this deliberate neglect, the Tlaxcalans promised to come to the Cuetlaxtlas' immediate aid and help defend them.

That portion of Duran's narrative I wish to cite here comes from his two-volume work *Historia de las Indias de Nueva España y Islas de Tierra Firme* (Mexico City, D.F.: 1867–1880):

> When the royal tribute ceased arriving and the tribute collectors no longer came, Tlacaelel was advised of this. He communicated the ill news to the king, saying, "O Lord, the people of Cuetlaxtla have failed to send their tribute, and the governor has sent no word of this. Let us find out to what this negligence is due." So the king sent messengers, his couriers, who immediately left for Cuetlaxtla. When they arrived there, they were well received and were taken to the governor's house, where they were told to rest while the governor was notified. Then the lords of Cuetlaxtla closed the door of the chamber where the Aztec emissaries rested and set fire to a great pile of chile peppers that they had placed next to that room so the smoke would penetrate it. The smoke from the chiles, flowing into the chamber, was so great and so pungent that the Aztec envoys, trapped inside and unable to defend themselves, were suffocated.

No one probably has a better idea of the full extent of their excruciating suffering than does Cokie Roberts, a political analyst for National Public Radio and one of the on-air intellects for the regular ABC News program *This Week with David Brinkley.* Sometime in 1994, her husband Steven brought into their kitchen a basket filled with purple, red, green, and yellow peppers. Usually, he would hang all his chile peppers in the window to dry over the long winter months. But he decided that would take too long, so he opted for a quicker method by drying them in the microwave.

"Don't try it," she warned this author. "Toxic fumes will be the result. It was like someone had lobbed canisters of tear gas through the windows into our home. We were coughing uncontrollably. It was simply awful. I tried through the tears, choking, and sinus discharges to get the animals out of the house. Fortunately, we have lots of windows and doors in the kitchen, so we could blow the deadly fumes out. Then about seven o'clock at night my husband decides to take a nap before dinner, goes upstairs, and he can't breathe on the *second* floor. All the fumes had moved upstairs. We had to blow it out completely. I think we must have gassed the entire neighborhood," she concluded with a hearty laugh.

Most of the time, chiles were utilized for beneficial purposes in ancient America. For instance, whenever the Aztecs were exacting tribute from other Mesoamerican nations they had just conquered, they were known to be very lenient to their captives if such a vanquished people made a solemn oath to provide them with chiles, beans, corn, chia seed, "and all the vegetables and seeds they were accustomed to eat[ing]," Durán reported. Whenever an Aztec emperor saw one of his large public works projects completed by workmen, he would reward them, in part, with plenty of *C. annuum.* Durán noted this in his history about one of the kings named Motecuhzoma:

> Turning to the stonemasons, he then thanked them and gave orders that they be paid for their work. They were given many loads of maize, beans, and chiles, also mantles and clothing for their wives and children. Some loads of cacao were also given, to be divided among them, and each sculptor received a slave to serve him. The stonemasons were happy with these compensations and considered themselves well paid. . . .

It is sufficient to say that through the skillful domestication of the capsicums, the early people of the Americas were abundantly provided for so far as food flavoring and medicine went.

The China Connection:
Did Cayenne Come from the Orient?

The first chiles came in the form of tiny wild berries that grew on vines beneath the forest canopy of the mighty Amazon jungle in South America several thousand years ago. That isn't to say they originated there. Some scientists—myself for one—are of the strong opinion that chiles may have come from Southeast Asia, more specifically from China.

There is a little archaeological evidence that lends support to our theory. The early ceremonial center of Chavín de Huántar, which appears to have been founded around 900 B.C., contains a large temple from ancient times. This great structure lies on the outskirts of a small town of the same name, which is located in a fertile valley on the northwestern slope of the main range of the Peruvian Andes at an altitude of 10,200 feet at the headwaters of the mighty Amazon River.

Early in this century, a farmer poking among these temple ruins found a carved, rectangular granite shaft, which he hauled home in a wooden-wheeled cart drawn by llamas. It was later moved to a church, where Peruvian archaeologist Julio C. Tello rediscovered it in 1919. The Tello Obelisk (as it has come to be called ever since) currently resides on display in the Museo Nacional de Antropología y Arqueología in Pueblo Libre in the Peruvian capitol of Lima.

This stela (carved stone monument) measures 8 feet 3 inches tall by 12-1/2 inches, but narrowing to 10-1/2 inches, in width. On the obelisk are depicted two representations of a mythical being in the form of a black caiman (a small crocodile indigenous to Central and South America). In the claws of one alligator-like caiman are the blooms, leaves, and four pods of the genus *Capsicum.*

Archaeologists such as Robert Heine-Geldern and Betty J. Meggers believed that this earliest of advanced South American cultures originated in mainland China somewhere and eventually spread their influence across the Pacific Ocean to the western hemisphere. Those espousing such an idea are called diffusionists within archaeological circles. Writing specifically about the art between both civilizations in *Actas Del XXXIII Congreso Internacional de Americanistas* (San Jose, Costa Rica: Lehmann,

1959; pp. 321–326), Heine-Geldern made these worthwhile observations in regard to some of their cultural similarities:

> The only reasonable and, therefore, the only scientific explanation seems to me to be the conclusion that during the 8th century B.C. some kind of contact took place between China and Peru and that . . . the Chavin culture was to a certain extent *influenced by that of China.*
>
> I may add that Chinese influence in Peru seems to have continued through several centuries. [Italics added.]

More recently, Richard L. Burger has hinted at the same things. This professor of anthropology at Yale University and curator of South American Archaeology at the Yale Peabody Museum in New Haven, Connecticut, did a beautiful and thorough book on the subject, appropriately entitled *Chavin and the Origins of Andean Civilization* (London: Thames and Hudson, 1992). In it, he makes a fairly strong case for China being the likely "mother culture" for the great Chavin civilization of ancient Peru.

Such evidence implies then that the *Capsicum* genus may have in fact, originated in China or somewhere else in Southeast Asia and then later on been imported to Peru by Chinese seafarers. Assuming a likely correctness for this theory, one may wonder how chiles eventually made their way up to Central America. Max Uhle, the acknowledged "father of all Peruvian archaeology," suggested at the beginning of this century that visits of Maya sailors from Mesoamerica could have been the critical factor in the appearance of so much Peruvian civilization there. Not only his conclusion but the conclusion of other archaeologists lends further credence to Uhle's idea. Donald W. Lathrap devoted an entire chapter to "Relationships between Mesoamerica and the Andean Areas" in the multivolume series *Handbook of Middle American Indians* (Austin: University of Texas Press, 1966; Vol. 4, *Archaeological Frontiers and External Connections,* Chapter 13). He asserted with definiteness that maize or corn is an "indisputable indication" of migratory contact between ancient cultures in both geographical areas. Might we not also assume the same pattern for chiles?

Oriental Health Benefits of Red Pepper

The Chinese have long utilized red pepper for a variety of food functions and medicinal uses. In 1980, I was part of a group consisting of 28 third- and fourth-year medical students and five faculty advisers (myself included) who went to mainland China. The nearly monthlong trip was cosponsored by the American Medical Students' Association and the American Medical Association. We went there to investigate Chinese medicine in all of its facets, including the well-known systems of acupuncture and herbal therapy.

I learned much while we were there. In some ways, I still consider it to have been "the trip of a lifetime" for everyone concerned. We visited such facilities as the Shanghai Second Medical College and the Soochow Chinese Traditional Medical Hospital, where we got to see Chinese doctors in action and had a chance to interview them and their patients. I made extensive notes of everything I saw and heard. A large portion of the following data came from this trip as well as a later medical expedition I made with a group of Canadian doctors to Taiwan, the other China. Most of this information is presented here for the first time.

Blood Clots. These are semisolidified masses that can be formed in or out of the body. They can produce aneurysms or lead to strokes. Some Chinese doctors have made a tonic for this by boiling 1/4 teaspoon chopped red pepper (and its seeds) in 1/2 pint milk from a cow, goat, mare, or yak and then giving to their patients in divided doses (one cup morning and evening) when sufficiently cool. The idea for using the milk as a liquid medium instead of water seemed to be in reducing the pepper's fiery properties.

Bruises/Hematomas. Any superficial injury to the skin but without laceration produced by an impact and resulting in some temporary discoloration is regarded as a bruise. A hematoma is any localized collection of blood (usually clotted) found in an organ, space, or tissue due to a break in the wall of a blood vessel.

The treatment in China and Taiwan used for bruises or hematomas was an ointment applied to them every day for a week or until healing became evident. In one Taipei hospital, doctors informed my Canadian friends and me that 10 of their 14 patients thus treated were entirely cured, while 3 showed some improvement and 2 others did not. An average of 7 applications was used to ensure good results.

The mixture consisted of 1 part ground red pepper mixed with 5 parts melted Vaseline. After the petroleum jelly had congealed again, it was ready for external application.

Chilblains/Frostbite.   Chilblains are recurrent erythematous, often localized, and doughylike swelling of the skin brought on by exposure to damp, cold conditions. Chilblains are often accompanied by an itching and burning sensation. In children, the hands, feet, ears, and face are usually involved; in women, it always seems to be their legs and toes (probably due to short dresses and open shoes); and in men it's pretty much their hands and fingers. Frostbite is so well known that it needs little or no explanation. Suffice it to say, though, that it is local destruction of body tissue resulting from exposure to intense cold or to contact with extremely cold objects. In milder forms, it parallels chilblains to some extent.

In the city of Soochow (west of Shanghai a couple of hours by train ride), I discovered that doctors in the local hospital there made a weak decoction from red peppers for this very thing. Hospital staff prepared this extract by boiling 1/2 cup of cut-up red peppers in 2-1/2 quarts of water for 7 minutes and then straining off the residue. The liquid was used while warm to wash all affected areas of the skin.

In the northern part of the country, where it can get very cold, an alternative remedy was employed for the same purpose. One cup of Vaseline was slowly heated over the fire until it was melted. Then 1-1/2 tablespoons of finely ground red pepper (seeds included) and 2/3 tablespoon of camphor were stirred into the solution. It was then permitted to reharden before being rubbed on the chilblains or frostbitten areas. Doctors in the hospital we visited in Inner Mongolia told us that the best results were obtained by rubbing the liquid decoction or ointment on the hands and feet of those suffering from either condition. In a study of 200 patients treated daily for 1-1/2 weeks with the decoction alone, 94 percent were reported cured; another 4 percent had modest response, while a mere 2 percent received no benefit at all.

Lumbago/Neuralgia/Rheumatism. Lumbago is a pain in the lower lumbar region (back and buttocks) of the body and is due to poor blood circulation. Neuralgia is a pain extending along the course of one or more nerves. And rheumatism can be any one of a variety of disorders usually characterized by inflammation, degeneration, or metabolic derangement of the connective-tissue structures of the body. It is attended by pain, stiffness, or limited movement.

Use either the weak decoction mentioned under **Chilblains** or the ointment recommended under **Bruises/Hematomas** for any of these conditions.

Sciatica. This is a syndrome marked by pain radiating from the back into the buttock and into the lower extremity along its posterior or lateral aspect. It can also have reference to any kind of pain along the course of the sciatic nerve itself.

Consult the foregoing **Lumbago/Neuralgia/Rheumatism** for ways of utilizing red pepper to bring relief to this syndrome.

Snakebite. I saw several different treatments for poisonous snakebites while I was in China and Taiwan on different occasions. Each method involved the use of red pepper in some way. In the Soochow Chinese Traditional Medical Hospital, patients were given eight chile peppers intact and told to chew and swallow them with some goat or yak milk. Soon their inflammations and pains subsided. Doctors showed me blisters that soon appeared over the bite marks; eventually runny, yellow matter was secreted through the blisters during the recovery process.

A slight variation of the same method was to have patients chew the chile peppers first and then apply them directly over the wounded areas; a little adhesive tape held these oral poultices in place. Doctors theorized that the combination of human saliva and the capsaicin itself within the peppers chemically interacted with the rich protein complex of the snake venom, rendering it inert.

Sprains. This may be defined as being a joint injury in which some of the fibers in a supporting ligament are ruptured but the continuity of the ligament remains intact. I was very impressed with the approach taken by the Chinese toward this problem. Two pans or buckets of water would be set before the patient. One of them was filled with a *hot,* weak decoction of red peppers (1/2 cup chopped red peppers boiled in 1 gallon of water for 15 minutes). The water was *not* scalding, however, so as to injure the skin, only hot. The other container consisted of cold water; sometimes ice or snow would be put into the water, if such were available.

Patients were then instructed to immerse their sprained limbs in the hot-pepper water first for about 45 seconds before plunging them into the cold water for the same length of time. This back-and-forth routine usually lasted until the hot water became cool and the cold water turned mildly warm. The procedure was repeated every 4 to 6 hours twice or three times daily for several days.

When a large portion of the body suffered serious strain (such as the back), clean hand towels were used instead. They would be immersed into either container of water, lightly wrung out, and then immediately placed upon the patient and covered over with a second, dry towel to retain the heat or cold as long as possible.

These methods worked equally well for severe contusions.

Thrombosis. This is the formation or presence of aggregated blood due to vascular obstruction at the points of its development. It is more than just simple coagulation of the blood or clot development.

I have always been intrigued with the extremely low incidence of thrombosis and clots in the Orient. Unlike Western cultures, which seem to have very high rates of them, Orientals are relatively free from thrombosis and clots. I remember reading some years ago in an old issue of *The Journal of The American Medical Association (JAMA)* a report from a group of medical doctors practicing in Thailand. They noted how thrombosis and clots were virtually absent in the Thai people. They attributed this to the frequent consumption of the *Capsicum* genus.

I believe that if those over the age of 50, who seem to be the most susceptible to those things, would take at least one gelatin capsule of powdered cayenne pepper each day with a meal or a glass of milk or tomato juice, they would be able to prevent the formation of thrombosis or clots within their systems.

Thumb Sucking/Nail Biting. This one comes from a number of old Chinese grandmothers I interviewed years ago while in China and Taiwan. A very weak decoction was made by simmering 1/4 teaspoon cut red peppers in two cups water. After the solution had sufficiently cooled, dutiful grandmothers would then paint some of this liquid extract on the *nails* of the thumbs and fingers of their infant grandchildren with any small, thin brush used by regular artists. They guaranteed it worked every time to keep thumbs and fingers out of young babies' mouths. And by doing it on their nails like this, it didn't injure their skin.

Varicose Veins. One thing that has forcibly struck me every time I've traveled to Southeast Asia is that the greater majority of Oriental women *do not* suffer from ugly and unsightly varicose veins the way American and European women do. Nor do the Mexican or Maya women of Central America whom I've interviewed in times past. I attribute this medical phenomenon in some way *directly* to their *daily* consumption of chiles.

Ranking the Chiles According to Their Heat Intensity

All peppers are members of the genus *Capsicum* and the family *Solanaceae,* or nightshade family, which includes eggplant, potatoes, and tomatoes. The name *Capsicum* comes from the Greek word *kapto,* which signifies "to bite." While many domesticated varieties of the *Capsicum* species, such as green bell peppers and paprikas, don't "bite," the wilder varieties range from mild to very pungent. This is an action of the substance capsaicin, an alkaloid that is the heat-producing agent in the pepper.

I asked Barry Green, a researcher at the Monell Chemical Senses Center in Philadelphia, exactly how this substance behaved in the body. He has studied capsaicin probably as long as anyone has and seems to know quite a bit about it. This is how he described its effect on the human nervous system. "Capsaicin activates pain receptors in the tongue, as well as neurons that respond to warmth, thereby giving a sensation of heat. Among the sequelae: watering eyes, running noses, sweaty foreheads, and mottled skin." (Apparently, barnacles have pain receptors too. There is a boat paint available from marine supply houses called Barnacle Ban that contains 22 percent cayenne pepper.)

Chiles can hurt, and cops know it. In a day and age in which many law-enforcement officers are being continually hampered from carrying out their full protective duties by the presumed rights of criminals, there are nonlethal weapons that can stop the bad guys cold in their tracks. I spoke with one Phoenix police officer by the name of Lt. Andy Anderson in the summer of 1994. He showed me a small 2-ounce canister of a cayenne-based spray called Punch II. The all-natural weapon contains a very potent dose of the oleoresin capsaicin. "Enough," noted Lt. Anderson, "to make even the toughest thug a whimpering, whining, blubbering idiot within moments after being sprayed with it."

Punch II is intended to be sprayed from a distance of 4 to 10 feet. A one-second burst is usually all that's necessary to stop a charging, 200-pound attacker. The 2-ounce canister holds 60 one-second bursts of spray. My informant observed that the acquisition of this pepper spray had been in the works for more than a year. The FBI Academy in Quantico, Virginia, tested an assortment of sprays and other chemical agents from 1987 through 1989 and judged pepper sprays to be the most effective.

The pepper spray irritates eyes, causing them to swell shut. It also temporarily restricts breathing. "It totally shuts the person down we want to apprehend," Lt. Anderson said. "It makes the individual want to stop and give up immediately without further resistance. We're able to deal with them more effectively this way."

The effects of this cayenne pepper spray last about 45 minutes; however, respiration clears up in a couple of minutes, and vision returns to normal within five minutes. Punch II has proven to be a much more effective nonlethal weapon than a stun gun or tear-gas sprays such as Mace. Lt. Anderson stated, for the record, that he would rather disarm an armed attacker with something like this than have to shoot him (or her) with his service revolver.

Also, he noted, "I don't need to use any choke holds to subdue an aggressive suspect. And anyone high on drugs or alcohol can just be given a squirt of this stuff in the face and brought down very quickly without any of us [the police] having to resort to a higher level of deadly physical force to do the same job."

Currently, there are more than 1,000 hot sauces sold in America. Some of them bear such names as Capital Punishment, Vampfire, 911, Bat's Brew, Hellfire & Damnation, Pure Hell, Devil's Tingle, Devil Drops, Hell-in-a-Bottle, Satan's Sauce, Lucifer Lingering, Fiery Inferno, and Mad Dog. It seems as if manufacturers these days have come a long way from the Tabasco sauce of yesteryear.

There is a nationwide organization called the Chili Appreciation Society International (CASI). Their Houston chapter holds monthly meetings during which time several of these aforementioned brands or others are routinely sampled by the membership. I attended one of their meetings sometime in 1994 just for the heck of it. The club president, called the Great Pepper, asked for silence. He then placed his left hand on his stomach and gravely intoned the chapter's CASI oath, which I found hard not to laugh through:

> I pledge allegiance to CASI and to the camaraderie for which it stands, one comestible indigestible, with heartburn and gas pains for all. So help me, Chiligula.

After finishing up there I next flew to Albuquerque, New Mexico, where I was guest of honor at the National Fiery Food Show. There was everything imaginable to be sampled, besides chile dishes: There was chile beer, chile ice cream, and even chile chocolate cake. But in all of my travels to such events, I have yet to find anyone who's come up with the ultimate form of *Capsicum* pain: a nonfiltered chile cigarette!

I should probably mention my recent encounter with David Letterman while in New York City on business in the spring of 1995. I was ushered into his office on the twelfth floor of the Ed Sullivan Theater at 1697 Broadway with a friend. We noticed that

Letterman has a shelf display of some two dozen brands of hot sauce. And they weren't there just for show either.

"I love food that does something to you other than make you fat," the CBS nightly talk show host explained when he finally came into the room a few minutes later. "I like to interact with my food: You bite it and it hurts you back r-e-a-l good!"

He told us of his experience with one of the hottest peppers on earth. "I got hold of some Scotch bonnet. Boy, are those babies hot, most powerful things I have ever eaten in my entire life. My first reaction was, `OK, that's not so bad.' And then my tongue went numb all of a sudden and I started to sweat like mad. I felt myself going down . . . down . . . down."

Dave then demonstrated for us how it felt, by slightly bending over, placing his hands on his knees, and slowly doing this crazed, hyperventilating thing. "It's great fun, though," he summed up. "And there's no weight gain afterwards," he said with a flashy grin.

Believe it or not, there is an exact science in determining how hot, hot, hot a chile pepper really is. The system was developed by Wilbur L. Scoville, a pharmacologist for the company that developed the muscle-treating salve HEET. Depending on the number of units given a particular mixture of ground chile, sugar water, and alcohol, he would grade each type of pepper accordingly.

Today, the process is done by computers using high-performance liquid chromatography, a method of analyzing chemical compounds—in this case the chemical capsaicin. Liquid chromatography tells, in parts per million, how much capsaicin pepper has. In simple terms, the Scoville test measures the strength of an individual pepper by dilutability; a ranking of 5,000 Scoville units means you could dilute a sample of the chile in question with 5,000 times as much water and still taste hotness.

Having given you the heat intensity of many of the world's leading chiles, it seems only fitting and appropriate now to conclude this section with the most effective antidote for a mouth burning from chile backdraft. Numerous studies have shown that dairy products such as milk, cream, sour cream, ice cream, and yogurt are the most effective cool-downs. The protein casein in milk and milk products acts like a detergent of sorts and literally

The Chile Heat Scale

Rating	Scoville Units	Chile Varieties
10	100,000–300,000	Habanero, Scotch Bonnet, Macho, Bahamian
9	50,000–100,000	Santaka, Chiltepin, Thai, Tabasco, Jamaican Hot, Brazilian Malagueta
8	30,000–50,000	Aji, Rocoto, Pequín, Cayenne, Tepín, Peruvian
7	15,000–30,000	del Arbol, Serrano Seco, Peter Pepper, Tuxtla, Amatista
6	5,000–15,000	Yellow Wax Hot, Serrano, Manzana, Fiesta/Fips, Pico de Pajaro, Korean, Pasilla de Oaxaca, Chiltepe, Dutch Red, Mora, Pulla, Santa Fe Grande, Fresno Red, Morita, Costeno
5	2,500–5,000	Jalapeño, Mirasol, Patzcuaro, Huachinango, Chipotle, Catarina, Pepperoncini, Pasado, Chilcostle
4	1,500–2,500	Sandia, Casabel, Onza, Güero, Chilhuacle Negro, De Agua, Chihuacle Amarillo, Costeño Amarillo
3	1,000–1,500	Ancho, Pasilla, Español, Chawa, New Mexico Greens and Reds, Chilaca, Poblano Greens and Reds, Chilhuacle Rojo
2	500–1,000	Mulato, Guajillo, New Mexico Eclipse, New Mexico Sunset, New Mexico Sunrise, New Mexico Miniatures, Anaheim Greens & Reds, Ají Mirasol
1	100–500	R-Naky, MexiBell, Hungarian Cherry Pepper, Ají Panca, Pimento
0	0	Sweet Purple Pepper, Hungarian Sweet Chile, Bell Peppers (Violet, Yellow, Orange, Red, Green, and Blond)

wipes or strips the chile capsaicin from its nerve receptors within the mouth. So, the next time you imagine yourself brave enough to try a hot chile and find your mouth instantly on fire, do what I've done: Hold a cup of cream next to your bottom lip and hang your tongue in it for awhile.

Chemical Composition of Red Peppers

As mentioned earlier, the pungent principle in many types of different chiles is capsaicin. This compound represents an extensively investigated group of compounds collectively known as capsaicinoids. Current cultivars grown in Mexico, Korea, and Thailand have a capsaicin (plus other capsaicinoids) content reaching and occasionally even exceeding 1 percent. Cultivars grown in Africa are more potent as a rule, with capsaicin contents reaching 1.5 percent or more.

The biological significance of capsaicin in the plant remains unclear, although a number of different proposals have included a role for the compound in defense of the fruit through deterrence of birds and insects. The capsaicinoid content is genetically controlled, but is subject to environmental variables such as light, temperature, soil moisture, and fertilization level.

The carotenoids are some of the most widespread and important pigments in living organisms. Although usually masked by chlorophyll, this group of compounds has been observed through-

out the plant kingdom and has been detected in insects, birds, fish, and other forms of animal life. As pigments, these compounds provide a range of colors from light yellow to dark red and, when combined with proteins into various chemical complexes, form green and blue colors. This wide range of possible colors makes carotenoids an important coloring agent in a wide variety of foods and feeds and in natural sources of food color extracts, including annato, paprika, saffron, and palm oil. The most recent compendium of carotenoids, according to the *Phytochemical Dictionary: A Handbook of Bioactive Compounds from Plants* (London: Taylor & Francis, 1993), lists some 563 pigments that have been isolated and characterized. More than 50 carotenoids are known to be metabolized into vitamin A by a variety of animal species.

As one of the richest sources of carotenoids among vegetable crops, red peppers have considerable commercial significance as colorants in the food and cosmetic industries. The ketoxanthophylls capsanthin and capsorubin are the major pigments contributing to the red color of the chile species, whereas betacarotene and zeaxanthin are responsible for the yellow-orange colors. During fruit ripening in the chiles, a rapid synthesis of ketoxanthophylls occurs, being formed from beta-cryptoxanthin, anthraxanthin, and violaxanthin.

Red peppers are particularly high in ascorbic acid, being the richest sources of vitamin C among the vegetable kingdom. They were used by the famous Hungarian scientist Albert Szent-Gyorgy for the first extraction of vitamin C; in 1937, he won the Nobel Prize for physiology and medicine. In some cultivars of paprika, the content of vitamin C can reach 340 milligrams for every 100 grams of fresh pepper fruit. Unhappily for chile lovers, though, the vitamin C content of dried chile or paprika is minimal due to an almost total loss during processing and storage.

The concentration of vitamin E in red pepper appears in a moderate amount of a collection of chemically related compounds known as tocopherols. The amount of alpha-tocopherol in paprika is usually double that for green bell pepper. The alpha-tocopherol content of red pepper is quite stable during storage, provided a relatively high water content is maintained. Indeed, the loss of alpha-tocopherol during dehydration is minimal, in sharp contrast to loss of vitamin C. (I am grateful to the Haworth Press for permission to use selected excerpts from a lengthy review of the capsicums by D. Palevitch and L. E. Craker, published in their *Journal of Herbs, Spices & Medicinal Plants* 3(2):58–64, 1995.)

Medicinal Applications of Cayenne for Other Disorders

Earlier in the text, there was a discussion of some of the health benefits of cayenne in various parts of the Orient. About 15 different disorders were cited for such possible benefits and explanations given as to how red pepper might be of some advantage to them. They included: blood clots; bruises/hematomas; chilblains/frostbite; lumbago/neuralgia/rheumatism; sciatica; snakebite; sprains; thrombosis; thumb sucking/nail biting; and varicose veins.

Beyond these problems, however, cayenne has some additional therapeutic possibilities with a number of other disorders. The following information has been gleaned from several different sources—my own investigative research conducted on numerous trips around the world and the published data of other scientists. The material being offered here is quite reliable and may be safely used, but should never take the place of regular medical care. Instead such folk remedies should become an *added* part of normal allopathic practices.

Alcoholism. Dr. Norman Felter, a Pennsylvania physician, treats alcoholics with his own version of what he calls a "virgin bloody Mary." It consists of an 8-ounce glass of tomato juice in which is mixed 1/4 teaspoon cayenne pepper, 1 teaspoon each of the citrus juices of grapefruit, lemon, and lime, and 1/2 teaspoon granulated kelp. One of these is drunk on an empty stomach in the late morning and again in the early evening hours. He has had much success with this procedure in helping alcoholics break their drinking habits.

Allergies. A homeopathic doctor from Philadelphia told this author a couple of years ago at a natural health convention in that city what he did for his patients who suffered from excessive mucus accumulations in their lungs due to food-related allergies (especially to dairy products and eggs). "I have them season their food with a pinch of cayenne pepper instead of using regular salt and black pepper," he said. "I find that it helps to strip the phlegm out of their throats and lungs and enables them to breathe better." He also puts them on a restricted diet, which omits the offending foods to which his patients are allergic.

Angina Pectoris. This same homeopathic practitioner also explained to me how he prepared a simple tincture of cayenne pepper for treating the presenting symptom in those of his patients suffering from coronary artery disease. "I combine 3 ounces of cayenne pepper with 1 ounce of powdered lobelia with about 10 ounces of Russian vodka," he said. "I then let this stand for two weeks, shaking it 2 or 3 times daily. Afterwards I strain the liquid through coffee-filter paper and then evenly distribute it into dark amber bottles, which helps it keep better." He instructs his patients to take 15 drops beneath the tongue twice daily.

Arteriosclerosis. To prevent a thickening and hardening of the walls of the arteries, my doctor informant mentioned that a combination of cayenne pepper (2 capsules), Japanese aged garlic extract from Hiroshima (3 capsules), and ocean kelp (1 capsule) each day with a meal is a good supplementary program to be on for this problem.

Arthritis. In the last half of this decade, roughly 1,327 scientific studies on cayenne pepper's most active ingredient, capsaicin, have appeared in numerous medical and scientific journals. The majority confirm what many lay people have known for years—that red pepper does, indeed, relieve the pain, inflammation, and joint stiffness of arthritis sufferers.

Lab chemists designate capsaicin as trans-8-methyl-N-vanillyl-6-nonenamide. This jaw-breaking chemical appears in different salves or creams that, when rubbed upon the surface of the skin, penetrate to arthritic joints, where capsaicin halts the destruction of bone cartilage, relieves excruciating pain, and increases joint flexibility quite a bit.

In order to properly evaluate the benefits of such topically applied products containing capsaicin, a team of doctors from the University of Miami School of Medicine in Florida conducted a double-blind study on almost a hundred patients suffering from either rheumatoid arthritis or osteoarthritis. Patients were instructed to rub a 0.025-percent-strength capsaicin cream or a plain cream to their swollen joints four times each day. The majority of them did so on their knees.

Patient responses were tracked through exact measurements and physical movement and pain, as well as through individual subjective reports about whether each patient felt better or worse. Those using the capsaicin cream had a clear reduction of pain after only two months; in three months better than 80 percent of the participants applying the cream containing this constituent of red pepper reported having remarkably fewer arthritic symptoms, including less morning stiffness. In contrast to this, though, fewer than 55 percent of those using the lookalike placebo or plain cream felt better.

The only unpleasant side effects to be observed in about 50 percent of the group was a localized burning sensation during the first several weeks of the study. But after three months, just a trio of the 96 patients said burning was still a problem.

A doctor from Case-Western Reserve University School of Medicine in Cleveland, Ohio, recommends that of the two strengths of capsaicin cream currently sold—0.025 percent and 0.075 percent—the latter one or higher strength cream ought to be the preferred cream if no relief is felt from the lower one. Chad Deal, M.D., the physician giving this advice, mentioned that only a small dab, about the size of a pea, should be squeezed onto the skin covering the affected joint and slowly massaged in using a circular motion of the fingers to do so until no residue remains. This procedure should be repeated about every 4 hours, 4 times a day, and up to 12 weeks at a time.

All of these capsaicin creams are quite expensive, though. Zostrix, for instance, one of the best-known brands, costs $25 an ounce for the treatment of arthritic pain. But you can make your own cayenne salve at home and save big bucks besides. How much? How about just *20 cents an ounce*! I am indebted to herbalist Jeanne Rose of San Francisco for an abbreviated version of a more lengthy recipe she formulated years ago and included in her book, *The Aromatherapy Book: Applications & Inhalations.*

Jeanne Rose Chile Cream

15 tbsps. chiles, finely chopped with the seeds intact
1 quart extra-virgin olive oil
2 tbsps. melted beeswax
40 drops of lavender oil

Combine the chilies and the olive oil in a saucepan and bring to a slow, rolling boil. Reduce the heat and simmer the contents very gently for 3-1/2 hours. Then let it cool down for the same length of time. Repeat this procedure twice more.

Place the mixture in a Vita-Mix whole food machine or equivalent blender and blend on high speed for 30 seconds. Strain the mixture through a wire sieve that has been lined with either muslin cloth or pantyhose.

Put into a ceramic or stainless-steel bowl and add the hot, melted beeswax and lavender oil. Stir thoroughly before pouring into small bottles. Cap with tight-fitting lids and store in a cool, dry place until needed.

Circulation. Priddy Meeks was one of the most famous frontier herb doctors in the early Utah Territory. He kept a very detailed journal of his many life's experiences. This "Journal of Priddy Meeks" was published over half a century ago in the *Utah State Historical Society Quarterly* (10:145–223, October 1942). The following episode appeared on page 207 of said publication, showing the use of red pepper reviving frozen limbs.

"An incident took place in Parowan, Iron County, the same winter [1857–1858] that Colonel [Albert Sidney] Johnston came against Salt Lake City with the United States Army [on orders of U.S. President James Buchanan]. There was a teamster by the name of James McCann, a young man, who started to go back to the states by way of California. He reached Parowan [18 miles northeast of Cedar City in southern Utah] with both feet frozen above his ankles. He was left with me to have both feet amputated as it was thought there was no possible chance to save his life without amputation. I was at my wits end to know what to do. I saw no possible chance for amputation. An impulse seemed to strike my mind as tho by [divine] inspiration that I would give him cayenne pepper inwardly and see what effect that would have on the frozen feet.

"I commenced by giving him rather small doses at first, about three times a day. It increased the warmth and power of action in the blood to such a degree that it gave him such pain and misery in his legs that he could not bear it. He lay down on his back and elevated his feet up against the wall for three or four days and then he would sit up in a chair. The frozen flesh would rot and rope down from his foot when it would be on his knee, clear down to the floor, just like a buck-wheat batter, and the new flesh would form as fast as the dead flesh would get out of the way. In fact the new flesh would seem to crowd the dead flesh out of the way to make room for the new flesh.

"That was all the medical treatment he had and to my astonishment and to every one else that knew of the circumstances, the sixteenth day after I gave him the first dose of pepper he walked nine miles, or from Parowan to Red Creek and back, and said that he could have walked as far again. He lost but five toe nails all told. Now the healing power of nature is in the blood and to accelerate the blood is to accelerate the healing power of nature and I am convinced that there is nothing will do this like cayenne pepper; you will find it applicable in all cases of sickness."

Melissa T. Stock shared this experience a year ago. "The truth of the matter is that I have extraordinarily poor circulation. Not a big deal, unless those frigid footsies happen to touch someone in the night. My loving husband still agreed to marry me despite the fact that I would probably wear wool socks to bed, winter and summer alike, for the next century or so.

"And then there was cayenne pepper. For the last month I have been taking cayenne pepper capsules (3 a day) and am happy to report that I have been virtually sockless since. My hands and feet *really* have warmed up. And I seem to have more energy, too. And since we don't have any children yet, I'm a little worried about taking any more cayenne—you never know what might happen!"

Cluster Headaches. A nasal application of capsaicin greatly relieved symptoms among 52 patients suffering from cluster headaches. Seventy percent of the patients benefited when the capsaicin was applied to the nostril on the same side as the headache. When capsaicin was applied to the opposite nostril, patients didn't improve that much, according to a report that appeared in the medical journal *Pain* (59:321–325, December 1994).

Common Cold. The following proven remedy comes from a geologist by the name of J. Michael Queen, Ph.D. He swears by the stuff and claims that it is the best thing he's ever tried for getting rid of mucus, drying up a runny nose, reducing fever, and stopping the pain usually associated with a common cold. He says that this tonic should be used during the cold and flu season to help ward off any impending symptoms.

Capsicum Cold Remedy and Tonic

1 inch-long piece of ginger
1-1/4 cups hot water
1 rounded tbsp. lavender flowers
frozen lemonade concentrate, to taste
1/4 tsp. cayenne pepper powder

Mash the ginger in a garlic press and place the juice and pulp into a small bowl. Add the hot water and lavender, and steep for 3 to 5 minutes. Strain the liquid into a cup and add the lemonade concentrate and cayenne. Drink the entire mixture.

Steve Worthington of Eugene, Oregon, passed on this little remedy that his grandmother has used for years to treat the colds that simply refuse to go away after being treated with everything imaginable under the sun.

Hot Cayenne Tea

1 quart distilled water
1 tsp. cayenne pepper powder
2 bouillon cubes, chicken or beef

Heat the water and add the other ingredients. Slowly sip one cup of this savory brew on an empty stomach every few hours. This is a simplified version of a Jewish grand-

*mother's chicken soup recipe for colds (assuming that
chicken bouillon cubes are used to make this tea effective
for a quick recovery).*

Cuts. Some years ago while eating a meal in a local vegetarian restaurant here in Salt Lake City, I met with a slight accident that required some quick thinking to immediately correct. I was cutting a garlic breadstick lengthwise with a serrated steak knife. While I was doing so, I kept on talking to my lady friend across the table from me and failed to watch my other actions more carefully. The result was that I sliced the web of skin between my thumb and forefinger about a quarter of an inch deep.

Blood started oozing out of the wound. I got up and walked over to the serving window from which waitresses picked up their orders. I asked the cook inside the kitchen to give me the cayenne-pepper box sitting on a shelf over the stove. He did so, and I took a clean tablespoon and dipped it into the container and got enough cayenne pepper to sprinkle on my injury. Within less than a minute *all bleeding had completely ceased.* I left the pepper in place for about two hours before gently washing it and the congealed blood away.

I was amazed at just how efficiently the wound had closed and healing ensued with something so simple as this wonderful flavoring spice.

Diabetes. Years ago, while scanning through some obscure medical journals in the vast archives of the huge National Library of Medicine in Bethesda, Maryland, I found in one of them a significant article on the effects of capsicum and other spices on blood-sugar levels. According to the *West Indian Medical Journal* (31:194–197, 1982), when a cayenne-pepper water extract was administered to anesthetized mongrel dogs via stomach tubes, it produced *significant* hypoglycemic effects upon their systems that lasted up to four hours.

This preliminary investigation tells us two things. First of all, those who have low blood sugar or already suffer from hypoglycemia need to *avoid* using cayenne pepper, as it will only aggravate their existing symptoms, making them feel more fatigued and cranky and restless while at sleep. (Along with cayenne pepper, garlic, onions, goldenseal, and pau d'arco also need to be avoided as they tend to plunge blood sugar levels dramatically.)

But the upside to this research strongly suggests that cayenne pepper and the other aforementioned herbs will be of definite benefit to those suffering from diabetes mellitus. An average of three capsules of capsicum per day is recommended. Keep in mind, however, that this doesn't mean cayenne pepper will cure diabetes. Instead, it will help the body to reduce the amount of glucose in the circulating blood plasma, which means *less* intake of synthetic insulin every day for those who have insulin-dependent diabetes.

Food Poisoning. If you've ever suffered ptomaine poisoning caused by contaminated raw oysters or bad sushi, then you won't want to miss this bit of valuable information. Scientists working out of the Louisiana State University Medical Center in the capital of Baton Rouge recently reported a series of tests performed on a bacterium, *Vibrio vulnificus.* It is found in some raw oysters and produces symptoms ranging from mild diarrhea to fatal blood poisoning.

An effective way of destroying this dangerous bacterium was revealed by these scientists at an American Society for Microbiology meeting in October 1993. There they recounted their experiments with test tubes full of oyster bacteria. Ordinary ketchup added to the test tubes did nothing. Lemon juice worked tolerably well, as did horseradish. But a well-known brand of hot sauce loaded with chile peppers killed *all* bacteria in one minute flat. Even when it was diluted with only 1 part to 16 parts of water, the red sauce still performed admirably and killed all the bacteria in five minutes.

"Some of the findings were a little astonishing to us," Dr. Kenneth Aldridge, one of the researchers, told the assembled conference delegates. "We had no idea these condiments would be so powerful." They also tested three other varieties of *Vibrio* bacteria, as well as *E. coli, shigella,* and *salmonella.* Hot sauce killed them all.

If seafood lovers ever needed a reason for using hot sauce, they have it now. Could there be a bright future for sushi and sashimi when cayenne pepper is simultaneously taken with them? Undoubtedly so, thought some of these LSU scientists when briefly interviewed by this author over the telephone.

Heart Arrhythmias. According to different news reports, researchers from the Bristol-Myers Squibb Pharmaceutical Research Institute in Princeton, New Jersey, conducted animal studies using capsaicin in which ventricular tachycardias and ventricular fibrillations were greatly reduced. For humans suffering from these types of serious heart arrhythmias, it should come as no surprise that capsaicin functions as a natural calcium blocker, analogous to the effect of some heart drugs routinely prescribed by many cardiologists for such symptoms. An average of 2 capsules of cayenne pepper daily with a meal is suggested.

Hypoglycemia. As previously mentioned under the entry for diabetes, cayenne pepper is *not* suitable for anyone suffering from the effects of low blood sugar.

Hypothermia. Carol Helfrick of San Jose, California, shared this with others in the latter part of 1993. "When I travel to cold climates, I carry gelatin capsules of cayenne pepper along. I open a capsule, pour the contents into my hands, and rub the pepper into my feet. Or, if my feet are cold, I will rely on the following remedy: I put finely ground capsicum in a box and use a powder puff to lightly powder my feet with the pepper. I then put my socks on, and I'm ready to go forth." She mentioned that the capsules of red pepper can be purchased at any health-food store or herb shop. She also warned that the hands should be thoroughly washed with soap and warm water after applying the capsicum. If this isn't done, then the red pepper is apt to be transferred from the hands to the face where it can greatly irritate the eyes and mucous membranes.

Influenza. Many years ago (in 1979, to be exact) I journeyed with other scientists on a historic trip to the then Soviet Union. We were there for almost a month as guests of the Soviety Academy of Sciences. We saw and heard a lot and had a chance to meet many interesting people. Among the things I came away with, related to my own field of medicinal plant expertise, was a recipe for a curious Russian folk medicine product designed espe-

cially for colds and influenza. It was called adzhiga (also spelled adjikha or adzhika) and was used in much the same way as we would use salsa today. It was terrific for curing the worst kinds of respiratory ailments, including the common cold, the flu, and even bronchial pneumonia. A little bit was spread on some dark rye bread or a saltine cracker and consumed that way by the sick person several times a day and always on an empty stomach. Recovery was generally very rapid after a few snacks of this.

Russian Salsa

3 red bell peppers, stems and seeds removed, chopped
3 red jalapeños, stems and seeds removed
2 miniature tomatoes, peeled and chopped
8 large cloves garlic, peeled and chopped
1/2 tsp. salt to taste (omit if you have hypertension)

Place all of these ingredients in a Vita-Mix whole food machine or equivalent blender and puree until smooth for about 1-1/2 minutes. Put into several small empty baby-food jars and keep refrigerated. Yields about 2 cups. (In the former USSR, peasant folks would put everything through a meat grinder due to shortages of electric food processors.)

Mouth Sores. Take a pinch of cayenne pepper and mix it with the oil squeezed from the end of two gelatin capsules of vitamin E that have been pricked with a pin. Then apply this mixture on top of a small square slice of white bread onto which a thin layer of creamy peanut butter has been spread. (The peanut butter is for helping it stick in the mouth longer.) This small bread poultice can then be inserted through the mouth directly onto a cold sore and left in place for an hour or more. Repeat the same procedure twice daily.

Neck Pain. Paul and Barbara Stitt run a bakery, Natural Ovens, in Manitowoc County, Wisconsin. But they also believe very much in the powers of hot peppers. After discovering and researching the properties of cayenne pepper, Stitt, a biochemist by training, decided to design a program to give away free cayenne capsules to anyone in their county interested in improving his or her health.

Since January 1995, more than a thousand families have signed up for the program, which includes recommended diet changes, a medical history, and follow-up meetings at the bakery with program facilitator Paula Wagner. Wagner, a longtime bakery employee, mentioned that she loved working with the people on the program and has seen incredible results from the participants.

"Each day brings with it more incredible news of the many different ways that people are being helped with cayenne. Just the other day a lady came in and told me that she had suffered a lot of pain from a serious whiplash injury she had sustained months ago in a rear-end collision with another car. But after getting some capsules from us and starting to take them, she noticed the pain beginning to diminish. She stated that after six weeks or so of being on the cayenne, the pain just disappeared. These are the kinds of things we hear around here on a fairly regular basis. Cayenne pepper must be one of God's gifts to humanity."

Old Age. One of the contributing factors believed by many doctors to be responsible for the aging process is the frequent consumption of oxidized foods, particularly things that include oxidized dietary fats. A husband-wife team of Connecticut-based analytical chemists cooked up batches of capsaicin, the key component of cayenne pepper, at about 400° F. for two hours—with and without oleic acid, the primary monounsaturate in both olive and canola oils. They analyzed the resulting heat-fostered breakdown products with gas chromatography and mass spectrometry. They noted in the November 1995 *Journal of Agricultural and Food Chemistry* that although oleic acid usually oxidizes readily when heated, this oxidation "appears to be inhibited by the presence of capsaicin." And though they used rich mixes of capsaicin to oil (10 to 50 percent by weight), they also heated the oil for a long time. Still, in batches containing capsaicin, they detected less than 10 percent of oleic's normal oxidation products—usually just 1 to 2 percent of those seen when the fatty acid was heated alone. The couple, David E. and Susan K. Henderson of Hartford, think they may have detected a previously undiscovered antioxidant within capsaicin. If this is the case, then it certainly lends weight to the theory of utilizing cayenne pepper more often in the diet as one gets older. Because the more antioxidants there are in an older body, the less amount of free radicals there will be, which is one of the main causes of aging.

Psoriasis. An interesting study on red pepper appeared in the September 1993 issue of the *Journal of the American Academy of Dermatology.* In research conducted on 200 patients with psoriasis, the application of a 0.025 percent capsaicin cream significantly reduced itching, scaling, thickness, and redness compared with patients who used a plain cream for placebo purposes.

Raynaud's Phenomenon. For those unfamiliar with this vasospastic disorder, a brief description might be helpful. This progressive disease involves the fingers and is nearly always found in women from ages 15 to 45, but sometimes occurs in men, too. Symptoms include a whiteness of the fingertips with cold exposure, accompanied by numbness, paresthesias, cyanosis, then redness and pain with warming. A slow ulceration of the finger pads may take place, especially during cold weather spells.

David Roche contributed the following experience he had with the healing benefits of red pepper for his own problem. "I was diagnosed as having Raynaud's phenomenon awhile back. I had tried using niacin, but encountered too many flushing symptoms to continue using it. Other treatments seemed to work pretty well for me, but were a real pain to do. In one of your herb books, you mentioned that cayenne is good for blood circulation. So I took your suggestion and went to a local herb shop and bought myself some gelatin capsules of cayenne pepper. I started taking two a day with food of some kind in November of one year. I noticed that all winter long my hands stayed nice and warm. This may help some of your readers out there if they suffer from this circulatory disorder."

Skin Injuries. Can something as extraordinarily hot as cayenne pepper actually be of potential benefit in relieving the excruciating pain of burn victims? That appears to be the consensus of opinion of a team of doctors at Johns Hopkins University School of Medicine in Baltimore, Maryland. Richard A. Meyer and his colleagues injected a capsaicin analog under the skin of one inner forearm of each of eight volunteers. The volunteers received a control injection of an inactive substance in the other inner forearm. The volunteers reported reduced pain in the capsaicin-treated forearm immediately after receiving a burn on each arm equivalent to touching a hot stove. Moreover, on the day after the burns, the subjects said the treated arm was much less sensitive to touch and heat than the control arm.

The doctors noted that capsaicin worked well this way by killing small-diameter nerve fibers, the ones responsible for pain. However, it had no effect on large-diameter nerve fibers. According to *Science News* (142:333, November 14, 1992), in which this story appeared, "physicians may one day slather capsaicin-like compounds on the skin of burn patients or smear it into the incisions of individuals undergoing surgery."

Ulcers. Remember the Stitts (mentioned under Neck Pain), who operate a Wisconsin bakery and give away tens of thousands of cayenne pepper capsules free? Well, Paula Wagner, one of their employees who is busily involved in this project of theirs, called to my attention another wonderful story that beautifully illustrates the superb healing properties of this unique spice.

Lee Klatt, 59, of Twin Rivers, Wisconsin, suffered with duodenal ulcers for 20 years, but after less than two weeks of taking cayenne, his symptoms were noticeably relieved. "It always felt as if I had a bobber in the base of my throat; it was like trying to swallow a cork," he said of the pent-up gas that was always in his stomach. "But now I can eat the rust off of nails again," he bragged with obvious exaggeration and some humor, too.

Klatt told me that he had tried many other remedies, including using goat milk to coat his stomach. But "nothing seemed to work for me," he said. Then "I heard Paul Stitts' offer on the radio, giving away free cayenne pepper capsules, that convinced me to give it a shot. I begin taking them in mid-December of 1994. I took four 500-milligram capsules three times a day with food or tomato juice. In six weeks I cut back to two capsules twice a day. Then, four months later, I cut back to just two capsules a day. I've been totally amazed at just how well cayenne pepper has worked for my ulcers!"

Cayenne for Self-Defense Purposes

In the early 1980s, I was affiliated for a short time with a company called Orion International. It distributed a line of herbal and nutritional products through a direct marketing system. In my capacity of service, I educated thousands of their dealers throughout the United States and Canada on the finer points of herbal medicine by means of numerous public lectures, a monthly newsletter, and a book.

But before getting into the health-care line, the company had its beginnings with a unique self-defense spray called the "Mugger Slugger." It was able to quickly subdue a person, in a way similar to Mace and tear gas, with noxious substances that burned the eyes, mucous membranes, and skin. The principal constituent was capsaicin. The company sold tens of thousands of units and made lots of money, which enabled it eventually to expand into health-food supplements.

Today there are similar products on the market, but with more aggressive potency to them. Some are designed only for animals, while others have been specifically intended for human beings. Bob Mottram, an outdoors writer for the *Tacoma* (Washington) *News Tribune,* reported in one of his columns about how such a capsicum spray saved the lives of two hunters by routing a hungry and ornery grizzly bear.

Mark Matheney, a general contractor from Bozeman, Montana, and his partner, Dr. Fred Bahnson, were bow hunting for elk in the Gallatin National Forest about 30 miles north of West Yellowstone, Montana. They accidentally surprised a female grizzly and her three cubs feasting on a freshly killed elk, and the grizzly mother instantly reacted to protect her cubs.

"She charged with incredible speed," recalled Matheny later on. "I had no time at all to do anything. I held my bow up in front of me for protection, and she just knocked it out of my hand with one mighty swat of her massive paw."

Matheny next recalled being knocked to the ground with great violence by the big bear, who then seized his head in her jaws. Meanwhile, his partner had drawn his can of 10 percent capsicum oleoresin spray and charged the bear, screaming unprintable obscenities at the top of his lungs. The bear turned and was hit directly in the eyes with the caustic spray.

Seemingly oblivious, the grizzly then knocked Bahnson to the ground, turned back to Matheny, and mauled him again. The good doctor recovered and charged the huge beast again, this time squirting the remaining contents of the can within inches of its beady little eyes. In fury, the grizzly knocked her aggressor down again, bit his arm, and was about to rip his throat out when the spray finally took effect. The animal's reaction was a loud roar of pain and sudden lunging from side to side as it tried to wipe its snout and eyes with both of its paws. It blindly ran away, hitting into trees, tumbling over dead logs, and lunging through bushes, all the while growling in pain.

Matheny suffered from 16 inches of bear bites on his face and head that required more than 100 stitches to close. But he made out okay, thanks to Dr. Bahnson, who just happens to be a plastic surgeon specializing in facial reconstruction.

Law enforcement officers are taught to use their guns only as a last resort, when other methods of subduing criminal suspects have failed. And with many of the nation's lower courts looking with greater disfavor at the discharge of firearms by such personnel, new self-defense weapons have been sought that are nonlethal and legal to use. The most common of such products are high voltage stun guns, CN and CS tear-gas sprays, and the new oleoresin capsicum (OC)-based pepper sprays.

But stun guns must be held in direct contact with the attacker. Most officers wouldn't want to allow their suspects to get this close if at all possible. And tear gas works only if the criminal can feel pain. For suspects who are crazy, or who may be high on drugs or under the influence of alcohol, CS and CN sprays have proven to be of little or no value. Also, it takes from 10 to 20 seconds for them to take effect, and a lot of damage can be done by a suspect in that amount of time.

OC pepper spray is an "inflammatory" agent. Thus, an attacker need not be sober or sensitive to pain for it to be effective. In a two-year study, the Federal Bureau of Investigation (FBI) discovered that when each subject was sprayed, he (or she) experienced an immediate involuntary closing of the eyes, severe gasping for breath, and gagging if the spray was inhaled. Some of those sprayed even became nauseous and several lost control of their upper-body motor skills. Symptoms lasted about three-quarters of an hour and there was no recorded evidence of permanent injury to people sprayed with OC.

Hot Flashes from the Southwest

There are a couple of very large gatherings every year in the American Southwest that attract tens of thousands of "chile heads" (as they're called by local folks), fans of chile peppers, who like their food *really hot* and spicy! These are the events at which to sample dozens of chiles and hundreds of sizzling salsas, not to mention a wide variety of other food forms in which chiles are cleverly used.

At the annual Santa Fe Wine and Chile Fiesta, held September 17–20, 1992, in Santa Fe, New Mexico, I got a chance to sample some cayenne pepper and bean pie a la mode, the topping being a scoop of capsicum-tomato ice cream. There was food and wine galore, not to mention a lot of interesting people with some very *hot* breath. Call (505) 988-7124 for a brochure or to make advance reservations for a real "fire-breathing" experience of a lifetime. Oh, and be sure to take along plenty of Maalox or whipping cream to drown the fire in your mouth and belly.

True chile aficionados also congregate by the thousands every August at the Hot Sauce Festival in Austin, Texas, which has been sponsored by the *Austin Chronicle* for almost three decades. Texans claim their chiles are superior to those grown in New

Mexico. But if the truth be told about the matter, Texas chile cooks are always soundly defeated at the Chile Wars cookoff competitions held annually in Las Cruces, New Mexico. Call the *Austin Chronicle* at (512) 454-5766 and ask the food editor for specific times and dates for this festival.

Two mail-order companies that specialize exclusively in chiles and chile products are both located in New Mexico, generally considered *the* chile state of the nation. They can provide you with whatever you need in the way of *hot* things.

> Old Southwest Trading Co.
> P.O. Box 7545
> Albuquerque, NM 87194
> 1-800-748-2861

> Salsa Express Corp.
> P.O. Box 3985
> Albuquerque, NM 87190
> 1-800-43-SALSA

Chileheads even have their own publication. It's called simply *Chile Pepper* and is issued six times a year. The subscription rate is $18.95. To order, write or call:

> *Chile Pepper* magazine
> P.O. Box 769
> Mount Morris, IL 61054-8234
> 1-800-959-5468

If you want to read up more on the capsicums, there are three books that I highly recommend you get. The first one gives a nice overview of the species and was written by the chef of Santa Fe's celebrated Coyote Cafe.

> Mark Miller. *The Great Chile Book* (Berkeley, CA: Ten
> Speed Press, 1991), $14.95.

The second work is an exquisite celebration in text and photos of the small, yet highly potent chile pepper. Assembled by a popular fiction writer and her world-renowned photographer husband, it is an enduring book that has been thoroughly researched.

> Susan Hazen-Hammond and Eduardo Fuss. *Chile Pepper Fever: Mine's Hotter Than Yours* (Stillwater, MN: Voyageur Press, Inc., 1993), $29.95.

The last of this trio is a more formal work. This handsome volume describes the taxonomy of the genus, the biology of the plant, how it is grown and used, and what makes it red and hot. Included with the text are full-color plates of 32 cultivars, representing the five domesticated species, handpainted at life size with scientific accuracy. The author is a scientist, an artist, a historian, a gardener, and a fine cook; she holds a Ph.D. in art from the University of North Texas.

> Jean Andrews. *Peppers: The Domesticated Capsicums* (Austin, TX: University of Texas Press, 1984). It has since been reprinted and updated. Write to the publisher for cost: University of Texas Press, P.O.B. 7819, Austin, TX 78713-7819.

Some Like It Hot

Awhile back, Jennifer Trainer Thompson described by telephone for me her own experience of testing hot pepper sauces. "For the food world, it's comparable to bungee jumping," she noted. "I introduce beginners to some of this liquid fire," she continued, "before pushing them off the culinary cliff for real dives of their own. What an adrenalin rush they must get!" she laughed.

Thompson is the author of *Hot Licks: Great Recipes for Making and Cooking with Hot Sauces* (San Francisco, CA: Chronicle Books, 1994). Her recipes and advice give you thrill-seekers—those who've never met a hot sauce that's hot enough—inspiration for many a new creation. But she also talks to lots of other people who've discovered that the subtle use of hot sauce can enliven food without obliterating anyone's taste buds.

Those brave or crazy enough to follow her on a culinary expedition will explore myriad hot sauces from different regions and lands as well as those made in different styles. This queen of "mouth surfers" described for me the waves of pleasure that follow the initial hit of pain: "Like acupuncture, jogging, and sex, chiles can induce a glowing sense of well-being, thanks to the physiological reaction to capsaicin, a chemical found at the stem-end of the chili pepper. Biting into it alarms the mouth and the brain, which then releases endorphins, which are the body's own pain relievers. It's like the plateau that joggers often experience when they've run for so long that they don't feel any more pain and then they're just coasting along comfortably."

Thompson authoritatively declared over the phone: "There is nothing salt can do that hot sauce can't do even better." Herewith is one of her all-time favorite "bungee-jumping" liquid-fire recipes that she guaranteed "will make you think you're a human volcano if you eat enough of it!"

Chipotle Red Sauce

5 dried chipotle chiles

2 dried New Mexico red chiles

1 dried ancho chile

6 medium garlic cloves, unpeeled

1-1/2 cups water or chile water

1/2 tsp. salt

6 tbsps. apple cider vinegar

1 tsp. unsweetened cocoa

2 tbsps. dark brown sugar

1/4 tsp. ground cumin

1 cup fresh orange juice

1/4 tsp. ground cloves

1/2 tsp. ground cayenne

Preheat oven to 250° F. Stem and slit all the dried chiles, removing half the seeds. (For a milder sauce, she suggested removing all the seeds.) Then roast the chiles in the oven just until you smell them, about 3 minutes maximum. Submerge them in a pot of hot water and soak until softened, about 20 minutes.

While the chiles are soaking, turn the oven up to 500° F. Roast the garlic on a baking sheet for 20 minutes, then peel it.

Taste the chile water. If it's not bitter, use it instead of water. Combine the chiles, garlic, chile water, salt, apple cider vinegar, cocoa, sugar, cumin, orange juice, cloves, and 1/4 teaspoon cayenne in a Vita-Mix whole food machine or equivalent blender and puree for 1-1/2 minutes. Taste and add an additional 1/4 teaspoon cayenne if greater heat is desired. Pour into a sterilized fruit jar and seal. Refrigerate; the sauce will keep for about 3 weeks.

Note: *Thompson mentioned that a person can substitute canned chipotles in adobo, which will make roasting and soaking unnecessary. Lift the chipotles from the sauce, but don't rinse, as the adobo adds flavor.*

To go along with her cliff-diving hot sauce, how about "the salsa from Hades"? This is a recipe that a Mexican police officer in Tijuana gave me a few years ago. His name is Hernando Antonio de Maria y Sanchez Guadalupe Rodriguez. But he asked me to call him by his nickname of "Harry," which was a lot easier for me to do. He utilized the hottest chiles on the planet to make this dynamite dish.

Harry's Habanero Salsa from Hell

1/4 cup plus 1 tbsp. extra-virgin olive oil
1 tsp. minced garlic
6 plum tomatoes, halved
salt
cracked black pepper
10 fresh or dried habanero chiles, stemmed
1/4 cup lime juice
1/4 cup chopped cilantro

Combine 1 tablespoon olive oil and garlic in a small bowl. Rub this mixture onto tomato halves. Season to taste with

*salt and pepper. Roast at 500° F. until blackened, approxi-
mately 15 to 25 minutes. Remove from the oven; permit to
cool; then dice.*

*Grill the habaneros over a medium-hot fire until lightly
browned. Remove from the fire and mince, but be sure to
wear rubber gloves to protect your hands from blistering.*

*Combine the roasted habaneros and chiles, the remaining
1/4 cup olive oil, lime juice, and cilantro in a medium-
sized bowl. Mix well. This can be kept covered in a plastic
bowl and refrigerated for up to a week. It makes about
1-1/2 cups of dragon-breathing salsa.*

Seldom has history ever produced a more schizophrenic per-
sonality than in the form of Diego de Landa. A Franciscan who
was eventually named the Catholic bishop of all of the Yucatan
Peninsula in 1572, later in his life, he incinerated at least 27 Maya
books. Yet he still managed to record an "alphabet" that provided
archaeologists and linguists with vital clues for the recent deci-
pherming of the ancient Maya writings that had escaped his holo-
caust. His portrait hangs in the vast religious complex that he built
on top of an ancient pyramid in Izamal, Yucatan, and depicts him
with downcast eyes and an attempt at a meek smile. But he over-
stepped the limits of his authority to such an extent that he was
sent back to Spain to be tried for breaking ecclesiastical regula-
tions. He subjected his Maya flock to hideous tortures, yet left an
exhaustive account of their daily life. It is to him, therefore, that I've
turned for the following unusual beverage recipe of the sixteenth-
century Maya.

Hot Chocolate with a Twist from the Classic Maya

1 small ripened macho chile
2 small chile pequin
1 pint boiling water
2 tbsps. chocolate (use broken pieces of a Hershey milk
chocolate bar for this)
1/2 tsp. honey

Turn oven to 275° F. and preheat. Stem and slit the dried chiles, removing two thirds of their seeds. Then roast them in the oven on a cookie sheet for about 3-1/2 minutes. Next submerge them in boiling water for 30 minutes until thoroughly softened. Strain the chile water and reheat. Slowly add the chocolate pieces and keep stirring until completely melted. Finally, stir in the honey, cool a few minutes until still very warm and slowly savor while sipping. This was one of the standard beverages enjoyed by the Classic Maya many centuries ago.

Red Devil English Toffee

This is an interesting candy recipe for those to chew on who are always up to a little bit of devilry of some sort.

3/4 cup finely chopped walnuts

1 cup unsalted butter

1 cup sugar

3 tsps. ground red chile

2 tbsps. water

1 tbsp. Karo corn syrup

1/4 pound semi-sweet chocolate, chopped, melted, cooled

Butter a 13" × 9" pan and sprinkle half the walnuts over the bottom of the pan. Melt the butter over low heat in a medium-sized heavy saucepan fitted with a candy thermometer. Whisk in the sugar and chile and cook over a low heat, stirring constantly, until the mixture comes to a rolling boil.

Stir in the water and corn syrup and mix well. Continue cooking, stirring often, until the mixture reaches 290° F. Pour the candy into the prepared pan, spreading it evenly with the back of a spoon. When the toffee has cooled, spread the melted chocolate evenly over the toffee with the remaining nuts. Refrigerate until set. When the toffee is hard, break into uniformly sized pieces. Store in a covered container. (I'm grateful to Mariah Stock of Albuquerque, New Mexico, for this recipe.)

Great Balls of Fire

This recipe has been reprinted with permission from Chile
Pepper Fever: Mine's Hotter than Yours *by Susan Hazen-
Hammond and Eduardo Fuss (Stillwater, MN: Voyageur
Press, Inc., 1993) $29.95 (1-800-888-9653).*

2 slices of dry French bread
about 1/4 cup milk
1 pound ground sirloin
1 onion
1 fresh jalapeño pepper
2 tablespoons olive oil
1 egg or 2 egg whites
2 ounces grated Parmesan cheese
about 2 tsps. chopped fresh cilantro
1/2 tsp. salt
1/4 tsp. coarse-ground black pepper
canola oil for frying

*Soak the bread in the milk, squeeze it lightly, and add to
the sirloin, discarding any extra milk. Chop the onion fine.
Using rubber gloves to protect your hands, wash the
jalapeño, remove and discard the stem, and chop the pepper extra fine. Open all the windows in the kitchen and
saute the onion and jalapeño lightly in the oil. (If the
fumes are too much, cover the pan; if they still bother you,
consider the mixture sauteed enough. Better still, saute
these ingredients outside over a hibachi stove or grill.)
Cool slightly and add to the meat mixture, blending well.
Beat the egg lightly and add Parmesan, cilantro, salt, and
black pepper. Add this mixture to the meat mixture and
blend together well.*

*Wearing rubber gloves, form the meat mixture into balls
approximately one inch in diameter and separate the balls
into two batches. Pour oil into a cast-iron skillet so that
half an inch of oil covers the bottom. Heat until a piece of
meat mixture dropped in the oil sizzles. Turn heat to medi-*

um high and fry the first batch of meatballs until the underside is brown. Roll them over so that the other side cooks. Remove from the oil with a slotted spoon and drain well on paper towels. Fry the second batch of meatballs in the same oil. Makes about 42 meatballs.

These mildly hot meatballs make excellent appetizers and can be served with some of Harry's Habanero Salsa From Hell (mentioned earlier) as a dip. They also go well in homemade or canned spaghetti sauces. As appetizers, they taste best if served within two hours of cooking. To make zippier meatballs with more daring fire in them, just add an additional jalapeño.

Jumpin' Jalapeño Marmalade

This marmalade is closer to a relish with its chunks of red and green bell peppers and raisins, spiced just right with cinnamon, cloves, and allspice. As a change from putting it on toast or muffins, try it alongside an entree. It's scrumptious with pork chops, beef, or poultry.

4 medium oranges

3 quarts water

3-inch piece cinnamon stick, broken into pieces

1 tsp. whole cloves

1 tsp. whole allspice

cheesecloth

1 medium lemon, thinly sliced, then chopped

2 green bell peppers, stems and seeds removed, finely chopped

3 cups granulated sugar

1 cup golden raisins

1/4 cup chopped jalapeño chiles

Peel the oranges, removing most of the white pith from the peel. Cut the peel into very thin strips. Cover the peel with 1-1/4 quarts of water, bring to a boil, and cook for 5 minutes; drain. Repeat with another 1-1/2 quarts water.

Remove the seeds and membranes from the orange pulp and chop; place in a heavy saucepan. Tie the cinnamon, cloves, and allspice in a square of cheesecloth and add to the saucepan along with the orange peel, lemon, bell peppers, sugar, and raisins, and add 1 cup water. Cook over low heat until the sugar dissolves, stirring frequently.

Bring to a boil and boil for 5 minutes. Cover and let stand at room temperature 1 hour to blend all the flavors. Bring back to a rolling boil and cook 10 more minutes, stirring every so often. Add the jalapeños and cook, stirring frequently, until the marmalade has thickened, about another 25 minutes. Remove and discard the cheesecloth bag.

Spoon the marmalade into hot, sterilized jars leaving 1/4 inch at the top. Wipe the rim with a clean towel, cover with a two-part canning-jar lid and process in a boiling water bath. Yields about 4 cups.

Chapter Three

Garlic
Nature's Own Antibiotic Weapon
Against Diseases

What's in a Name?

Through the ages, garlic has earned for itself a prolific reputation on account of its odor. And because of this unforgettable aroma have come a variety of names as well. The most famous of them all has been "The Stinking Rose." But numerous others abound, as the list below readily indicates:

Poor Man's Treacle	Fruit of Love
Devil's Posey	Hell's Passion Flower
Poor Man's Camphor	Dragon's Perfume
Devil's Rose	Billy Goat's Cologne
Lucifer's Tulip	Witches' Poison
Hades' Aphrodisiac	Devil's Madness

All of these names have their origins steeped in many centuries of lore and legend. Just about all of them had their beginnings at some point in the distant past with common people, most of whom were usually quite superstitious to begin with. Therefore, it wasn't unusual for their superstitions to become intertwined with the names that have been variously assigned to garlic.

The name *garlic*, however, is believed to have come from the Gaelic: "gar" was meant for a spear or lance, while "lic" was a common name assigned to a leek or type of onion. Hence, garlic was probably intended to describe a "spear onion" by its uniquely tapered shape. The scientific name *Allium sativum* comes from the Celtic and Latin: *all* meant "smelly," and the Latin *sativum* has always stood for "grown" or cultivated. Hence, the herb's proper name really means "smelly cultivate."

A Spice or a Drug?

Some of life's most intriguing questions have never been fully answered by men and women of science. One of those is the oft-quoted brain teaser, "Which came first, the chicken or the egg?" Another, equally puzzling head-scratcher is this: "Is garlic a spice or a drug?" Although the former question remains to be resolved, it can be said that the latter can be answered that garlic is *both* of them.

In one of my other books, *The Healing Benefits of Garlic* (New Canaan, CT: Keats Publishing, Inc., 1994), I mentioned in the first chapter that the uses for garlic began some five millennia ago. But it was actually the Egyptians who did more to make this smelly spice highly prized and very popular than anyone else.

The Greek historian Herodotus traveled extensively in the middle part of the fifth century B.C. He happened to be down in Egypt on one occasion and stood before the great pyramid reared to Cheops. A local guide interpreted some of the hieroglyphics—cheap Egyptian wallpaper—etched in the stone. Among other things, it told that this mighty monument of ambition and pride had cost this particular pharaoh 1,600 silver talents—in modern parlance that would be the equivalent of 40 *tons* of silver!

Now, the market value for a 1,000-ounce bar of silver in 1996 was somewhere close to $5,000. There are 32,000 ounces in a ton—the pyramid old Cheops built for himself cost 1,280,000 ounces of silver. That's a grand worth of $64 million, give or take a few million. These 1,600 silver talents not only included food, clothing, and iron tools for the hundred of thousands of slaves who labored on this gigantic project, but also the cost of *a lot of garlic,* red onions, and black radishes to keep them healthy!

Garlic figured in as a helpful *aromatic* in ways you would never believe possible. It was told on the same block wall in hieroglyphics how Cheops put his own daughter in a brothel to bring in extra income when funds for the project started running low. She was smart enough to charge all of her customers silver and *garlic* for her services of pleasure, so the story goes.

Another Greek author, Charmidas, reported that Egyptian men chewed garlic on the way home from their mistresses, so that their jealous wives wouldn't think anyone had come near them. The sulfurous odors of eaten garlic permeated not only the breath but also came through the skin, thereby hiding any detectable hints of dainty perfume these guys might have still had on them when they reached their dwellings. Presumably, they had concocted stories of equal potency to explain away their late arrivals home.

More often than not, ancient Egyptians employed garlic interchangeably as a spice *and* a drug at the *same* time. Case in

point are the "bitter herbs" mentioned in Exodus 12:8, which the children of Israel partook of during the night that the angel of death "passed over" them, while destroying all of the firstborn among the Egyptians. (The noted Jewish religious holiday, the Passover, is in celebration of this event.) Garlic was one of the prominent herbs featured, along with chicory, endive, sorrel, and dandelion. But this wasn't just a one-time thing, as ancient writings clearly demonstrate that the Egyptians in the days of the pharaohs regularly ate salads or bitter herbs with their meat dishes.

So, here we have garlic being routinely used as a spice in meal preparations, while at the same time serving as an effective drug in a *specific* event of mass infection on a grand scale. It comes back to the original question posed, of course—"Is garlic a culinary agent or a valued pharmaceutical? Other examples could be cited to show that it is more *both* than one or the other. Take, for instance, the business of embalming, which the ancient Egyptians perfected to an art. Garlic was a common ingredient used with their dead pharaohs to help preserve their mortal remains for the afterlife that followed. But garlic was *also* used to flavor the foods that were prepared in advance and placed inside the tombs with the dead pharaohs. *An X-Ray Atlas of the Royal Mummies* of Egypt by James E. Harris and Edward F. Wente (Chicago: University of Chicago Press, 1980) shows us that this was the case.

Hence, for the record, we can say that garlic is, indeed, a spice *and* a drug, either separately or, more often, *together* at the same time.

Roman Contributions to the Spread of Garlic

Ancient Rome is remembered more for its many military engagements and its long line of Caesars than for anything else. The Romans themselves weren't what historians or anthropologists might exactly refer to as a cultured people. In fact, come to think of it, there weren't too many intellectuals among them either. All of the great poets, dramatists, and philosophers came from the Greeks, and most of the great medical men (save for Hippocrates) and building engineers came from the Egyptians. Rome could never boast very much of its literary figures or men of science as the Greeks and Egyptians could.

Rome was and still is best known for its generals, legions of foot soldiers, and clever politicians. It also was all over the ancient world with its armies. Whenever Roman legions marched to some distant place, they took along with them the necessary supplies that armies of this size usually commanded. Standard to a soldier's rations was an adequate amount of garlic, which came in handy for improving the flavor of bad military chow and for doing self-doctoring whenever the occasions warranted it.

The Romans actually borrowed this idea of taking garlic with them everywhere they went from the Greeks and Egyptians, whom they periodically conquered and dominated. Although some of their medical uses might seem rather preposterous to us today, there was a certain amount of actual sophisticated theory behind them. Further probing into what they prescribed has usually turned up many grains of medical truths.

For example, the Romans mixed powdered garlic with goose grease and ashes from a camp fire to smear on boils, carbuncles, and abscesses. Now although this may appear to be terribly messy, it is, in fact, extremely practical. The ashes would abrade the wound and clean out purulent matter. The grease would, in turn, ensure that the site was constantly exposed to the antibiotic qualities of the pulverized garlic. From what we currently know about garlic's wonderful antibacterial properties, it would be fair to say that this curious remedy worked effectively against infections.

It was Roman legions who carried garlic to the British Isles when Julius Caesar invaded the place. That land was known for its damp cold and frequent mists, due to vast tracts of fen and marsh. Being privy to this information enabled Roman physicians such as Galen, Dioscorides, and others to strongly recommend garlic in order to reduce the health risks of their troops to fevers, colds, and other diseases such as typhus, cholera, and dysentery.

The spread of garlic by Roman legions throughout much of Europe and Asia Minor has been documented in a number of histories. The pharmaceutical and medical uses of garlic by Roman doctors has been extensively covered in specific chapters on Roman medicine in two very excellent books that I highly recommend to those interested in doing additional research on this intriguing subject. Jürgen Thorwald's *Science and Secrets of Early Medicine* (New York: Harcourt, Brace & World, Inc., 1963) is a tightly written, thoroughly entertaining book that covers ancient medicine and garlic in broad brushstrokes. On the other hand, *The Healing Hand: Man and Wound in the Ancient World* (Cambridge: Harvard University Press, 1975) by physician Guido Majno, M.D., focuses more concisely on the specific ailments for which garlic proved itself, over and over again, to be a timeless remedy of worthy merit.

Garlic Cures from the Middle Ages

The noted historian Edward Gibbon described in his *Decline and Fall of the Roman Empire* (London: Methuen & Co., Ltd., 1914, 7:338) the collapse of this mighty civilization as being "the greatest, perhaps, and most awful scene in the history of mankind." And with that demise came an end to the sciences of that empire, including its entire branch of medicine (much of it heavily borrowed from the Greeks, of course).

Many of the healing arts were lost for a number of centuries. It was a gradual rather than rapid disintegration. Gibbon attributed "four principal causes of the ruin of Rome, which continued to operate in a period of more than a thousand years": (1) the moral decay of its citizenry; (2) the domestic quarrels among the Romans themselves; (3) the waste and abuse of materials; and (4) the hostile attacks of German barbarians such as the Goths and Vandals (from which the word "*vandal*ism" came) as well as Christian intruders.

Between A.D. 350 and 900, garlic all but vanished from the medical scene. Lovingly cultivated in the medicinal herb gardens of the monasteries, however, it was still around and kept in pretty active use. Those were the times when wild garlic was more in use for ailments in humans and beasts alike. Hildegarde of Bingen was one of few healers who routinely relied on this important herb to do much of her healing with. Hers is an interesting tale worthy of relating.

This remarkable woman was born in 1098, of noble family, in Brocktheim Castle, whose ruins still stand high above the Rhine, at Kuesnach in Germany. At the age of 8 she was taken to the convent at Disibodenberg, to be reared by the pious Dame Yutta. At 30 she became the head of this monastery. A few years later, having gathered about her a group of women of noble birth, she founded the monastery at Rupertsberg, the scene of her long life, and where she was laid to rest at the age of 81—something quite incredible for those short-lived times.

This Benedictine abbess was born a spare, sickly child, but was cured of her undisclosed malady with garlic soup (Dame Yutta having had a dream of the girl's cure). She grew into a tall woman, stately in mien, haughty in demeanor, with a kindly, piercing eye, a heart filled with love for the church and for humanity. But, more than all of this, she bore the burden of spiritual powers seldom ever understood by common folks. You see, Hildegarde was a mystic of sorts and enjoyed continual revelations, visions, and dreams from heaven on a fairly regular basis. In fact, she declared in the last of her theology books, *Liber Divinorum Operum,* the true author of all her medical works: "In all creation, trees, plants, animals, and gem stones, there are hidden secret powers which no person can know of unless they are revealed by God Himself." Thus, at age 70 she could truthfully say, "*Everything* I ever wrote came wholly from the source of my heavenly visions."

All of this is well and good, of course, for those who are themselves adherents to mysticism in general. But do her numerous remedies—many of which include the use of garlic somewhere—really hold merit when applied to the rigors of twentieth-century medicine? The answer, as unlikely as it may seem, is an absolute and unqualified "Yes!" Not too many people may be aware of the clinical work of Gottfried Hertzka, M.D., and his pharmaceutical chemist colleague, Wighard Strehlow, Ph.D., in the city of Konstanz.

According to them: "For the past forty years now, we have clinically tested more than 500 remedies and methods of treatment of Abbess Hildegarde, and have proved them to be an unqualified success for thousands of patients!" Their "Hildegarde Practice" (as they've called their clinic), has verified more than enough the effectiveness of her numerous recommendations, which obviously leads one to conclude that her visionary information must have come from a "good source," if it has helped so many people through the years.

Hildegarde's principal "secret" for good health lay in a special diet based on *viriditas,* or "nature energy." Garlic, it was shown to her, contained a high degree of this vital life force found within all living vegetation. It could simply be chewed, used in salad dressing, or else cooked in a soup, stew, or warm broth for healthy rejuvenation of the body.

In her many medical writings, which were also laced with considerable theology, Hildegarde suggested chewing one-half a clove of garlic every day "to invigorate the liver and spleen." And her standard dressing for salad contains the following few ingredients: one tablespoon pure wine vinegar, three tablespoons sunflower oil, a bit of honey, and, of course, one-quarter crushed garlic clove. Lemon juice and yogurt can be added, if desired, which improves the flavor and gives it somewhat of a modern touch. The Abbess prescribed "one drink in moderation during a meal." Her favorite tea was a blend of fennel and garlic—"the one flavors the strong medicine in the other." Spring and well water were the preferred choices over mineral water.

As head abbess, she had the duties and powers of a baron, ruling over lands and estates, over monks, nuns, peasants, and people. She attended synods, attested decrees, and counseled rulers. A medieval example of feminine supremacy she was, in a community both prosperous and eminent. She and her female associates practiced music, chanted in choirs, studied, performed the duties of cooking, cleaning, weaving, and spinning, not to mention tilling the drug gardens, making up the medicines, and tending the sick in the hospice.

Seven hours a day, nuns and monks labored with their hands; seven monastic offices were recited and sung, beginning with night office in the cold, dark church choir at two in the morning and ending with the evening complin. "Two hours or more must be given over to sober and Godly recreation," she soberly wrote of their religious duties every day.

Through the day, and far into the night, nuns and monks translated, copied manuscripts, and wrote commentaries in fair, round script, ornamented the initial letters and illumined the sheets. I've seen some of Hildegarde's ancient manuscripts. Around one carefully hand-drawn picture of garlic was painted a golden halo. "This is one of God's finest creations," she wrote, "and must always be cherished as a sacred thing most holy."

Up and down the Rhine and across the Valley of the Nahe, this wonderful woman of God—a prophetess and seeress in her own right—preached and healed on a daily basis. With her own hands she washed and dressed the sick, made their beds, and gave them food and medicine. She was in the habit of boiling two chopped cloves of garlic in "a flagon of wine" (about a quart) and using that liquid to disinfect her hands before touching a sick patient. She hung bunches of garlic bulbs over the beds of the sick to kill whatever contagious germs may have been in the air, although knowing nothing about bacteria or viruses as such—"I do this because God told me," she simply offered without further reason. She shrank from no disease, not even something as hideous and dreadful as leprosy. Had she been alive today, this woman would surely have followed in the steps of Mother Theresa, or maybe vice-versa.

In the gossip of the time, and in the records of the Medieval bishops to the monasteries, we can read the shortcomings of this particular abbess, whom some complained "stank of Devil's Rose" on account of the garlic she used. It is known that Hildegarde was charged with "gadding about" too much by some jealous bishops, who apparently had neither the time, means, nor desire to travel as much as she did. She went on many journeys to small villages and larger cities, to the castles of the nobles and the hovels of the poor. She visited church dignitaries and atheists. Rulers, who were the politicians of the days, and their serf subjects alike enjoyed her company.

It is recorded that she visited one German duke who was ailing with a terrible infection in his right leg. Hildegarde bathed the wound with some of her garlic wine vinegar and then applied a poultice of crushed garlic clove upon the same for several days straight. Soon the duke was up and around and off pursuing his favorite sport, namely that of hunting wild game with his men. She went from his castle to the squalid hut of a serf, whose young son was burning with a fever. Again, she bathed the child's face and body with more of her garlic wine vinegar and managed to get some of it into him also. A while later, the child sat up and asked for something to eat, the first nourishment he had received in days.

This is how she lived and practiced her craft, frequently using garlic by itself or with other herbs to work her healing magic. She went on tours of preaching, teaching, expounding, and prophesying. Some of the very predictions she uttered many centuries ago have come to pass in our time: "Strange machines will replace the will of God in healing" and "Moving wagons without horses shall poison the land everywhere" are typical of her amazing utterances.

When she was 42 years and 7 months of age, a voice from heaven told her sometime in A.D. 1141 to commit her visions to writing. With a most unusual trait for a woman, in each work she informs the reader of her exact age at the time of the writing of the book, and she continued this record of her age even after she had passed three score and ten.

Some of her most remarkable writings have to do with the liver. Her medical insight into its function without the benefit of modern scientific research is nothing short of astonishing. In her own language, she described the circulation of the portal vein, which causes blood from the liver to flow back to the heart and, from there, on into the lungs. And how did she ever know that the liver is supplied and purified through the liver artery with arterial blood, as well as through the portal vein with venous blood. Read now her own words of the liver and its function.

"The liver is like a bowel in a person into which heart, lungs, and stomach pour their juices, which the liver in turn lets flow back into all members of the body, just as any container placed under a fountain will let the water received flow out elsewhere. But if the liver is full of holes and fragile, it will be unable to absorb the good juices from heart, lungs, and stomach. These juices and liquids return back to the heart, lungs, and stomach and cause there a kind of flood. If this sickness ever begins in a person, he or she will not be able to live very long."

Her recommendation for reversing this process was a simple tea made from dandelion roots and garlic clove. Though no precise measurements were given for the ingredients, it would be fair to assume that to one pint of boiling water would be added one tablespoon of dried dandelion roots and one small clove of garlic, both chopped, of course. The material was left to brew for a few minutes before being covered and set aside to steep awhile. She administered one-half cups of this strained liquid to patients with liver disturbances with apparently very good results.

This abbess with the "healing touch" also seemed to recognize that liver problems and mental or emotional upsets could be traced back to inherited characteristics or could even be dependent on the moment of conception within the womb. Of this, she wrote the following remarkable passage.

"There are also persons who were conceived by the waning moon and under the turbulence of changing air currents. Some of them are always sad and have a restless character. Because of their sadness, their liver becomes weakened and perforated by many very tiny holes like cheese. Therefore, such persons do not eat very much and have no desire for food and drink, but rather eat and drink with restraint. Because they eat and drink so little, their livers become fragile like a sponge and shrink."

In a vision from heaven, she wrote, "God showed me quite plainly that dandelion root, fenugreek seed, thistle seed, and garlic were of practical benefit for closing these holes and making the liver whole again." Though no further instructions were given as to how these herbs could be used for this problem, it is assumed that either a tea made of them (as previously described) or else their being taken in gelatin capsule form (2 each daily with a meal) would work equally well.

Elsewhere Hildegarde described metabolic imbalances as the cause of liver illnesses, whereby bad juices (*mali humores*), harmful juices (*noxi humores*), and disease-related infection juices (*infirmi humores*) confuse the complete metabolism. Sometimes a person suffers for years from "bad juices" (as she called them), without being able to find the actual cause.

"Sometimes the aforementioned juices can pour into the chest of the person in profusion and eventually overflow the liver too. Excessive and diverse brooding arises in such a person, so that the person thinks he or she is going crazy. Thereupon these juices ascend to the brain, invade it, and then go back again to the stomach and cause fever. In this way a person can also become sick over a long period of time," she wrote with clarity. No doctor I've ever known could even begin to describe to an allergic person, as well as Hildegard has done, the connection between metabolism and the psychological causes of that same illness.

Furthermore, she adds: "Through these particular floodings, the intestines begin to move around the navel of the individual. Juices ascend in this matter to the brain and make the person angry. If they also upset the vessels of the loins area, then they will affect the black bile, so that the person becomes confused and falls into an unmotivated sadness."

Clearly, the ancient idea that the liver was the seat of nearly all human emotions still prevailed in Hildegarde's time. It may not be too much of a stretch of the imagination to venture here to say that doctors and patients should begin to consider the role of the *liver* in the disease state as well as the current mind-body connection. In other words, the more correct approach would be to look at the "mind-body-*liver* connection."

Hildegarde developed several different remedies to treat not only the liver, but also the lungs and blood. She described "the *complete* plant of dandelion" (flower, leaves, stalk, and roots) as being "helpful to the liver, the lungs and the blood. Take the complete plant and boil it in *garlic* wine, add pure honey and boil it again. Add long [black] pepper and twice as much cinnamon powder to the prepared wine and boil once again. Strain it through a cloth to obtain a clear drink. Drink often after eating, as well as before eating, and it will benefit the liver, heal the painful inner organs, cleanse the lungs, and take away inner decay and slime."

The base for this wonderful elixir is, of course, garlic wine. To make it the way Hildegarde did, simply add one-quarter cup coarsely chopped garlic cloves to one quart of wine vinegar and let the material set for ten days, being sure to shake the contents vigorously once a day. "Best to do during a full moon," she advised. Then strain off and use with the other previously mentioned ingredients to make a great liver tonic.

Hildegarde was never certified as a saint by the Vatican, and she did not need to be. In her century, saints were made by popular choice of the common people and not by ecclesiastical decree of the Vatican. The people whom she cured and served while she lived lifted her into the fellowship of the saints. She is enrolled in the Martyrologium Romanum, with September 17 as St. Hildegarde's Day. Her philosophy about life in general could best be summed up from one of her writings: "All things that stand in God's order correspond with one another. The stars sparkle from the light of the moon, and the moon shines from the fire of the sun. Everything serves a higher purpose, and nothing exceeds its measure."

The Oriental Approach to Garlic Use

A common thing for many of us is to read or study a particular thing and then go back to it later on and rediscover something entirely new that we may have missed in previous perusals. This is what finally happened to me one time after having gone over the use of garlic in the Orient umpteen times, I suppose.

There I was, one day, examining the usual materials, when it suddenly struck me like a bolt out of the blue that *most* of the recipes in the historical Chinese Herbal Code (issued about five centuries ago) and calling for garlic usually mentioned it in some type of *processed* form. At first, I blinked like an owl when the impression hit my brain dead-center. Then, as I went back and carefully reread many of those recipes, sure enough, they called for cooking, pickling, or aging of raw garlic, but seldom—now get this—ever for *raw* garlic. In fact, *raw* garlic was the *least* desired; the *aged* or processed garlic was the more preferred. Aging has been the unique and traditional method used to increase the effectiveness of many different herbs, besides just garlic, and to decrease and eliminate any toxic effects. Hundreds of sulfur-containing compounds formed through chemical and biological reactions, in addition to non-sulfur compounds, contribute to the benefits of the internal use of this noble spice (but more about that later).

First of all, a very simple test to show you that the aging of garlic does away with some of its side effects that in garlic's raw form would cause problems. Anyone who has hypoglycemia may wish to conduct a simple experiment to prove my point. Chew a whole clove of garlic and swallow it. Or, better still, include it well minced or chopped in a Caesar salad. Or eat a plate of pasta thoroughly saturated with raw garlic. Within a short time, the hypoglycemic will begin to experience a headache, a loss of energy, and a reverse in mood. This typically happens when the individual's blood sugar begins dropping like crazy, all due to the negative impact of *raw* garlic in the system.

After measures have been taken to bring the blood sugar back up to normal—eat some whole-grain foods, beans or carbohydrate vegetables—take some aged garlic extract (the Kyolic brand from Wakunaga of America is the only one of its kind in the world that I ever recommend). I suggest 4 capsules at once with a meal. Then wait awhile and see what happens. *Nothing* will occur that is even remotely eventful. In fact, waiting for something to take place will get pretty boring. And *that's* my whole point: By aging the garlic, its strong hypoglycemic activity is totally removed.

A bit earlier I had cited the three different ways that most Orientals prefer to have their raw garlic *processed* before consuming it—cooking, pickling, and aging. The following information will enable readers to prepare their own forms of processed garlic, just as they do in the Orient.

Cooking. Roasting the cloves is the best method of cooking, since it creates a fragrant, nutty-sweet garlic that can then be incorporated into other dishes such as garlic mashed potatoes, for instance.

You will need the following for this: 1 head garlic; 1/2 cup extra virgin olive oil; 3 sprigs of thyme; 1 bay leaf; and some granulated kelp. Preheat the oven to 250° F. Break the garlic head into cloves, leaving the inner skins on. Place the garlic in a small oven-proof dish and add the olive oil, thyme, and bay leaf. Season lightly with the kelp and bake until it is quite tender. This usually takes about 35 minutes. Turn the cloves over occasionally with a fork. Remove the dish from the oven and let the garlic cool to room temperature.

The roasted cloves can be consumed individually, but they work better when added to other things. Squeeze the roasted cloves into a small bowl, add a little of the flavored oil in which they were roasted, and add to mashed potatoes. For use as a sauce with grilled vegetables, just add a few drops of wine vinegar to the squeezed cloves and the oil in which they were baked.

Another very versatile way of cooking them is to make a delicious garlic soup from the cloves. I'm indebted to Susan Belsinger of Baltimore, Maryland, and Carolyn Dille of San Jose, California, for this recipe. They experimented for a number of years with many different kinds of garlic soup recipes from all over the world before finding one that they liked.

You'll need the following ingredients for making this: 1 head of garlic; 1-1/2 quarts chicken broth; 2–3 slices stale whole-wheat bread (4 days old); granulated kelp (my addition); a few green garlic leaves, cut very thin; and some extra-virgin olive oil.

Peel the garlic and poach the cloves in 2 cups simmering broth. When the garlic is totally soft (about 12 minutes), puree the mixture in a Vita-Mix whole food machine or equivalent blender. Next, cut the stale bread into cubes. Soak them in warm water until quite soft, then squeeze out the excess water and crumble them.

Add the pureed garlic to the remaining broth and whisk in the softened, crumbled bread. Sprinkle in the kelp (about 1/4 teaspoon) and simmer for 10 minutes. Drink or eat hot, garnished with garlic leaves and good olive oil drizzled in, if you like.

Pickling. The best way to pickle garlic is usually with something else. The Koreans prefer doing it with cabbage, one of their very favorite vegetables. Kim chee is a condiment that Koreans serve with nearly every meal and always with rice. Because many people can't tolerate extremely hot flavors, I've eliminated the chiles and cayenne pepper to make it more palatable. Many fans of kim chee whom I've spoken with throughout South Korea in past years informed me that they obtained good health and longevity from using it often. Be advised and forewarned, however, that during the pickling process, kim chee gives off very strong odors that will affect the rest of your refrigerator contents.

To make kim chee, the following things will be required: 2 pounds of Napa or Chinese cabbage; 2 tablespoons sea salt; 8 cups cold water; 10 garlic cloves, minced, to equal almost 1/4 cup; 3 tablespoons minced fresh ginger root; 2 bunches green onion, trimmed with 2–3 inches of green and cut crosswise into 1/2-inch slices; 1-1/2 teaspoons sea salt; 1 teaspoon sugar; 2 cups water.

Cut the cabbage lengthwise into quarters. Cut it crosswise into slices about an inch wide. Place about half the cabbage in a large stainless-steel bowl or ceramic crock. Sprinkle it with 1 tablespoon of the salt. Add the rest of the cabbage and sprinkle with the remaining tablespoon of salt.

Next, pour 8 cups of cold water over the affair. Press the cabbage down so that it is all moistened and place a plate and a weight on it to hold it down. Place the cabbage in a cool place for 24 hours, stirring once and replacing the plate.

Drain the cabbage and rinse it well with cold water. Drain it again and squeeze out any excess liquid. Place the cabbage in a bowl and add the garlic, ginger, and green onions. Toss everything well with two forks. Then add the remaining ingredients—the other salt and sugar—and toss thoroughly again.

Now pack the cabbage mixture into two sterile quart glass fruit jars. Cover the cabbage with cold water, about 1 cup per jar, and use a chopstick to distribute the cabbage evenly and release any air bubbles.

Cover the jars with a double layer of waxed paper or cheesecloth and screw a canning ring on top. Place the jars in the refrigerator and leave them for five days.

Then go ahead and taste the kim chee to see if it is "pickled" enough for your liking. If not, leave it in for two more days or one week. Replace the waxed paper or cheesecloth, cover with a metal canning lid and ring, and keep the kim chee in the refrigerator for as long as six weeks.

Aged Garlic. The Japanese wrote the book on garlic, as far as I'm concerned. Nobody, but nobody, has done more in this world to perfect the processing of garlic than these people have. The Japanese form of aged garlic extract that is superior to all other commercial forms of prepared garlic is marketed worldwide under the Kyolic brand name.

But it all starts in Hiroshima, Japan, at facilities owned and operated by the Wakunaga Pharmaceutical Company, one of that nation's large suppliers of natural drugs and other medicinal agents. About six years ago, I had the opportunity to go to Japan with others to see exactly how the people at Wakunaga were able to "age" their garlic.

Not everything was given to us; there were certain valuable pieces of information deemed "proprietary" that obviously couldn't be handed out indiscriminately. And certainly not for publication to the world in a book such as this. But with what I saw and heard during the time our group was there, enough data was recorded to make some general conclusions about how the Japanese "age" their garlic.

It all starts in their fields where the herb is grown. My nose detected a distinct "fishiness" to the soil; no wonder, since a certain amount of ground-up fish scraps were regularly added to the earth. This produces a more intense garlic, which, when picked and randomly sampled by naive visitors, can set the mouth on fire and the brain's alarm signals clanging like crazy.

There is a short drying process that follows next. But as to the specific length of time involved here, I could never determine from those I casually interviewed. But the *brief* drying *is* critical to the aging itself.

Next comes the actual part of the process wherein semi-dried garlic cloves are prepared and then soaked for several months in a special solution in round, gigantic tanks almost resembling an oil refinery. After this, the "mother liquor" of garlic is strained off and put into its final forms—liquid or capsulated powder—for distribution and consumption.

Kyolic aged garlic extract is available worldwide in some 91 countries. It just happens to be *the* premier-selling garlic on the planet because of its high quality and medicinal/nutritional effectiveness. Kyolic is sold in health-food stores throughout North America and comes in several different formula varieties for specific health needs.

Buying the aged garlic extract is, of course, the simpler and more convenient thing to do. But if you want to try your hand at making your own aged garlic, then here are some time-consuming and labor-intensive steps to follow. Bear in mind that the final result won't be exactly like products offered by Wakunaga, but it will come reasonably close thereto.

First and foremost is the preparation of the ground the garlic is to be planted in. Always choose a sunny location and prepare the soil well by working in the *same* organic matter that the Japanese do, namely *old* fish material. I know this is bound to stink, but don't worry—it's *critical* to growing *good* garlic that can be aged well. Both sandy soils and heavy clay are definitely improved by adding dead, ground-up fish as well as rice hulls (if you can get them). They improve aeration and drainage in heavy clay soils.

Be aware, though, that garlic is subject to fungal attacks in damp and poor-draining soil. Large garlic fields have had sometimes to be abandoned because they were cursed with soil-borne fungal diseases that were virtually impossible to get rid of. If the soil you intend planting garlic in is heavy, you will want to construct a raised bed for your plants.

Choosing healthy bulbs also tends to reduce the risks of incurring fungal disease. Garlic bulbs should always be nicely firm and plump, not shriveled or discolored by any means. And stay away from those with soft spots or mildew—"whatsoever you sow, so shall you reap!" Purchase quality garlic bulbs from a local nursery or by mail order.

The people who worked in the huge garlic fields owned by Wakunaga Pharmaceutical Co. told me in confidence that the *very best time* for planting garlic bulbs was sometime in the fall, usually between mid-September and mid-October, just before the ground freezes. Spring-planted garlic will invariably yield smaller bulbs than those that have had a chance to lay over the winter.

When you're ready to plant, be sure to break your healthy heads of garlic into individual cloves, leaving the papery inner skins intact. Now here's another little planting secret from my friends in Japan: you *do not* need to hand-plant each clove, root down. Because, they told me, "Garlic is smart enough to right itself every spring with the assistance of the shifts and settlings of soil and the pull of the sun. So, in other words, you can safely plant each clove with the pointed end *down* and the root end up or slightly on its side.

Whether you just aim the cloves at furrows, or hand-set each one with the root to the side, be sure and plant them deep enough, somewhere between 3 and 4 inches. Plant the cloves 6 inches apart in rows about a foot apart to give them plenty of room to feed. Garlic does well among ornamentals, so don't hesitate to plant them in and among your flower beds. They do particularly well around roses, believe it or not.

In the spring, fall-planted garlic sends up green shoots that become flat leaves. Flower stalks appear in late spring in some varieties; the flowers are edible and taste great in salads. Interspersed among the individual flowers are tiny bulbs called bulblets. The farmers in Japan remove them in order to encourage the growth of larger bulbs. The bulblets shouldn't be discarded, though, since they are also tasty. Or, they can be saved and planted later on; expect a wait of two years, however, before they will produce harvestable garlic bulbs.

Be sure to keep your garlic patch weeded at all times. Some Japanese garlic growers use strong solutions of black and green tea, which they spray on their garlic plants to keep the weeds down. (See my other books, *Heinerman's Encyclopedia of Healing Herbs and Spices* and *Heinerman's Encyclopedia of Juices, Teas and Tonics* for more on them. They are available through Prentice Hall, Englewood Cliffs, NJ 07632.)

Summertime is when most of the bulb development occurs. Eventually, the leafy tops wither. Once most of the tops fall and turn brown, harvest the bulbs. Dig them from the dry soil rather than attempting to pull the tops.

Where you intend drying your garlic is *very important*. It should be done in a cool, dry place with good air circulation. You want to avoid dampness and direct sunlight, however. And *how* they're put out to dry is equally important. Some prefer to spread the heads with their foliage intact on old screens in a shed for several days. If the bulbs are to be braided, then their dried foliage should be removed and excess dirt brushed off as well. Some Japanese farmers like to put individual heads in little bags made from cheesecloth, tie the tops with string, and hang them from rafters in a shed. They claim this is the *best* way of all to dry the bulbs for top-quality garlic. After all this, you may store your garlic bulbs in a basket of some kind in a dark, cool, dry place.

Now that you've been through the growing, harvesting, and drying phases of this wonderful spice, I'd like to lead you through the remaining steps that are necessary for "aging" your garlic. You may choose one of two soaking mediums for accomplishing this—extra-virgin olive oil or apple cider vinegar.

Take ten *heads* of your cultivated and dried garlic and separate them into individual cloves. Then coarsely chop them with a French knife or thin Oriental cleaver (such as the kind Chinese and Japanese chefs routinely use). Put them in a large *ceramic crock* (the best for this) and add 1-1/2 quarts of *either* olive oil or apple cider vinegar. Cover with a *loose-fitting* lid of some kind and set aside in a dark, cool, dry place for 3 to 5 weeks. Stir occasionally, every few days, with a wooden spoon and then replace the lid.

Strain through layered pieces of cheesecloth or a fine wire-mesh strainer. Store in a clean, sterilized fruit jar and cap with a screw-on lid. Keep in the same cool, dry place and use as needed.

Therapeutic Applications of Raw and Oriental Processed Garlic

Because the Chinese, Japanese, and Koreans have done more in furthering the advancement of garlic therapy than any other culture or nation, I'm strongly inclined to lean their way in recommending *processed* garlic for a variety of health disorders. Beside each of those given in the following list, I've specified *which* form(s) may be best suited—cooked garlic, pickled garlic, or aged garlic. And I have provided suggested amounts wherever appropriate. In instances where cooked or pickled garlic might be suggested, no specific amount will be mentioned, since they would appear more in foods rather than as a dietary supplement such as aged garlic would be.

Still, each of them in their own way is practical for the problems presented. Perhaps a quick discussion of just how each one benefits the body may be in order here. Cooked garlic always imparts a *stronger* flavor on account of the heat, which causes a separation in the essential oils of the plant. Pickled garlic, on the other hand, is chock-full of enzymes, due to its fermentation. And aged garlic usually *reduces* the odor of the spice, which always seems better for many people in social settings.

Keep in mind that each of these methods of processing alters or changes the chemistry of garlic. It has numerous sulfur compounds (discussed a bit later), which are always being transformed in many interesting ways. The *stronger* sulfur taste of cooked garlic not only improves the flavor of certain foods but also greatly benefits the heart by lowering serum cholesterol and triglyceride levels within the blood. The vigorous enzymatic action of pickled garlic always helps the entire gastrointestinal tract, ranging from easier digestion to quicker elimination of waste materials from the colon later on. Aged garlic stands somewhere between the former two in terms of what it can do for the heart, stomach, and colon. But, in more subtle ways, aged garlic can work to increase energy, stimulate appetite, sharpen memory, and lengthen life spans.

One final thing that all three forms of Oriental *processed* garlic have in common is this: They give an unbelievable boost of power to a flagging immune system. Think about it for a moment—*no other* herb or spice found in nature can do for body immunity what this wonderful plant can do. Garlic stands alone as nature's ultimate weapon against infections. Bacteria and viruses just don't have a chance of existing for very long whenever garlic is present in the system (this holds true for raw and processed garlic alike).

It is those incredible sulfur components that go to make up garlic's highly interesting chemistry, that account for its penicillin-like actions. Long before conventional medicine ever discovered the magic of synthetic antibiotics, there was garlic. It was known to Egyptians 4,500 years ago, long before Alexander Fleming discovered the mold that led to penicillin. In modern times, the herb has become even more remarkable for its incredible ability to subdue new strains of so-called "super bacteria" that have proven very resistant to all forms of conventional antibiotic therapy. Where these drugs fail, garlic comes through time and again, proving itself invincible to almost anything around.

The health problems covered in this particular section are fairly common to most people. They can be remedied with garlic in the three major forms previously suggested: cooked, pickled, or aged. However, where still another form of prepared garlic (such as an alcoholic tincture or dried powder) may be more desirable, then that will be mentioned instead. Occasionally, I might even advise using a piece of the *raw* garlic itself (as in the case of a toothache). But in all instances, instructions will be provided where they haven't been; however, the reader is reminded again to refer to pages 111–117 for details regarding the preparation of cooked, pickled, or aged garlic.

Aging. Aging is a natural consequence of living in mortality. In modern times, however, the process has become somewhat accelerated due to free radicals. These are scavenger molecules lacking the necessary electrons that run amok in the system, creating in the process a great deal of biochemical havoc in our cellular tissues.

Now garlic is one herb that happens to check the erratic behavior of these delinquent molecules very nicely. Garlic can be chewed, one-quarter of a clove a day, or used raw in foods such as Caesar salad, in which not only the salad itself contains slivered bits of the spice but the wooden bowl it's to be served in has also been well rubbed with an extra piece of whole garlic for added flavor. Cooked garlic is more advantageous here than the pickled kind would be. Kyolic or homemade aged-garlic extract can be taken regularly (2 capsules or 1 teaspoon daily with meals).

Arthritis. Rheumatoid arthritis is an autoimmune disease wherein the body's immune functions turn against itself. Osteoarthritis, on the other hand, is an age-related deterioration of cartilage within the joints that is gradual and eventually causes pain and occasional deformity. And unlike rheumatoid arthritis, this kind lacks the joint inflammation that is so typical for the other.

A news report featured in an April 1980 edition of Tokyo's largest paper, *Yomiuri Shimbun,* mentioned that arthritis and lumbago patients reported feeling much better after being administered Kyolic aged-garlic extract. The news item didn't mention, though, how much they were given or for how long the treatment lasted. A safe guess might be ventured here in the amount of 2 capsules or 1 teaspoon of Kyolic garlic daily; double these amounts for homemade aged-garlic extract, however.

Boils. Boils, pardon the pun, can be "a real pain in the neck," which is where they frequently occur anyway. The Old Testament figure Job was afflicted with them all over his body and had to resort to scratching himself with a pottery shard in order to find some relief from their itching. He is lauded for his incredible patience in the midst of much suffering, as the account goes.

Boils usually represent an accumulation of different poisons within the body that have to break through the skin somewhere in order to come out. A clove of raw garlic daily will certainly help to remove some of these toxins, as will cooked garlic and aged garlic (3 capsules or 1-1/2 teaspoons).

Burns. Not quite a decade ago, a Chinese medical doctor, Xu Rongxiang, M.D., attracted considerable interest in the West with his remarkable burn ointment that had even the worst burn cases showing total recuperation within a matter of months without the benefit of tissue transplants or hormonal therapy. Although not making a full disclosure of all the ingredients, he did tell reporters and other scientists that one of the chief ingredients was garlic (others were onion, sesame seeds, honey, salt, and so forth).

The best way to utilize either garlic or onion for this is one of two ways. First is to procure a small garlic press and actually squeeze the juice out of garlic or onion, which is then lightly sprayed or sponged onto injured tissue several times a day. Another method is to use liquid aged-garlic extract. The amount intended depends, of course, on the size of the area to be covered. Mixing the liquid garlic juice with a small amount of white sugar seems to increase the healing (probably due to an enzymatic reaction between the two and oxygen in the air).

Calluses. Slice two pieces of peeled garlic lengthwise. Put them together on a Band Aid and affix to the callus. Leave in place for 10 hours and then repeat the same procedure. Do this for several days or until the callus disappears.

Cancer/Aids. Any malignant diseases such as these deserve medical care and supervision while using the appropriate natural remedies. Raw garlic, of course, is clearly the first line of defense if the patient's digestive system is capable of handling something this strong. A minimum of one whole clove per day is recommended (with food, of course). Cooked garlic is also of definite benefit here. Pickled garlic, though, may be useful for some forms of cancer (colorectal) but not for others (bone marrow or brain). Aged-garlic extract will certainly help here, too—3 capsules or 1 teaspoon three or four times daily with meals is not excessive by any means.

Garlic works well against cancer on account of its mineral contents. Its antitumor strength resides primarily in two of them, namely sulfur and germanium. Garlic is rich in numerous sulfur compounds, which explain its potent odor. A garlic bulb contains germanium in very miniscule amounts—no more than 2 or 3 parts per billion—but it is still enough to be of some significance when put to work with sulfur and other trace elements.

Cholesterol (Elevated). Different studies that have been done with both raw garlic and aged garlic extract have shown a curious thing in regard to levels of serum cholesterol in the blood. At first, they increased, to the astonishment of medical researchers, but thankfully they did start plummeting after a few weeks of continuous administration. So, technically, yes, garlic does reduce serum cholesterol levels, but only after raising them a bit in the beginning. But during this brief climb, good (HDL) cholesterol is also raised, which helps the heart. All forms of garlic are useful here. Supplementation of 2–3 capsules or 1-1/2 teaspoons daily of aged-garlic extract should, in time, give more normal cholesterol readings.

Clots. A protein called fibrin is essential to the clotting of blood. Without it, blood will simply not coagulate. Garlic is able to split or divide this protein so harmful blood clots won't form. In the few cases of hemophilia that prevail, however, it may be wise to avoid garlic altogether. Those most at risk from clot formation are over 50 and under 75. Also those who are inactive, overweight, have circulatory disorders, or heart problems are at risk. They should be taking garlic in some form pretty regularly. Maintenance doses of 2 capsules or 1/2 teaspoon daily of aged-garlic extract is suggested.

Common Cold. Here is an instance in which garlic in *any* form is going to do a sick person a lot of good. In fact, in trying to

recover from a cold, one would be well advised to double or triple his or her intake of this important spice. Probably the best way to take it for something like this, though, is in a cooked form, most likely as a hot soup. I have one of my own recipes for this, which I've included here. It will knock a cold every time, g-u-a-r-a-n-t-e-e-d! You've undoubtedly heard of the familiar "Grandma's chicken soup," by now. Well, I took my Grandmother Barbara Heinerman's favorite chicken soup recipe and turned it around several times until I came up with this, which I call "Grandson's Soup Recipe."

Grandson's Soup Recipe

Needed:

1/4 cup butter

2 garlic cloves, peeled and minced

1/2 lb. russet potatoes, cleaned, not peeled though and thinly sliced

2-1/2 cups chicken stock

pinch grated nutmeg

pinch grated ginger root

pinch horseradish

4 bunches decent watercress, washed and trimmed

3-1/2 tbsps. heavy cream (optional)

What to Do:

Melt butter in large pan and sauté garlic until transparent. Stir often to prevent burning.

Add spuds, stock, and other spices in pan. Boil, cover, and simmer for 20 minutes.

Add cress and simmer another 7 minutes.

Cool soup to very lukewarm. Then pour everything into a Vita-Mix container or equivalent blender and liquefy on medium speed for 1 minute. Rinse the pan and stand a fine-meshed sieve next to the pot.

Push the pureed soup through the sieve using the back of a wooden spoon. Discard tough materials. Soup in pan should be a fine puree.

Gently reheat but don't allow to boil. Add cream if desired and eat warm. Makes two generous servings.

Complexion Problems. A nifty lotion can be made from garlic that might help to eliminate blackheads or pimples from the skin. Peel and coarsely chop one garlic clove; boil in one cup of water for 10 minutes, uncovered; let stand until cool. Tape three Q-tips together and dip in this solution and dab on blemishes. Let dry naturally. Or with the same amount of garlic, make a small amount of tincture by soaking it in an equal amount (1/2 cup) of alcohol for 5 days. Keep covered, however, and shake daily. Apply in the same fashion. You'll be surprised at how well this works—either garlic solution (but especially the tincture) will soon dry up the acne.

Corns. See under **Calluses** for same treatment.

Cuts. I've used this myself on different occasions through the years and find it works well for nicks, cuts, abrasions, and small wounds that don't hemorrhage very seriously. Mix together equal parts (one teaspoon each) of cayenne pepper and powdered garlic (not to be confused with garlic salt or powder, but rather garlic emptied out of gelatin capsules). Then generously sprinkle this on any cut in the skin and leave in place. The bleeding will stop quickly, and the garlic will prevent infection from setting in. Healing will ensue rather rapidly after that.

Cysts. See under **Boils** for identical treatment.

Diabetes. Garlic, onions, cayenne pepper, goldenseal, and pau d'arco (an herb used for cancer) are all strongly hypoglycemic. What this means is that they *dramatically* lower blood-sugar levels. For those suffering from hypoglycemia, taking such herbs can be very problematic. But for diabetics, such news is actually a godsend. Garlic, especially, when taken faithfully every day, will actually help to reduce the amount of daily insulin a diabetic requires. Garlic won't necessarily cure the disease, nor take a diabetic completely off insulin (some will always be needed). But at least the amount injected each day will be gradually reduced over a period of time.

Cooked garlic and aged-garlic extract both work to a diabetic's advantage here. Meals in which garlic has been generously incorporated will assist the pancreas in turning out more natural insulin of its own. Four capsules or one tablespoon of aged-garlic extract are recommended for additional supplementation.

Diarrhea. Often, watery stools can be caused by bacterial invasion of the lower intestinal tract. Raw garlic as well as pickled garlic present a potent force in killing such harmful microorganisms. One garlic clove should be carefully chewed twice daily. At least one-half cup of pickled garlic should be consumed twice daily with meals, too. Diarrhea will cease very soon after this is done.

Earache. Where serious ear infection and pain prevail in a child or an adult, a medical doctor specializing in ears, nose, and throat disorders should be consulted. Garlic oil can be used to advantage here, but one should be careful about not overdoing the amount used; here a case can be made for "smaller is better."

Peel one clove of garlic and then slightly bruise it with a heavy object; after this finely chop it. Put the garlic into one-half cup of extra-virgin olive oil and let it stay there for several days. Then, using an eyedropper, place *no more* than four drops at a time in the canal of an infected or painful ear by tilting the head sideways. Insert a piece of cotton to keep the oil from running out. Repeat this procedure every 24 hours, if necessary. Be advised, however, that you should probably consult with a medical doctor before doing this to get his or her input on the matter. At least you'll then know whatever inherent risks there might be from such a thing and can choose according to your own conscience in the matter.

Flu. See under **Common Cold** for same method of treatment. A garlic enema may also be necessary here. Follow the directions given under **Complexion Problems** for making an enema solution, only double the quantities given for making this. Allow to get lukewarm before filling a hot-water bottle with it. Attach the hose and syringe part and place in an elevated position (on a door clothes hook or held up by someone else). Lie down on the floor after having lubricated the end of the syringe with a little oil or petroleum jelly and carefully insert it into the rectum. Slowly release the warm garlic water into the bowels until they can hold no more. Retain for two minutes before sitting down on the toilet to discharge. You'll be surprised at just how effective this method is for reducing fever and helping you get over the flu a lot quicker.

Fungus. Nail fungus on the fingers or toes and skin fungus (like athlete's foot) can be easily corrected with daily applications of raw garlic juice, pickled garlic juice, garlic tincture, or Kyolic liquid garlic extract. Look under **Complexion Problems** for how to effectively apply it topically using Q-tips. Instructions for making a simple garlic tincture are given there also. Doctors in India have treated soldiers suffering from skin fungus by applying thin slices of raw garlic directly to the infected surface and leaving for 24 hours. At first the area will become inflamed, but will soon subside as the sulfur components in garlic go to work to attack the fungus and kill it. It may take ten days to two weeks to clear up a stubborn case of skin fungus, but without garlic treatment nail fungus usually takes a lot longer to disappear.

Hardening of the Arteries. See under **Cholesterol** (Elevated) for similar information relating to this problem. Be advised not to expect too much from garlic, however, when problems of arteriosclerosis and atherosclerosis have prevailed for many years. Garlic may be a "wonder herb" for many health problems, but even it has limits to what can be expected against something that has taken a long time to accumulate.

Heart Attack.   Myocardial infarction is the fancy medical term for this medical emergency that occurs whenever a portion of the heart chamber is deprived of oxygen due to blockage of one of the coronary arteries that supply the heart muscle with blood. Heart attacks are more common when arteries have already been greatly narrowed through the years by coronary artery disease. *Warning—No attempt at self-treatment should be pursued if such an event occurs. Immediate hospitalization is required.*

One third of all cases occur suddenly and without advance notice. But with the remaining portion, attacks of chest pain (called angina) brought about by stress and tension or overexercise routinely occur for months or even years prior to a big heart attack. In many instances, a mild heart attack goes completely unnoticed, earning for it the term "silent heart attack."

Since blood clots blocking a coronary artery are the most common cause of heart attacks, reading the information given under **Clots** in this section will be helpful. Also the entry preceding it under **Cholesterol** (Elevated) should, likewise, be consulted. The reader will find material about the use of garlic that will be of benefit here.

Lifestyle changes are essential for avoiding a situation this critical. Eat less fatty and salty foods. Exercise more, especially by walking every morning or evening for 30 minutes. Get on a good weight-loss program, if necessary. Incorporate garlic, cayenne pepper, ginger root, and horseradish more frequently into the diet. Use these spices in their raw forms in meal preparations. Additional supplementation with them in capsulated forms is needed, too. I recommend a minimum of 1 capsule of each once a day with a meal for general maintenance of the heart, coronary arteries, and blood circulation.

Heart Disease.   Valuable information pertaining to this serious health condition is scattered among several different entries in this section: **Cholesterol** (Elevated), **Clots, Hardening of the**

Arteries, and **Heart Attack**. Consult each of them in the order given.

The specific term for this medical problem is coronary artery disease. It happens to be the leading cause of death in America. Besides other lifestyle advice previously given under **Heart Attack**, it is strongly suggested that a person susceptible to this avoid the inhalation of smoke or frigid air and not permit himself or herself to become emotionally wrought up.

Other health tips include the daily intake of Kyolic or home-made aged-garlic extract—4 capsules or 2 tablespoons of liquid—and the frequent use of raw, cooked, and pickled garlic in different meal arrangements. For some reason or another, daily consumption of *warm* peppermint tea seems to be of definite benefit as well, but just how it works isn't exactly known. It may be that the herb is a great oxygenator on account of the menthol present. There certainly is a synergism, though, when peppermint and garlic interact in the system together. (Look under the next entry, **Herpes,** for more information on the use of garlic wine or garlic vinegar in the prevention of heart disease.)

Herpes. Here is a viral disorder that is as old as the dinosaurs, some paleontologists think. Let's face it, the herpes family of viruses has been around longer than we have. It's one of those things that, when you get it in childhood (in the form of chickenpox), it will stay with you for life. It never dies but lies dormant in the nerve cells that extend from the spinal cord to the brain for many decades. But, eventually, it can be reactivated due to a severe psychological trauma or a serious infectious illness of some kind. Then it recurs in the form of shingles, which can prove fatal if not carefully attended to.

Garlic works in a number of different ways to weaken the activity of this virus within the body. First, it can bolster the power of the immune system. Taking 4 capsules of aged-garlic extract or 1 teaspoon of the liquid every day is good for this. Another way is by taking or using either garlic wine or garlic vinegar for this. Making either one is simple. Over low heat, simmer one entire bulb of peeled, raw, and coarsely cut garlic in one quart of red wine or apple cider vinegar until the cloves become somewhat mushy. Poaching garlic in either of these mediums not only softens it, but also helps to sweeten the flavor so that surprisingly large amounts can be used without proving to be offensive to our tasting or smelling senses. One tablespoon twice daily of either garlic wine or garlic vinegar between meals will give the body more power to resist herpes.

Second, the sulfur components in garlic and the phenolic compounds in wine and vinegar are going to help prevent the accompanying pain of shingles from ever reaching the brain. And either liquid extract may be applied topically to the small, red, fluid-filled blisters that appear on one side of the torso, arms, legs, or face. The liquid can be put on using several cotton Q-tips taped together.

High Blood Pressure. Frequently I get asked the question at many public-speaking engagements across the country, "What do you recommend for high blood pressure?" Invariably, the answer is garlic. And then I quickly add a follow-up explanation as to how it works for this condition. While doing so, I obviously keep my tongue planted firmly against my cheek and at the same time try to maintain a sober appearance so as not to betray my lighthearted intentions.

"Well," I begin to reason with my audience, "high blood pressure is usually caused by stress. And people, very much like ourselves here, are the reason behind most of this tension. Therefore, it seems to me that if you chew a couple of garlic cloves each day, it will keep annoying folks away from you, which produce the stress that elevates your blood pressure in the first place." I have yet to see a crowd fail to enjoy the mirth of the moment when I'm finished playing my little gag.

On the serious side of things, though, garlic is simply wonderful for bringing down high blood pressure. It has to be one of the most useful herbs for doing so in the entire plant kingdom. I know of nothing else that works so rapidly or so well for this common problem. Any of the processed forms of garlic will do nicely. The Kyolic aged-garlic extract (or its homemade counterpart) can be taken in 4 capsules or 1 teaspoon daily. Also, don't overlook the garlic wine or garlic vinegar mentioned under the previous entry, **Herpes**. One tablespoon every day of either helps a lot.

Infection (General). Infection, when it occurs, can be either bacterial or viral in nature. It is an assault on the body, which can be a direct frontal attack, or it can come sneaking in the back door under more suspicious circumstances. At first the problem is localized within a specific region, but it soon becomes more widespread if left unattended for very long. The immune system scrambles to get enough infantry cells out there to do battle with the bad guys. Depending on just how strong the body's immune reserves are will largely determine the outcome of the fights involved. If not enough reserve cells are fully active because of poor diet, too little sleep, and lack of exercise, then the enemy bacteria or viruses can overwhelm the body.

But by taking lots of garlic internally, it becomes the equivalent of quickly mobilizing more men into the military to deal with an emergency situation somewhere in the country or the world. Those wonderful but not necessarily pleasant-smelling sulfur compounds in this herb assist the body in recruiting more immune cells for its frontline defenses. Once this happens, other microbial invaders are quickly routed or else destroyed, thereby restoring a measure of integrity and safety to the body's own immune system.

I realize that what I've largely explained has been put in rather plain terms that may be too simplistic for some readers. But at least the language employed enables the average person to comprehend what is going on when garlic is used. In a true chemical sense, however, a much more sophisticated and scientific description would be utilized to accurately convey exactly what is going on inside the body. But I believe that the other portrayal suffices for our needs here.

When it comes to infection, garlic in *any* form or preparation is highly advisable. You don't need to be a rocket scientist or brain surgeon to understand thatnature's *ultimate antibiotic* will work no matter how much it is sliced, diced, freeze-dried, or overcooked. Average supplementation for a general infection can be as high as 6 capsules daily and as low as 4, but I wouldn't go below that until the problem has sufficiently passed. A good garlic enema is also recommended to help evacuate toxins that may have accumulated in the body long before and actually provided the environment in which the infection began. Consult under the entry **Flu** in this section for details on how to take an enema for this purpose.

Insect Bites/Stings. Garlic makes a nifty insecticide, whether planted near other vegetables more susceptible to insects or made into a spray and applied over them. But the subject here has more to do with the topical application of garlic than anything else. It has been said that "necessity is the mother of invention." I've found this to be true in many of my travels to remote parts of the globe. I've had more than my share of bites and stings from small flying, creeping, or crawling creatures that have left me in pain, swollen, and itching like crazy.

It was somewhere near the Tibetan border a number of years ago that I, quite by accident, happened onto the combination of chewed raw garlic and saliva as one of the quickest forms of relief for insect bites or stings. I don't know what bit me on my inner right thigh, but it was the cause of much grief and annoyance for the next few hours. That is, until an old Buddhist monk clad only in an orange sarong methodically chewed two cloves of garlic and then quietly slapped this wet material, saliva and all, onto my afflicted site before walking away saying nary a word to me. Within minutes the area felt 100 percent better, and by the end of the day my miseries down there had ceased. I truly recommend this for anyone who has ever suffered from insect bites or stings. Never venture outside very far without carrying a few garlic cloves in your pocket or purse.

Itching. See the foregoing entry for information relating to this. A mild solution of garlic and peppermint tea is also ideal for obtaining desired relief. To 1-1/2 cups boiling water, add 1 chopped garlic clove and 1 teaspoon peppermint leaves. Simmer, covered, for 10 minutes. Strain and spray on when cool.

Liver Disease. Members of the *Allium* and *Brassica* families are wonderful food therapy for liver distresses. These would include garlic, onion, leek, and scallion from the first and cabbage, kale, kohlrabi, Brussels sprouts, cauliflower, and mustard greens. Nor should be overlooked nasturtium, watercress, horseradish, or radish.

I always prefer a combination of Kyolic aged-garlic extract (3 capsules or 3/4 teaspoon liquid) and the marvelous turmeric-derived C-3 Complex product (2 tablets daily) from the Sabinsa Corporation for treating any disturbance in this organ (other than cancer). Also incorporating tomato and carrot juice into the diet is a good idea. Mix 1 level tablespoon of Mighty Greens and Beet Root Juice Powder from Pines International into either juice and drink with a meal. (See Product Appendix for information on how to get these fine products if they aren't available in your local health-food store.)

Lung Problems. A little nip of garlic wine or garlic vinegar (1 tablespoon) every day in some *warm* peppermint tea (1 cup) will help to facilitate breathing better where an allergy, asthma, bronchitis, or emphysema may persist. The same solution is quite effective for mild cases of tuberculosis. An old drifter, who has ridden the rails all over America, once told me that he held his own TB in check by taking a swig of garlic whiskey a few times every day. He made it up by soaking one entire peeled and coarsely chopped garlic bulb in one pint of sour mash whiskey for a week or more.

Oral Problems. Cold sores are common to teenagers and adults and can be a source of much annoyance. They are usually caused by the herpes or some other virus. Thrush is a fungal condition in the mouths of infants and very young children. Both problems can be treated with garlic preparations, but in very different ways. The first can be treated with a strong garlic-vitamin-E oil and the latter with a garlic tincture.

To make the oil, peel and coarsely chop one garlic bulb and set in a glass jar. Pour over it about 1-1/2 cups of Rex's Wheat Germ Oil or an equivalent brand of vitamin-E oil until the garlic is covered. Loosely screw on a lid and let set in a cool, dry, dark place for ten days, shaking vigorously once a day. Strain, add 10 drops of glycerine to preserve, and store where it was before until needed. Using Q-tips or a cotton ball, apply some of this special garlic-vitamin-E oil to cold sores around the corners of the mouth and lips. For holding in place inside the mouth somewhere, apply some of this oil on top of a square-inch slice of white bread smeared with a thin layer of peanut butter, before inserting with your thumb or fingers. (*Note:* To order Rex's Wheat Germ Oil, send $65 to John Heinerman, Ph.D., P.O. Box 11471, Salt Lake City, UT 84147. A one-quart metal can of it will be sent by fourth-class mail to you. I carry it as a service to readers who have difficulty getting it.)

You can make the garlic tincture by adding 1 chopped bulb of peeled garlic to 1-1/2 pints of good alcohol in a bottle of some kind and sealing with a lid. Shake morning and night and let set for nearly a month. A young child's mouth can be swabbed with a cotton ball that has been saturated with some of this solution. Several applications are necessary, however, to totally eliminate the fungal problem on the tongue and insides of the mouth.

Toothache. I came up with a simple solution for this many years ago while in New Orleans to speak at a National Health Federation convention. I had one of the amalgam fillings in a back molar drop out by accident. Within a few hours my tooth started hurting. I went to a market near my hotel and bought a garlic bulb. I took it back to my room and peeled one clove with my pocket knife. I then crushed it with a heavy glass ashtray and packed it into the hole and around the tooth where the filling had been. Within minutes the throbbing pain ceased and remained so for about 15 hours until another change of garlic was necessary. But the remedy worked satisfactorily until I returned home and could see a dentist to get the problem corrected for good.

Triglycerides (Elevated). Raw, cooked, pickled, and aged garlic extract are all good for controlling excess triglycerides in the body. I advise taking 2–3 capsules of Kyolic or 15 drops of the liquid each day for this. The garlic wine and garlic vinegar mentioned under the entry for **Herpes** also works well here. See **Cholesterol (Elevated)** for further data.

Warts. Warts are common, benign skin growths caused by a viral infection. There are a number of different kinds of warts, named for their location on the body and their appearance. Most of them disappear spontaneously within a couple of years. But recurrence is common, since the virus may be present in neighboring tissues.

Garlic is one of the best things for checking the spread of the human papilloma virus (HPV) that causes warts in the first place. There are some 60 types of HPV that can be transmitted from person to person or even something as simple as contact with shed skin from a wart found on a shower-room floor, for instance. Together with garlic, overripe banana skins are suitable for their removal. A combination of the two makes an unbeatable cure for warts.

Cut several wafer-thin slices of a garlic clove with a sharp knife. Or else squeeze a tiny bit of juice from several garlic cloves by using a garlic press. Then lay the garlic strips or drop the garlic juice on an inch-square *inside* section of nearly black banana skin. Place this directly over the wart and tape in place, making sure the *inside* portion of the banana peel is touching the skin. Leave it on for about 15 hours before changing; repeat this procedure for up to 10 days. By then, the wart should have disappeared for good.

Worms. Parasites such as roundworm, pinworm, hook worm, and tapeworm occupy the intestinal tracts of many people. Raw garlic and pumpkin seeds, thoroughly chewed at the same time and swallowed in small amounts will do more to get rid of them than just about anything else around (except for the noxious herb wormwood). Garlic in other forms can be used by itself, but won't prove nearly as effective as the foregoing combination will. Getting young children to chew both may take more effort than actually getting rid of the worms themselves. It may be necessary to pulverize a garlic clove and a few pumpkin seeds in advance and then stir them in with applesauce or a similar delicious medium to entice kids to take it.

Yeast Infection. The body always harbors a tiny amount of the fungus *Candida albicans,* in addition to some harmless bacteria that compete with this fungus and thus keep it under control. But if the number of such bacteria diminish very much (say, due to antibiotic drug therapy, the fungus will proliferate without restriction and soon cause symptoms. When it occurs in the vagina, it is known as yeast infection, and in the mouth it is called thrush. Sometimes it can enter the bloodstream; when this happens it produces chronic fatigue syndrome and can severely weaken a person's physical capacity to do much. Women are more susceptible to this than men are.

Now garlic is going to be of definite benefit in such cases. The advantage here is that the garlic's many sulfur components destroy this fungus but don't necessarily affect the adjoining bacteria that usually restrict Candida. Raw, cooked, pickled, and aged-garlic extract are all sensible forms of therapy to inhibit this fungal activity. The aged-garlic extract (Kyolic or homemade) can be taken in 3 capsules or 1 teaspoon of liquid each day with a meal.

There is a downside, however, to using raw, cooked, or pickled garlic. Quite often, those who suffer from Candidiasis also experience fatigue from hypoglycemia, which compounds the problem that much more. And since garlic in these other forms is decidedly hypoglycemic, it's obviously going to be a deterrent with low blood sugar, although serving the individual well on the yeast control side of things. Fortunately, though, Kyolic aged garlic isn't going to disturb a person's blood-sugar level in the event that the individual has hypoglycemia besides Candidiasis.

An important thing I mentioned in one of my earlier books, *Double the Power of Your Immune System*, is to always practice a rotation diet, wherein no identical foods are consumed within a week of one another. This helps to regulate the spread of *Candida albicans* so that it can't adapt itself more easily to a familiar food schedule and thereby grow more quickly.

Robust Recipes to Savor and Sample

No chapter on garlic would be complete without the inclusion of some recipes. But not just any ordinary recipes. Instead I have selected a few that are different in several ways. First, they offer a tantalizing aroma when made up. Second, they taste terrific to the palate when eaten. And third, they inspire the appetite and satisfy hunger pangs. But, most of all, *they are good for you*. (I am indebted to Susan Belsinger and Carolyn Dille for the original recipes from which these revisions were made. Susan lives in Baltimore and Carolyn in San Jose.)

Tuscan Whole Wheat Garlic Bread

Needed:

One dozen slices of whole-wheat bread from an uncut loaf;
   use an electric knife to slice pieces about an inch thick

2/3 cup extra-virgin olive oil

3/4 teaspoon granulated kelp (a seaweed obtained from
supermarkets or health-food stores)

5 garlic cloves, peeled

What to Do:

Toast each bread slice on both sides under the oven broiler until nicely browned. Mix the oil and kelp together in an aluminum pie tin. When the toast turns lukewarm, rub both sides of each piece with a garlic clove. Then dip one side into the kelp-oil mixture and enjoy the eating experience.

Garlic-Yogurt Sauce for Vegetables and Meat

Needed:

3 garlic cloves

1/2 tsp. granulated kelp

1/2 tsp. crushed peppercorns

1 cup plain yogurt

1/2 cup sour cream

2/3 cup finely cut cilantro and parsley

1/4 tsp. aniseed

1/4 tsp. lemon juice

What to Do:

Mash the peeled garlic between sheets of waxed paper aluminum foil, or in a plastic sandwich bag that has a zip-lock top to it with a rolling pin or hammer. Put the pulpy mass in a wooden bowl and add the rest of the ingredients. Mix together thoroughly with a wooden spoon. Cover with plastic wrap and refrigerate for four hours. Makes two cups of sauce that impart a wonderful taste to cooked vegetables, some squashes, meat, fish, and poultry.

Garlic Lamb with Spuds

Needed:

A leg of lamb (about 7 pounds in weight)
7 garlic cloves
Granulated kelp
Pinches of cumin and coriander
1 tsp. sweet basil
1 whole lime
4 medium-sized red potatoes, coarsely cut

What to Do:

Peel and crush the garlic cloves to a pulpy mass. Add the cumin, coriander, and sweet basil. Cut small, deep slashes all over the lamb and stuff some of this garlic-herb paste into them. Season the meat with kelp, then rub it all over with both halves of the cut lime. Place the meat in a roasting pan and firmly squeeze the remaining juice from both lime halves and drizzle over the top of the lamb.

The meat should be cooked for approximately 20 minutes in a preheated oven set at 425° F. Then turn the oven down to 350° F. In about 30 minutes add a cup of water. Then arrange the spuds around the lamb and continue cooking another hour. Remove the pan from the oven and let its contents stand for 20 minutes before cutting the meat into thin slices. Pour the cooking juices over the served meat and potatoes for extra flavor. There's enough here for four generous servings.

Lentil-Vegetable Curry with Garlic

Needed:

1-1/2 cups whole green lentils
2-1/2 tbsps. canola oil
1 tsp. granulated kelp
1 tsp. ground coriander
1/2 tsp. ground cumin
3 garlic cloves, peeled and finely minced

1 carrot, peeled and sliced diagonally

1 potato, peeled and cubed

7 okra, topped and tailed, then cut into 1-inch pieces

1 small eggplant, halved and sliced

1 small zucchini, sliced diagonally

2 cups water

1 tbsp. curry powder

1-1/2 tsps. fresh chopped peppermint leaves

1 tbsp. fresh chopped cilantro

1 tsp. finely cut radish leaf tops

What to Do:

Wash the lentils and drain thoroughly through a sieve. Put them into a large stainless-steel saucepan and pour 2-1/2 cups of water over them. Simmer on low heat for 20 minutes. When they become soft, pour into a Vita-Mix machine or equivalent blender and puree until they have a smooth consistency.

In another large saucepan, heat the oil and gently sauté the coriander, cumin, and garlic together for no more than 2 minutes. Turn the vegetables into the pan and cook another 2 minutes, stirring constantly. Add the 2 cups of water and the smooth lentil puree to this vegetable mixture and stir with a wire whisk.

Finally, add the curry powder and leaves of peppermint, cilantro, and radish. Continue cooking for 15 minutes. Makes about four servings.

Liver and Garlic

This is my own variation of the familiar liver and onions. Those who can't tolerate the latter may find my own garlic version something of an eating adventure.

Needed:

One garlic bulb

1 lb. lambs' liver, thinly sliced

Granulated kelp to taste

1/3 cup whole-wheat flour
4 tbsps. canola oil
2 tbsps. butter
2 tsps. fresh chopped cilantro

What to Do:

Peel the individual garlic cloves and slice them very thin with a sharp paring knife. Combine the kelp and flour together on an empty pie plate. Proceed to lay the slices of lamb's liver into it, turning each one and pressing gently to coat evenly all over.

Put the oil and the butter into a large frying pan. Heat gently until foaming commences. Add the garlic slices and sauté for about 2 minutes. Then add the liver slices and fry for 4 minutes on each side until well cooked. (Cooking time will vary depending on the thickness of each slice.)

Stir the cilantro into the liver and garlic and then turn out onto plates to eat. Serves about four people.

Garlic Honey Ice Cream

Needed:
4 garlic cloves, peeled
1/2 cup clover honey
1 cup whipping cream (which is double cream)
2 cups half-and-half (Which is single cream)
3 egg yolks

What to Do:

In a small saucepan bring the honey and garlic to a gentle boil for about five minutes. Be sure, though, that the honey doesn't boil over the top. Set aside, cover with a lid, and let contents steep overnight. Remove garlic cloves the next day.

Dissolve the honey in both creams over a low heat setting. Beat the egg yolks in a separate bowl, adding about one-half cup of the cream to warm them, then pour the yolk mixture into the pot. Stir the mixture over low heat until the custard just coats a metal spoon.

Strain the custard through a sieve into a bowl and chill it, covered, overnight in the refrigerator. Pour the chilled custard into an ice cream freezer and follow the manufacturer's instructions. Believe it or not, the honey will draw out the garlic's moisture and flavor to the point that you won't be able to detect the garlic, although you'll know the taste is definitely unusual.

The Chemistry of Garlic

I am grateful to Harunobu Amagase, Ph.D., for the following information on the interesting chemistry of garlic. Dr. Amagaso is the senior manager in charge of Research and Development for Wakunaga of America Co., Ltd., in Mission Viejo, California. Wakunaga Pharmaceutical Co., Ltd., of Hiroshima, Japan, manufactures the world's premier-selling aged-garlic extract, which its American subsidiary markets globally under the trademark name of Kyolic. So popular is this brand of garlic that in many parts of the world Kyolic and garlic have become virtually synonymous.

Although garlic has been used in traditional medicine for many centuries, plenty of new findings on garlic in chemistry and pharmacology have been revealed within the last 50 years or so.

A garlic bulb contains alliin (S-allyl cysteine sulfoxide) and the enzyme, alliinase. The cutting and/or crushing of garlic cloves activates alliinase, catalyzing the conversion of alliin to allicin. Alliin itself is not an odorous compound. But once garlic cells are ruptured by cutting or crushing, they start smelling because of the generation of allicin.

Allicin is an essential odor of garlic and is an unstable and highly reactive compound that readily decomposes to other sulfur-containing compounds. Allicin was discovered to be a component of garlic in 1944. At that time, doctors were just beginning to discover the antibiotics that have since then treated many infectious diseases. So the discovery of allicin in garlic at that time became sensational enough to warrant garlic being patented in the United States for its incredible antibiotic and antifungal properties.

The plan of medicinal or antiseptic use of allicin soon faded, however, because of its instability and toxicity. Allicin, a highly reactive compound, reacts with many substances such as amino acids and proteins. When allicin is mixed with blood, almost all allicin disappears within a few minutes. It has also been demonstrated that no allicin can be detected in the bloodstream after the ingestion of raw garlic or pure allicin. These findings clearly suggest that allicin doesn't contribute to any of the beneficial effects belonging to garlic when it's taken into the human body.

Currently, allicin is believed to be a transient compound that is rapidly decomposed into many different kinds of sulfur compounds. Thus, allicin hasn't been established as the main ingredient in garlic, although some garlic companies would like to have you believe otherwise.

Processed garlic that is aged for awhile is, however, very rich in a variety of sulfur-containing compounds, which can act synergistically or antagonistically with one another to provide the health benefits we've come to expect from this herb. Since aged-garlic preparations contain little or no allicin, due to the instability of allicin itself, they will cause no untoward effects when taken internally. Fresh garlic preparations, however, may invoke stomach distress and allergic reactions in some people who test out hypersensitive to raw garlic.

In the 1990s, other sulfur-containing compounds, such as S-allyl cysteine, ajoene, vinyldithiins, (gamma)-glutamyl S-allyl cysteine, and others have been demonstrated to exhibit respectable pharmacological activities within animal and human models. S-Allyl cysteine (SAC) has been shown to be bioavailable in biological systems. Besides this, various kinds of effects of nonsulfur components, such as saponins, phenolic compounds, mono- and oligosaccharides, fructose, and protein from garlic preparations have also been reported.

Garlic is rich in arginine. This amino acid is a source of nitric acid, which is a chemical transmitter of macrophages, blood vessels, and nerves. Likewise, garlic has some trace element content of germanium, albeit extremely minute. This rare element is crucial in the body's defense against cancer cells. Other unique compounds with some interesting behavior include allixin and assorted saponins (soaplike chemicals).

Recent scientific interest in garlic has risen considerably due to the impressive results of many research experiments conducted in numerous laboratories around the world. As previously mentioned, a number of other chemical substances and their derivatives have been discovered in garlic besides the much ballyhooed allicin. Some of the most acclaimed oil- and water-soluble sulfur compounds as well as other nonsulfur compounds are enumerated as follows:

Oil-soluble compounds:	Diallyl sulfide
	Diallyl disulfide
	Diallyl trisulfide
	Dithiins
	Ajoene
Water-soluble compounds:	S-allyl cysteine
	S-allyl mercaptocysteine
	S-methyl cysteine
	gamma-glutamyl cysteine
Nonsulfur compounds:	Arginine
	Allixin
	Saponins
	Polysaccharides

It isn't necessary to tax the reader's patience nor weary the brain further with jaw-breaking names that make no sense at all without some kind of a background in medicinal chemistry. Save to say that the preceding chemical constituents in garlic have overlapping responsibilities in the respiratory system; the digestive tract and colon; major organs such as the heart, liver, spleen, and pancreas; certain glands such as the thymus, hypothalamus, and thyroid; and in the immune and nervous systems. These are things that make garlic the incredible health wonder of the plant world that it has been for millennia on end.

Chapter Four

Eternal Ginseng
The Revealed Health Mysteries
of the Orient's Greatest
Medicinal Treasure

The Components of Life

I've read many treatises on ginseng through the years from Oriental as well as Western authors. But none has ever taken the *introductory* approach that my herbal colleague and friend Christopher Hobbs has in his recent user's guide on *The Ginsengs* (Santa Cruz, CA: Botanica Press, 1996, pp. 10–11). Near the beginning of his little guide, he features a sidebar discussion about "Qi, Blood, Yin & Yang— . . .", which he calls, ". . . The Components of Life" (the same one borrowed for this section subheading).

He starts out informing readers that Western medicine recognizes blood as a fluid substance "that carries oxygen, sugars and other nutrients, immune substances, and waste products in and out of the cells of the body." But traditional Chinese medicine (TCM) looks at the same blood plasma in a totally different manner. It is the way of yin and yang that matters the most here.

As I learned in my different trips to mainland China and Taiwan over the last couple of decades, this pair is basic not only to Chinese medicine and food, but to the rest of their culture and lifestyles. For them it is a "world of cause and effect" in which existence itself "is divided into pairs of opposites that balance and complement each other" to form a sum total.

A ready illustration I've always liked to use in explaining the concept to others is the moon. In its full state, we see it in the

145

night sky in its *whole* form. But it goes through different cycles of expansion and contraction in order to get there; this we call "the waxing and waning" phases. Another way of looking at this bit of philosophy is to consider how every 24-hour period is broken up: there is a morning phase for light increase and darkness decrease (dawn) and an evening phase wherein light ebbs away and night ensues (dusk). How about the four seasons of the year—aren't they really just merging opposites of sorts? We have fall-winter (cool to colder) and spring-summer (warm to hotter).

Hobbs writes of similar analogies, "Each has its own nature and can be defined by the pairs that relate with it." In a comparable way, yin and yang are similar. "For instance, Yin is associated with coldness, the feminine aspect, darkness and inward movement, and thus nurturing." On the other, he states, "Yang is associated with heat, light, action or activity, and outward movement."

The ancient Chinese strongly believed that for sound health to be present, these two factors must always be in balance. And when they aren't, then imbalance exists, which invariably sets the stage for organic weakness and eventually the disease process. There can't be "too much heat or cold, not too much activity or nourishment (catabolism versus anabolism)," Hobbs declares. He suggests that if we view yin as matter and yang as energy, it might help us better to comprehend just how the Chinese regard life in general and specifically. "Matter is solid and represents a denser manifestation of energy, whereas energy is active and expansive and represents matter breaking down to release energy, like wood burning to produce heat and light."

Yin and yang are beyond being theoretical; they are, in fact, "the primary law of physics: by way of Chinese reckoning and, therefore, constitute "everything in the universe [being] governed by this." In order to preserve one's health or correctly treat an illness, it is necessary for every individual to try to find "balancing pairs of opposites that are considered important to the function of the body." Yin and yang balance is the alpha and omega of human health—"the Beginning and the End," "the First and the Last"—by which harmony is accomplished and *wholeness* finally achieved.

The judicious use of botanicals is a significant step toward changing "the Yin-Yang balance of the cells, organs, and tissues" while on the road toward health restoration. Hobbs is of the firm opinion that "various ginsengs can promote either Yin or Yang, depending on the type, how much is taken, and under what circumstances."

So far we've discussed yin and yang only in general terms. But now for some specifics regarding the pair. If someone is into excessive jogging, drinking espresso, or taking an herbal energy stimulant every day, that person's body metabolism becomes "too active." In such instances, "the Yin substances (moisture, blood, sexual hormones, etc.) can be depleted, causing one to become 'dried out.' " Under such circumstances, it is highly desireable to "tonify the Yin."

A different scenario from this might be considered for the opposite factor. If someone suffers from an underactive thyroid gland, has hypoglycemia, chronic fatigue syndrome or yeast infection, is plain lazy, experiences coldness in the lower extremities due to poor circulation, is obese, full of mucus, or constipated, "there is lack of movement and release of energy." Therefore, in order to recharge certain "master glands" and organs of the body such as the liver, pancreas, and spleen, "we need to 'tonify the Yang.' "

Hobbs also gives focus to the Qi, which can be given "to mean energy or vitality." But, "in Chinese medicine, there are a number of types of Qi." He recommends two books for those wishing to better acquaint themselves with it: T. J. Kaptchuk, *The Web That Has No Weaver* (New York: Congdon & Weed, Inc., 1983) and H. Beinfield and E. Korngold, *Between Heaven and Earth* (New York: Ballantine, 1991). But for our own purposes here, "Qi will be taken to mean vitality, mainly." Hobbs explains that "Qi is the force that causes the blood to move through the vessels, the lungs to take air in and out, the body to move, the mind to think, and the immune systems to ward off pathogens."

In classical Chinese medicine, the immune system's entire ability to cast off pathogens that induce disease is referred to as the "Antipathogenic Qi." "Conversely, the power or vitality of the pathogen is known as the 'Pathogenic Qi,' " Hobbs writes. Hence, to overcome most health problems such as influenza and the common cold, it is desirable to "tonify the anti-pathogenic Qi." For many, many centuries, countless Chinese doctors, herbalists, and acupuncturists have, more or less, claimed that "if our anti-pathogenic Qi is stronger than the pathogenic Qi, we will *get better.*"

We definitely need "all the Qi we can get!" Ginseng is one of the finest botanicals in the entire plant kingdom for helping us to achieve this. When the root is used consistently in the body, all system functions "work better." We look better, feel better, think better, and move better because of it. Through ginseng root, our Qi levels gradually increase. It's almost as if the very pulse of life has been quickened. This inner quickening of sorts manifests itself outwardly in a number of different ways. Not only are we more alert and energetic, but in more subtle ways, too, our spiritual comprehension is keener, our feelings more sensitive, and our thoughts more ingenious.

This, of course, doesn't imply that ginseng root is going to enhance our appearance, or make us smarter, or more athletic. But the "action force" of Qi behind all these things will certainly be enlarged within our beings once we get on a regular program of ginseng supplementation. The purpose of this chapter, therefore, is to reveal the health mysteries of this, the Orient's greatest medicinal treasure—eternal and everlasting ginseng—in order to bring out the Qi in you!

Nomenclature

The Latin name for ginseng is *Panax ginseng,* and it has a somewhat interesting background as to its historical origins. First of all, the botanical generic name *Panax* hails from the Greek word for "panacea." This certainly hints at the root's broad spectrum of medicinal applications, from all that we know about it. Panacea is on par with the term "cure-all"; ginseng seems to have earned its well-deserved scientific moniker *Panax,* after all.

An even more intriguing tail lies behind the specific herb name of ginseng, however. This name relates to the somewhat anthropomorphic appearance of the root itself. The story first appeared sometime during the reign of the Chinese Emperor Wenti of the Sui Dynasty (from 581–601 B.C.). The setting is said to have been in the city of Shangtang in the Shensi Province. According to the ancient Chinese herbal *Pen Ts'ao* (published in 1578 by Li Shih-chen from an even older manuscript), the following happened one time:

At the back of a certain person's house, was heard each night the imploring voice of a man. And when search was made for the source of this sound, at the distance of about a *li* there was seen a remarkable ginseng plant [by members of the search party].

Upon digging into the earth to the depth of five feet; the root was secured. [It was found to have] the shape of a man, with four extremities perfect and complete. And it was this that had been calling out in the night with a man's voice. It was, therefore, called T'u-ching or "spirit of the ground." It is said that the best ginseng formerly came from this Shangtang [region].

'Seng hunters, as they are frequently called by those in the herb business, insist that the more humanlike the roots appear, the stronger and more potent are their medicinal properties. Some older herbalists with whom I have visited in times past throughout the Orient insisted that their *greatest* health miracles came from using roots that were at least eight years old and had the *general* outlines of a man's torso.

One man, in fact, by the name of Wu Lin, who resided in the city of Soochow on mainland China, told me in the summer of 1980 about several remarkable "back-from-the-grave" experiences involving some of his nearly gone patients and ginseng root. He noted two cases in particular—that of a 57-year-old man, whose weak heart had almost given out and that of a 33-year-old farm laborer, who just about died while delivering her child.

Wu Lin said that he administered copious amounts of the root tea to both, for many hours. But he could never give me specific amounts nor frequency of these administrations. Suffice it to say, though, that the man pulled through his coronary ordeal and the young woman gave birth to a healthy baby boy without further complications. He did specify, however, that *old* roots made for *stronger* tea. He claimed that they had more "ground spirits" in them than younger roots did.

My Oriental informant stated that for himself, gathering up the old roots in the late fall was the best time for obtaining the highest-quality ginseng. And when he couldn't find the time to go and dig it up himself, he would carefully purchase some from other 'seng hunters whom he trusted. But this wily old gentleman had developed an unusual but proven method to determine if what he was buying, was, in fact, true Panax or some inferior ginseng. He and a friend or relative who accompanied him on such buying trips would take a brisk walk together for about a mile or so. Wu Lin would place a small piece of the root in his mouth and be chewing on it the entire way; the other person's mouth remained empty. If, at the end of the distance, Wu Lin didn't feel as tired as his companion did, then it was true Panax he was getting. On the other hand, if he was also out of breath, then he immediately knew he was being sold a lesser-quality ginseng.

The finding of ground sources for patches of this herb were usually preceded by or accompanied with dreams, visions, invisible voices, even shooting stars and other supernatural phenomena. I asked Wu Lin if he had ever had such mystical guidance himself while searching for the root. He denied having any of these, but did admit that he had inherited from his father and grandfather before him a special "gift" (as he called it) or inner "sixth sense" for always knowing where to look for growths of old plant roots, without previous knowledge of their location.

Wu Lin stated in no uncertain terms that the true older root was good for character building besides the more obvious ones of physical healing and restoration of body health. "Ginseng root tea," he told me through my government-provided interpreter, "tonifies the five viscera. It quiets the animal spirits in man," referring, no doubt, to the animal lusts in each of us. This "establishes the soul, allays fear, expels evil debris, brightens the eye, opens up the heart," and thereby "benefits the [human] understanding." He also promised that "if taken for some time ginseng root will invigorate the body and prolong life."

On one level, my own scientific training as an anthropologist had taught me that whatever information a folk healer imparted would naturally have some fables intertwined with the fact. But, on another level, my gut reaction was that just about everything the old gent had been sharing with me was true, at least to a greater than a lesser extent. I mean, how could I question the validity of some of the unscientific things he told me about this root, when he said them with such sincere emphasis and a straightforward look in his eye?

I grant you that drinking ginseng root tea several times every day may not transform you into "the picture of perfection" that many imagine Pope John Paul II or Mother Theresa to be. But it definitely should help "clear out the debris" within in order to make you a better human being spiritually and emotionally, besides physically, of course (as Wu Lin insisted it does).

Giving Clarity to Types of Ginseng

Christopher Hobbs has some thoughts on the many variations of ginseng. "There are different varieties of true ginsengs, as well as differences in cultivation and manufacturing processes, each of which is relevant to how the herb affects the body and for which kinds of conditions it is best suited. Other herbs are not true ginsengs at all but are classified functionally in [traditional Chinese medicine] with the ginsengs, because they have similar effects." The *only* true ginsengs, he points out, are those belonging to the genus *Panax* from the ginseng family, Araliaceae. This is how botanists and Western herbalists, at least, characterize things. Unfortunately, though, "Chinese herbalists . . . often do not draw distinctions between herbs based on botanical characteristics alone, but on other properties such as taste, temperature, and actions in the body." Hence, we have the many variations in ginseng, with a few of them being the true kind and the remaining majority being merely *pseudo* "ginsengs."

Starting with true ginseng from the genus *Panax*, there is *Panax ginseng,* also commonly referred to as Oriental ginseng, Chinese ginseng, and Korean ginseng. This is the most common one and the chief ingredient of most ginseng products originating in China, Hong Kong, Taiwan, and Korea, or else manufactured in the United States and Canada. It comes in many forms, ranging

from whole root and coarsely cut crude drug for tea-making purposes to encapsulated powder and liquid tonic. All of these contain a guaranteed amount of ginsenosides, Hobbs assures us.

The two principal types of *Panax ginseng* are white and red. This has nothing to do with their botanical differences, but instead refers to the manner in which each one is manufactured. The white kind, which can be Korean or Chinese, is the root that has been peeled and dried. Red ginseng, on the other hand, is mostly Korean and has been steamed with the peel left intact and then dried. This process is quite effective in preserving the root from insects, but it also creates some chemical changes. Scientific studies confirm that red ginseng contains different ginsenosides, which helps explain its different effects in the human body.

When I was in mainland China in 1980 with the American Medical Students' Association and visited with Wu Lin in the city of Soochow, he explained to me the difference between red and white ginseng. He bade me and my government-provided interpreter to follow him outside his simple dwelling to a small backyard, where the embers of a dying coal fire still glowed beneath a heavy iron pot supported over it on a metal tripod. "My dinner," he joked with us in Chinese. Reaching for a stick lying nearby, he pointed to the embers and said that red ginseng was for those folks past 50 whose "fires" of vigor and vitality had started to extinguish. For anyone using addictive stimulants, such as tobacco, tea, coffee, colas, wine and beer, or mahuang (ephedra), or for anybody under 50 years of age, however, it could prove discomforting, if not somewhat harmful. In fact, instead of serving as a soothing tonic, it could actually aggravate the stresses these other substances induced.

White ginseng, on the other hand, was always intended to be a somewhat "cooler" ginseng. It has more universal appeal because of its "all-purpose" properties. Although nowhere near as stimulating as the red kind, white ginseng, nevertheless, contributes energy to the body by improving the digestion and assimilation of food. Its effects, Wu Lin noted, were more subtle and gradual on the system and not as easily detected as red ginseng could be. The white kind also yielded longer-term effects than the white did, especially when it came to promoting longevity.

As Hobbs explains in his *User's Guide* of the ginsengs, "the next . . . true ginseng is American ginseng, *Panax quinque-folius*

. . ." It can be found only in the United States and Canada, however, and nowhere else. It looks something like *Panax* and favors "the hardwood forests of Eastern North America, commonly occurring on cool north slopes along with sugar maple and red and white oaks." This type of ginseng was originally used by some Native American tribes for getting rid of fevers, promoting fertility in women, removing headaches, relieving cramps and hoarse coughing, overcoming shortness of breath, curing earache and throat pain, and to stop vomiting.

American ginseng was introduced to China by a Catholic Jesuit priest residing in Sault Saint Louis, close by Montreal. His name was Père Joseph François Lafitau (1681–1746). He had come from France in 1711 to work for six years with the Caughnawage division of the Mohawk tribe. He read an account of the use of *Panax ginseng* in China by another French Jesuit, who published his "Description of the Tartarian Plant Ginseng" in the *Philosophical Transactions of the Royal Society of London* in 1714. That author, Father Père Jartoux mentioned that if this herb might be found anywhere else in the world "it may be particularly in Canada, where the forest and mountains . . . very much resemble these here [in China]." After reading these words, Lafitau began a diligent search for some ginseng in the territory where he lived. One day, as luck would have it, he came across a patch of it growing in the back of his primitive log cabin. He sent samples of this American variety back to China. Within just a couple of years, a vigorous trade began in this herb between both countries. Indians, frontiersmen such as Daniel Boone, French fur traders, and others began harvesting this plant in great quantities and shipping it to the Orient.

A young Swedish explorer, who happened to be visiting in French Canada at the time, described just how ambitious this activity became. In his *Travels in North America* (II:436–37), Peter Kalm reported:

> The trade which is carried on with it here is very brisk, for they gather great quantities of it and send them to France, whence they are brought to China and sold to great advantage . . .

> During my stay in Canada all the merchants in Quebec and Montreal received orders from their correspondents in France to

send over a quantity of ginseng, there being an uncommon
demand for it this summer . . .

The Indians especially travelled about the country in order to collect as much as they could and sell it to the merchants at
Montreal. The Indians . . . were likewise so taken up with this
business that the French farmers were not able during that time
to hire a single Indian, as they commonly do to help them in the
harvest.

[Ginseng root] formerly grew in abundance round Montreal, but
at present there is not a single plant of it to be found, so effectual-
ly have they been rooted out. This obliged the Indians this summer to go far within the English boundaries to collect these roots.

This incessant plundering of one of our continent's most
abundant natural resources in the name of greed eventually put it
on the endangered species list in both countries; however, it is virtually impossible to find American ginseng growing wild anywhere
on Montreal island at present. In their mad and eager pursuits to
dig it all up, these early Indians and French colonists simply forgot to replant it or, at the very least, leave the younger plants
intact for future harvesting. Today, much of the American ginseng
being exported from the United States and Canada to mainland
China and Taiwan is cultivated.

I should mention here that there is a considerable difference
between wild-grown American ginseng and wildcrafted American
ginseng. The former root is grown in the woods under natural conditions, without fertilizer or herbicides, by planting the seed or
young transplants in areas where American ginseng has been
found growing before. The wild-grown kind sold for an average of
$450 *per pound* in 1996! On the other hand, though, wildcrafted
American ginseng sold for an average of $225 per pound in the
same year. Upper New York State is one of the leading suppliers of
this kind of American ginseng; in 1996, about 17,300 pounds were
exported from the state. According to an article on the subject in
the *Sunday Times Union* of Albany for April 30, 1989, it then cost
"about $30,000 per acre to set up a ginseng farm, and [that] the
venture is fraught with high risk, the crop being subject to various
diseases (like root rot)."

A terrific breakfast juice drink devised by Jim Long, an Arkansas herbalist residing in the Ozark Mountains, calls for the following ingredients and methods of preparation:

Pineapple-Ginseng Wake-Up

Piece of American ginseng the size of two pinto beans
1/2 cup boiling water
1 can pineapple juice
1 cup apple or mango juice
1 tsp. fresh lemon juice
1 tbsp. honey

Mash the piece of ginseng root slightly. Pour boiling water over the ginseng and cover, letting it steep 5 to 7 minutes. Remove the root and save for use again. Combine the ginseng tea with the remaining ingredients, shake or mix well, and refrigerate. Makes about 2-1/2 cups.

In his wonderful book, *Chinese Herbal Remedies* (New York: Universe Books, 1984, p. 76), biochemist Albert Y. Leung draws a sharp and clear distinction between American ginseng and Oriental ginseng. "In Chinese medicine . . . American ginseng is regarded as having cooling or even cold properties as opposed to the warming or invigorating nature of Oriental ginseng." He recalls when he was a child that neither he nor his brothers and sisters "were allowed to take Oriental ginseng because . . . we were young and strong and should not overdo what nature was already doing for us." He goes on, though, to relate that "we took American ginseng on numerous occasions in the summer to cool down. And when one of my sisters had scarlet fever and was under the care of a physician who practiced Western medicine, my grandmother gave her American ginseng to help cool her fever, with the consent of the doctor. My sister recovered with no complications."

Finally, he warns that because of "the opposing natures" of both ginseng, "if one takes [it] without knowing which type [the ginseng] is, one may use the wrong type and not derive benefits from its effects." The fact alone that American ginseng contains only ginsenosides but not the panaxosides found in Oriental ginseng suggests a strong chemical difference right there. And the behavior of each in the human body, Leung writes, is bound to be significant enough to make a noticeable difference.

A few other ginsengs from the genus *Panax* are worth considering briefly in passing. One is *Panax pseudo-ginseng* or *Panax notoginseng* (also called Tienqi ginseng). Chinese herbal doctors utilize it primarily for improving blood circulation in the elderly and to control unwanted hemorrhaging. On the surface, these actions may, at first glance, seem quite contradictory but upon closer examination have been proven to be physiologically correct.

There is also *Panax japonicum,* or Japanese ginseng, which is used in the Orient as a digestive aid and for the removal of excess mucus. *Panax majoris,* known as Pearl ginseng, is used for deficient Qi and upper respiratory problems.

One of the newest ginsengs of the genus *Panax* that has been catching on like wildfire throughout much of the Orient is *Panax vietnamensis.* It was discovered in 1973 in Ngoc Lay, Gia Lai-Kontum, in central Vietnam. At the time it was being used as a folk medicine by the Sedang ethnic minority who inhabit the high mountains of the South Annamitic Range. This Vietnamese ginseng has been found to contain 18 ginsenosides, which are the same active chemical constituents occurring in regular *Panax.* What sets this remarkable ginseng apart from other ginsengs is its strong antibacterial properties. It has been the subject of a number of pharmacological and clinical studies conducted throughout the Far East. This Vietnamese ginseng has been found to be strongly antistreptococcal and thus is now being used to treat sore throat caused by strep. Some London medical researchers are currently examining its role in the treatment of flesh-eating bacteria and other supergerms that have become resistant to conventional antibiotic drugs. It appears to hold great promise in this area, based on the preliminary work I've seen.

As cited earlier in this section, there are also several other herbs that aren't botanically related to the true (*Panax*) ginsengs, but are used for similar purposes. Two of the most important of these are Indian ginseng or ashwagandha and Siberian ginseng. The former (*Withania somnifera*) was mentioned almost a millennium ago in the ancient Ayurvedic medical text *Charaka*

Samhita as being a marvelous "vitalizer" for the body. Since antiquity, Ayurvedic doctors have successfully employed it as a rejuvenative tonic, both alone and in other herbal formulas. It is "as good as rain . . . to a [parched] crop," for "imparting strength [to an] emaciated body," reads a passage from the *Charaka Samhita*. Indian researchers have found that ashwagandha reduces stress and tension, helps relieve stomach ulcers, and reverses low-grade malignant tumors. It is distributed by the Sabinsa Corporation of Piscataway, New Jersey (see Product Appendix).

The other herb, Siberian ginseng, is a somewhat ugly-looking plant on account of its deformed roots and leaves. In far eastern Russia, it has been called Don't Touch Me or Devil's Bush because of its sharp thorns that inflict some pain when coming into contact with the skin. I met the discoverer of this other ginseng when I traveled to the former Soviet Union in 1979. I found Professor Israil Brechman to be a soft-spoken, rather modest but friendly man with an Old World charm to him. At that time he was serving as the Laboratory Chief of the Research Institute for Biologically Active Substances of the USSR.

He was the one who made this herb famous with his rat-swimming test. Rodents were given varying amounts of *Eleutherococcus senticosus* (the scientific name for Siberian ginseng) and then subjected to water until nearly exhausted. As the amounts of Siberian ginseng kept increasing, so too did the animals' stamina. Later on, a rope-climbing test was used in which rodents were made to climb an endless loop of rope to avoid a 25-volt current applied to the floor of the test chamber. The test was controlled and used three doses on an algebraic scale. Dr. Brechman conducted some 16 different experiments with every dosage to learn what the amount of each preparation would be in order to increase the climbing time by 50 percent or better. It took about a month for all these experiments in which the animal models were given allotments of Siberian ginseng twice daily.

Brechman told me something in our lengthy interview (he spoke English but with a heavy Russian accent) that I had never before nor since heard concerning any of the ginsengs mentioned here. He said there was an aspect to Western medicine that he never fully understood and certainly had a great distaste for. Western medicine, he noted, "divides people into two groups—the sick ones and those who are well." But it was his contention that "everybody should be divided into *three* groups: those who are sick, those who are well, and those who are *in between* both of these other states. This is where the largest group always seems to be. Western medicine doesn't seem to consider this state. "You certainly can't diagnose it, so how can you expect a cure for it?" he asked reflectively.

The solution for this great majority of folks in the *third* state was to take adequate amounts of Siberian ginseng on a daily basis. Unlike other true *Panax* or unrelated species, this ginseng could keep the body going for a very long time since its constituents "build up the body's resistance to infection, control stress, and manage blood sugar levels in a most wonderful way." Its primary function, Brechman soberly observed, with glasses removed and his head resting on folded hands as he sat at a table across from me, "is to *manage* the most important functions of the body." In other words, "to keep everything running smoothly, and as you Americans are fond of saying, taking the kinks out of things." We enjoyed a good laugh at this attempt to quote an American colloquialism.

Combination Therapy

One of the many unique properties about true ginseng is that it goes so well with many other herbs and nutritional substances. This blending together of several botanicals that usually called for ginseng as a major ingredient stretches far back into the distant past. It is said that whenever a Chinese nobleman was about to die, a strong dose of ginseng and garlic would be administered to prolong his life so that his far-off relatives might attend.

The ginseng-garlic vapors from the corpse would then condense on the coffin interior, forming over a great period of time a mushroomlike solid protuberance known euphemistically as "the mushroom of the dead." This was highly sought after by grave robbers, who could turn around and sell it to physicians for large sums of money. The doctors would then use it on their wealthy patients to ward off tuberculosis, smallpox, syphilis, and other infectious diseases. Foreign missionaries who were teaching in China in the early part of this century mentioned seeing these alleged mushrooms on sale in the open marketplaces of Shanghai.

Borrowing from this bit of fascinating history, the Wakunaga Pharmaceutical Company of Hiroshima, Japan, decided to fully investigate these strange claims. After some years of diligent research and considerable expense, they came up with Kyo-Ginseng, a product containing 600 milligrams of Kyolic aged-garlic extract and 100 milligrams of *Panax ginseng* extract powder (including 6 milligram of thiamine for good measure). This product helps the body several different ways. First, it prepares the nervous system to withstand greater amounts of stress. Second, it boosts the powers of the immune system to better resist viral or bacterial infections. Third, it works to increase the activity of certain "master glands" of the body, such as the pituitary, hypothalamus, adrenals, and so forth. But, most of all, it is able to accomplish these things by assisting the gastrointestinal tract in its digestion and assimilation of consumed foods. This is where the real benefit and value of this wonderful ginseng-garlic formula comes from. Kyo-Ginseng is available in most health-food stores (see Product Appendix for additional information).

Westerners who are in the habit of taking ginseng for different reasons usually do so without including it in other supplements. But for many years now, both Russian and Chinese doctors have known that the inclusion of ginseng root with drug or nutritional therapies makes such prescribed treatments perform even better within the system. When I went to mainland China back in 1980 with the American Medical Students' Association, we paid a short visit to the Hua Shan Hospital of the Shanghai First Medical College. There we were told by members of the medical staff the results of treating acute myocardial infarction treated with traditional Chinese and Western medicine. Two types of dangerous cases were pointed out to us: (a) arrhythmia with shocklike condition and (b) hypotension and shock.

Ginseng alone or with other Chinese herbs was given with very encouraging results. Two illustrative cases come to mind, after I reviewed some of my old notes taken on that historic trip. In the first case of acute myocardial infarction with shock, when a Western drug was used the blood pressure of the male patient went up temporarily and came down again; the same thing happened after each medication. But when ginseng root was given at the same time, the blood pressure went up, stayed up at a normal level, and didn't come down anymore. In the second case, a female patient with hypotension and a tendency to develop shock (the patient's face was white and her limbs were ice cold), ginseng alone was given. Two hours after the herb was administered, nothing happened, so another dose of ginseng was administered, only this time in conjunction with dong quai (an herbal tonic for females). Within 1 hour and 37 minutes, the woman's blood pressure went up by 20 millimeters of mercury and shock was prevented; her face became red and her limbs regained their natural warmth.

A clinical report from an old Soviet medical journal illustrates the advantages of combining Siberian ginseng with conventional drug therapy in the treatment of certain infectious diseases. The report was entitled, "Increasing of Antibiotic Therapy Efficacy with Adaptogens in Children Suffering from Dysentery and Proteus Infection" and appeared in the January 1982 issue of *Antibiotiki Ministerstvo Zdravookhraneniia SSR* (27:65–69).

Some 258 children from infancy to 14 years of age, who suffered from acute dysentery and enterocolitis, were evaluated by doctors. Doctors treated 157 of them with monomycin and kanamycin in combination with Siberian ginseng, and the other 101 patients were treated with the antibiotics alone. It was clearly demonstrated from the tests conducted that the use of Siberian ginseng "decreased the periods of the diseases." Furthermore, doctors concluded that adaptogens such as Siberian ginseng "increase the efficacy of antibiotic therapy in children with dysentery and Proteus infection."

One area of the body on which I have focused a lot of my own research attention within the last decade has been the human gut. Within it float somewhere around 500 different species of bacteria with a total bacterial count approaching 100 billion per gram of fecal matter. They outnumber even the cells in the rest of your body.

Now, most of these bacteria in your gut are beneficial. They help in synthesizing certain vitamins such as K, B-12, folacin, and thiamine. They keep your internal ecosystem inhospitable for such nasty bacteria as *Salmonella* and other harmful microorganisms. These friendly bacterial flora help to neutralize potential carcinogens and thus prevent cancer most of the time. They also help to stimulate the immune system.

One thing is certain: A high population of certain good bacteria is essential to health and longevity. And the health of intestinal organisms, such as your own health, depends in large measure on what is taken into the gut. Greasy, sugary, spicy junk foods, soft drinks, colas, coffee, and alcohol disrupt the complex ecosystem in the digestive tract. Antibiotic drugs, likewise, have an adverse effect on your intestinal bacteria. Small wonder, then, that people with indiscriminate eating habits or who are taking prescription medications will tend to have more unfavorable gut reactions than do those who are more particular in what they consume or who avoid drug therapy altogether.

In working with a number of natural substances that could restore natural bacteria to the gut, I came up with the following: wheat grass, barley grass, ripe papaya and mango (or their juices), ripe pear, ripe melons, raw carrot, shredded raw cabbage, and enzyme supplements. This was in addition to the already recognized dairy foods of live yogurt, kefir, and cultured buttermilk. But something very interesting happened in my experiments with the foregoing items: When I decided to combine some ginseng with each of them, they worked twice or thrice as well!

With liquid items, such as the cereal grasses and fruit juices, I would use one-half cup of ginseng root tea or liquid ginseng tonic to one 8-ounce glass of any of the others. But with consumed solids (several different fruits and vegetables) as well as with the enzyme supplements, I would recommend 2–3 Kyo-Ginseng capsules instead. The effects were phenomenal whenever ginseng, in some form, was added: Bacterial counts in different gastrointestinal systems skyrocketed dramatically where there had been very little flora present before. This told me that ginseng in some way was able to get more activity out of these other substances to produce greater amounts of useful bacteria.

Finally, an interesting German study published almost three decades ago underscores the value of ginseng in combination-therapy programs. Dr. P. Luth's report, "Erfahrungssbericht über eine Ausprobung ginsenghaltiger und Ginsengfreier Darreichungen von Geriatric Pharmaton in alternierender Reihe bei altern Menschen" appeared in the German medical journal *Medizin Heute* (11:340–41) for 1968). The good doctor reported that a combination of trace elements and vitamins were administered to one group of elderly patients. But the same combination plus ginseng root was given to another group of seniors. The gin-

seng group demonstrated more improvements with the nutritional therapy than did those without the benefit of ginseng.

Another study published two dozen years ago in the
American Journal of Chinese Medicine (1:2:268, 1973) reaffirms
the point being made here: Nutritional therapy without ginseng
isn't as good as vitamins and minerals taken with it. Dr. R. Vigue
did clinical observations on 145 geriatric cases. Here are the side-
by-side results of both groups.

Nutrients Without Ginseng	*Nutrients With Ginseng*
Little improvement in diminished memory due to old age.	Mental clarity observed within one week and considerably sharpened memory felt within two months.
Gradual show of physical and mental strength in first month with a general leveling out by the end of the second month.	Immediate vim and vigor realized within days. This was followed by a rapid rise in both physical stamina and mental energy that was consolidated at the conclusion of the second month.
Some improvement shown in patients suffering from hyperchromic anemia.	Substantial improvement noticed in patients with hyperchromic anemia.
Moderate decrease in convalescent time from medical or surgical illnesses within one week.	Substantial reduction in convalescent time from medical or surgical illnesses within less than a week.
Some slight toxicities observed with several trace elements in a few patients.	No acute or chronic toxicities reported in any patients.

The case is pretty clear-cut from all the evidence just given:
Ginseng in combination with nutrients and herbs makes these
items work better than when they are taken alone. And Kyo-
Ginseng from Wakunaga is the best source of ginseng to use in
conjunction with other supplements.

Ginseng Formulas for Igniting Desire in Both Men and Women

No one really knows just when the first Chinese discovered ginseng root, but it is generally understood by historians and other scholars to have been a very long time ago. Some have estimated that a knowledge of this particular plant has been around for at least 2,500 years. It is said on good authority that near the beginning, people in the Orient were already aware of its wonderful aphrodisiac properties. By medical definition, an aphrodisiac can be "anything that arouses or increases sexual desire."

This somewhat dubious distinction has at times relegated ginseng to the realms of quackery, because doctors simply didn't believe it could possess any such properties. But modern research has proven it to be otherwise. Most of the investigative work conducted in this area has been done by Oriental scientists and published in Oriental medical journals. The following table briefly lists some of the more important studies that have appeared over the years. They leave no doubt whatsoever that ginseng does, indeed, live up to its reputation of being a potent aphrodisiac.

Year	Study	Summary
1929	Min, B. K., "Experimental study on Korean *Panax ginseng* (Japanese text only)," *Chosen Igakkaishi* 19:68–96.	Ginseng extract facilitated lordotic (backward bending) response in female rats.
1931	Kim H. S., "Influence of Korean *Panax ginseng* on blood picture of rabbit (Japanese text only)," *Chosen Igakkaishi* 21:1131–42.	Ginseng extract facilitated lordotic (backward bending) response in female rats.
1941	Lee, Y. K., "Influence of Korean *Panax ginseng* on male gonad and on blood pressure especially the Arneth index (Japanese text only)," *Nippon Nailbumpi Gakkaishi* 17:82 (abstract).	Ginseng extract promoted the growth of testes and spermatogenesis in rabbits.

1964 Brekhman, I. I., *"Panax ginseng:* Its pharmacological problems (Japanese translation from Russian) (Matumoto, Japan: Shinshu Ginseng Growers' Cooperative Union, pp. 80–85).

Ginseng extract accelerated the growth of the ovary and ovulation in frogs.

1964 Hong, S. A., et al., "Effects of *Panax ginseng* upon production of hens' eggs (Korean text only)," *Journal of Korean Modern Medicine* 1:43–45.

Ginseng extract stimulated egg laying in hens.

1970 Moon, Y. B. and Park, W. H., "Influence of ginseng on the weight of viscera in rats (Korean text only)," *Korean Journal of Physiology* 4:103–05.

Ginseng extract increased gonadal weight in young male and female rats.

1973 Suh, C. M., et al., "Influence of ginseng upon testicular nucleic acid content in rats (Korean text only)," *Korean Journal of Physiology* 7:37–40.

Ginseng extract increased testicular nucleic acid content in rats.

1976 Kim, C, M. D., et al., "Influence of ginseng on mating behavior of male rats," *American Journal of Chinese Medicine* 4:163–68.

Male albino rats under the influence of ginseng extract began ejaculation earlier and repeated the action more often and deposited more copulation plugs in 10 days in receptive females.

Still, there are enough skeptics out there who would declare after reading all of the foregoing, "Well, this data applies only to animals; how about showing us some evidence that the root might do the same thing for humans?" A brief article headlined "Ginseng and Male Erectile Dysfunction" caught my eye in the

September/October 1995 issue of *Alternative & Complementary Therapies* (p. 340).

It mentioned the work of a chemist, Russell Bell, who is affiliated with McMaster University in Hamilton (near Toronto), Canada. Working with wild American ginseng root, he discovered a new type of steroid compound called saponin (a total of 13 different saponin molecules called ginsenosides have been isolated so far by other researchers). Bell seems to think that his saponin in particular may be the potent vasodilator that gives this plant its well-deserved aphrodisiac reputation. He pointed out that since erectile dysfunction in men is caused by poor blood supply to the penis, this ginseng steroid might, indeed, help to dramatically improve men's libidos.

I asked by what mechanism this could happen. He was of the opinion that his newly discovered ginseng saponin would cause an expansion of the blood vessels within the penis, thereby bringing in a sudden rush of blood and inducing a rather quick and firm erection. But he also seemed to think that this root steroid might produce a type of nervous or mental energy within a man that would increase his sexual drive. He also speculated that the plant compound could stimulate women's sexual desires by causing increased blood flow to their pelvic regions.

His isn't the only saponin that contains vasodilating activities; three other saponins do too. He felt that the agent that dilates the vascular system may not actually be a saponin as such, but instead some other component of ginseng that is carried along with the saponin molecule. If it can be located and synthesized into a pill, it would make a terrific anti-impotence medication or sex stimulant. A lot of men and women would then have happier sex lives.

In my own work with ginseng and some of its saponin compounds, I've been leaning more toward the idea that some of these ginsenosides could actually affect certain brain neurotransmitters that govern the reproductive organs of men and women. When these few brain neurotransmitters become agitated enough by these ginsenosides, then signals of mental excitement are rapidly transferred across the central nervous system to the sex organs. So what we have here is a dual effect from some of these ginseng compounds: there is first a brain arousal, followed by nervous excitement, and finally by physical action in the form of blood rushing to each gender's sex organs.

Some years ago, the Anthropological Research Center here in Salt Lake City, of which I've been a director for the past 25 years, participated in a study aimed at determining just how effective ginseng root extract was on *enhancing sexual desire* in men and women. We were more interested in the social ramifications than in any physiological responses. Our partners in this project were some medical researchers affiliated with Ying Ming University in Taipei, Taiwan. We provided the major portion of funding for this intriguing work.

Thirty-seven healthy men and women of Oriental background, between the ages of 19 and 34, volunteered themselves and their time for this research. They were each given a supply of ginseng extract capsules (enough to last for two weeks) and instructed to take three capsules every night, at least 45 minutes *before* engaging in sexual activities with their husbands or wives or boyfriends or girlfriends. They were interviewed on the third day, the fifth day, the eighth day, the eleventh day, and the fourteenth day of the test period. Thirty-three of the participants reported feeling *stronger* sexual desires or mood elevations of lust toward their sexual partners.

During the second phase of this research, the same group was given another set of capsules with an inert powder that closely resembled ginseng root (to serve as the placebo). They took it the same way for the same length of time as they had done with the ginseng, never once suspecting that what they were taking was *not* the root but something entirely different. Oral interviews were conducted on the same days as had been done with the herb. Twenty-nine respondents reported minimal sexual arousal; information from the remaining eight participants was ruled invalid since some kind of mechanical or physical stimulation was initiated by one or both partners in order to become sexually aroused.

The information gathered from this particular study suggested to us that ginseng root can, in fact, act as a *mood elevator* and raise the sexual interest index in both men and women to surprisingly high degrees. We felt that ginseng's effects were rather subtle toward achieving this; hence, my theory about a few of those ginsenosides triggering brain response that is then channeled through a number of neural pathways to the sex organs themselves.

In recommending *Panax ginseng* for more passionate lovemaking between the opposite sexes, I've always suggested that another ginseng-related plant be used with it, in this case Siberian ginseng or Eleutherococcus. The reason for this is simple. Since true ginseng is an obvious brain-nerve-organ stimulant of dynamic proportions, something else is needed to cope with all of the nervous and emotional stresses that usually accompany aggressive lovemaking.

A number of years ago, Dr. Steven J. Fulder, who was then doing biomedical research in Oxford, England, explored the relationship between arousal, stamina, and stress in mice. Those continually fed small amounts of ginseng every day throughout their short laboratory lifespans tolerated frequent sexual encounters with each other a lot better than did other mice receiving no ginseng. When the ginseng-fed rodents were later autopsied, it was noticed that ginseng saponins gravitated to certain regions of the brain. The greatest increase in ginseng sensitivity occurred in the hypothalamus, pituitary, and adrenal glands. Dr. Fulder and his associates concluded "that ginseng and eleutherococcus remove tiredness and fatigue and increase the feeling of well-being through the vitalizing effects of *psycho* hormones and *not* by direct action on neurones . . ." This lends further support to my own hypothesis about the brain-nerve pathway link to the sex organs. (Dr. Fulder's complete report appeared in the *American Journal of Chinese Medicine* 9:112–18, 1981.)

A while back I consulted with Dr. Roger Libby, a noted sex therapist, who has some rather remarkable ideas of his own for improving the sexual health of his male and female clients. Several of his most powerful prosexual formulas he labels as "potency insurance," comparing them to life insurance policies; only, in this case, they keep a person's sexual *life* insurance in great shape at all times. And, while he was obviously somewhat coy about giving me too much information, he did, at least, provide enough *general* data to help guide men or women toward igniting more sexual sparks between them.

For men, his advice can be summarized as follows:

- Drink plenty of fluids.
- Ejaculate regularly to empty the prostate of fluids that could make it infected.
- Don't sit on hard surfaces.
- Stay away from alcohol, coffee, colas, soda pop, and greasy and spicy foods.
- Take the following herbs and supplements (amounts were never specified): ginseng extract, ginger, ginkgo biloba, stinging nettle, L-arginine, niacin, zinc, and vitamins B-6, C, and E. (I would like to modify his recommendation of vitamin E and suggest that it be taken in the form of wheat-germ oil. Our research center in Salt Lake City has been supplying readers of my books a special brand of vitamin E called Rex's Wheat Germ Oil. But you won't find this in any health-food store, since it is sold only for animal and livestock use. However, it is the *purest and strongest* form of vitamin E you'll find anywhere. Send $65 for a one-quart can of it to: Anthropological Research Center, P.O. Box 11471, Salt Lake City, UT 84147.)

For women, Dr. Libby's suggestions go something like this:

- Drink fluids frequently.
- Avoid alcohol, caffeine, sugar, fat, and hot spices.
- Avoid high heels and wear flat-soled shoes instead.
- Don't sit for long hours at a time; instead, get up and move around every 30 to 45 minutes.
- Take the following health-food supplements (amounts were never specified): ginseng extract, ho-shou-wu, damiana, wild yam, licorice root extract, oat, stinging nettle, red clover *tea,* orthinine, niacin, chromium picolinate, and boron. (Although he didn't mention it, I would certainly add vitamin E to this list; Rex's Wheat Germ Oil is the best source for this. An average daily intake might be one level tablespoon for a man or woman.)

One other very important item that needs to be cited here in passing has to do with clothing, particularly undergarments. A man or woman should *never* wear any type of underclothing that is tight-fitting or constricting; this can severely hamper blood flow to the sex organs. This means that a man should switch to boxer shorts and forever discard his briefs (as I did a number of years ago). For a man this is especially important, as air needs to constantly circulate in and around the testicles at *all* times.

For daily supplemental purposes to maintain *reasonably* good sexual health, I recommend taking Kyo-Ginseng (2 capsules) and Gingko Biloba Extract (2 capsules), both from Wakunaga of America, zinc (75 mg.), stinging nettle (3 capsules), dandelion root (2 capsules), B-Complex (high-potency kind, 2 tablets), vitamin C (nonacidic, 1500 mg.), and Rex's Wheat Germ Oil (1 tbsp.). This way the sexual spark in you will never die out, but be there ready to ignite desire whenever love is rekindled.

Ginseng Do's and Don'ts

The September 1996 issue of *Sassy* magazine—a publication geared toward young high school and college-age women—featured a report on "The Dirt on New-Age Diet Aids," under its Anatomically Correct column. The article began with a statement followed by a rhetorical question, in the somewhat cocky, hip style of writing that the magazine's core audience has come to expect: "There's a ton of weight-loss gimmicks out now. Do they work? Fat chance!"

Ginseng was one of the leading ingredients examined. *Sassy* stated that the herb was marketed "under the guise of teas, protein drinks and 'herbal ecstasy' compounds." One of the main claims assigned to it, the magazine said, was that it "is sold as an appetite suppressant" as well as an energy stimulant. In presenting the true picture of what the plant really does, the publication reported: "The mild stimulant may balance male hormones and cause sexual desires, but it certainly does NOT cause weight loss. No adverse effects have been noted—but since it isn't a diet miracle either, why bother?" The final advice given was framed in the form of some alternative options. "Protein drinks are OK as long as you eat square meals too. Drink tons of H_2O if you're trying to lose weight, and stay active."

Although this magazine for young and liberated women took a somewhat flippant approach to a very serious subject, it did point out a problem that is inherent in other herbs besides ginseng—some plants are overhyped by the herb industry and, consequently, overused by consumers. Not only does ginseng fall into this category, but so do kola nut, ephedra or mahuang, yohimbine, pau d'arco, and a few others. Hence, from the rather ungracious put-down given by *Sassy*, it would seem that ginseng doesn't fit into weight-loss formulas. From the historical and folk uses we have of this herb, it would be fair to say that ginseng doesn't belong with the treatment of obesity, at least not as a primary herb.

To illustrate the problem further, I recall an incident that happened several years ago while I was attending one of the country's largest health-food-industry conventions in Anaheim, California. It was at the Natural Foods Expo West in the Anaheim Convention Center, where I questioned several manufacturers of weight-loss aids as to their particular reasons for including ginseng in their respective products. One fellow wisecracked: "Well, we think it looks good on our label." Another replied: "Consumers are apt to have more confidence in our product if they see ginseng among the ingredients." A third respondent simply asked me, "Why not?" Their cavalier ways of answering may have seemed funny and cute to them at the time, but revealed to me, a scientist well-trained in medicinal plants, the depth of their ignorance regarding herbs in general.

All of this leads me, of course, to the first rule of thumb: DON'T buy a product if ginseng is buried among a label's ingredients. The label is simply telling you that the manufacturer decided to put in everything, *including* the kitchen (read ginseng) sink! But DO buy a product in which ginseng is the sole ingredient, such as the Ginsana products, or a second primary ingredient, as it is with Wakunaga's excellent Kyo-Ginseng formula (aged-garlic extract plus ginseng-root extract). This way you'll know the difference between *serious* ginseng products and those that include a little bit "just for the heck of it."

The next thing worth scrutinizing are the reasons that people take ginseng in the first place. Ask yourself this question the next time you're about to purchase a ginseng product: "What am I getting it for? Do I really need it?" If you can answer both questions in an honest and straightforward way, then you probably have a *legitimate* purpose in using the herb.

But, more often than not, people buy something for the least important reasons:

- "It was on sale."
- "I read about it in the tabloids."
- "My friends tried it, liked it, and said I should."
- "I heard about it on [talk] radio."
- "[Name of famous person] endorses [or uses] it, so it must be something I need to be taking too."

Ronald K. Siegel, a psychiatrist formerly with the UCLA School of Medicine, termed it "ginseng abuse syndrome" in the *Journal of the American Medical Association* (241:1614–15, 1979; 243:32, 1980). In his study of 133 ginseng users, those who took it regularly for long terms reported experiencing hypertension, nervousness, and insomnia. This led Dr. Varro E. Tyler, a former dean of the Schools of Pharmacy, Nursing, and Health Sciences at Purdue University in Indiana, to issue this warning in his book *The Honest Herbal* (Philadelphia: George F. Stickley Co., 1982; p. 108): "If large amounts of ginseng are to be taken over an extended period, use caution!"

Another potential health impairment from long-term ginseng use can be chronic renal failure. The trace element germanium, frequently associated with cancer prevention and treatment, is "an ingredient in many ginseng preparations" according to the *Journal of the American Medical Association* 276:606–07, August 28, 1996). And this mineral can induce unwanted resistance to diuretic medications prescribed by doctors to their patients suffering from gout, edema, congestive heart failure, or hypertension. The result could eventually be a serious shutdown of kidney function. In the case cited by JAMA, a 63-year-old man had been taking nearly a dozen Korean ginseng tablets for almost two weeks, while on diuretic therapy from his doctor. Two sensible suggestions emerge from this evidence: First, consult with your doctor when intending to take *any* herbal supplement; and secondly, do so in *moderation*.

A more serious problem for the consumer may be in finding an authentic ginseng product that really *does contain* ginseng.

Quality ginseng root is terribly expensive, but plenty of cheap imitations abound. And the lack of quality control in many segments of the health-food industry also accounts for the astonishing variability in the actual content of many commercial ginseng products (capsules, tablets, tincture, teas, and powders).

Two independent studies have underscored this dilemma. One of them analyzed 54 different ginseng products and found that a full 60 percent of them were utterly worthless and that 25 percent of the sampled products contained absolutely *no* ginseng at all. (The full accounts of both studies appeared in the *Journal of Pharmaceutical Sciences* 67:1487–89, 1978, and *Whole Foods* 2(4):48–53, 1979.)

Here are several tips that will help in your next ginseng purchases:

1. Look at the company behind the ginseng ads. Does it back up its claims with hard science? Or are they mere hype and clever marketing ploys instead?

2. Check out the label *and* the price. Does it say "Ginseng" only or mention *"Panax Ginseng" specifically.* Remember that there are *many* kinds of so-called "ginsengs," but only one *true Panax ginseng.* The cost also reflects whether something has an inferior ginseng (by the cheap price) or a better-quality ginseng (by its expensiveness).

3. Does the label indicate *Panax ginseng* only, or does it list *Panax ginseng extract,* as in the case of Wakunaga's Kyo-Ginseng, for instance? An extract will invariably have *more* ginsenosides and, therefore, will be *more* active than the whole root will be.

4. When buying herb products from a direct marketing or multilevel company, always make sure that the business you're dealing with uses top quality ginseng. For instance, Total Life Concepts International (see Product Appendix) only uses domesticated American ginseng root from the state of Wisconsin in two of their excellent health products: Complete Renewal (a body makeover formula) and Proactivin (an antioxidant detoxifier).

5. If you're still a bit skeptical, then visit a Chinese herb shop in any large city's Chinatown district, where your chances of

getting *real* ginseng products are much better. Or else buy them from a health-supplement company owned and operated by Orientals, such as the Japanese-operated Wakunaga of America.

6. Finally, if truly in doubt, then do *without*!

Earlier in this chapter, I dwelled at length on combining ginseng with other herbs. I presented evidence that showed the positive benefits for greater health enhancement that could come from such botanical combinations. There are, however, some things that ginseng should *not* be mixed with. While not proving to be harmful necessarily, these items can severely weaken the healing integrity of the herb itself. The information presented in the next couple of paragraphs covers this aspect of ginseng, which is seldom dealt with in other herb books. Not even Christopher Hobbs's *User's Guide to the Ginsengs* (which I've periodically cited in this chapter) mentions anything about this subject.

In 1976, I spoke with Shiu-Ying Hu, who was then working at the Arnold Aboretum at Harvard University in Cambridge, Massachusetts. He kindly provided me with the following list of herbs that "tend to weaken ginseng." "One-half ounce of some," he said, "can destroy the function of a whole ounce of ginseng."

Herbs That Can Destroy Ginseng Function

Agrimony	Juniper
American hellebore	Kola nut
Black hellebore	Lobelia
Black pepper	Mexican chiles
Buchu	Milkweed
Bugleweed	Mistletoe
Cayenne pepper	Tansy
Eucalyptus	Tea tree oil
Henbane	Thistle
Hollyhock	Wild lettuce
Jalap	

If you would like to check out the herbal knowledge of individual formulators who came up with different ginseng combinations, just conduct this simple test. Examine the label of any herb product that contains ginseng among its many ingredients. Then look for any of the above herbs. If even one of them appears, then you'll be able to determine two things: one, that whatever portion of ginseng there may be in the product has been rendered fairly inert by the presence of a contraindicating herb; and two, that the product formulator didn't know his herbs too well.

Finally, you need to understand "that your dietary composition is of prime importance in determining the effect of ginseng saponin[s]" in your system. So stated four Japanese scientists in their report examining the effect of ginseng saponins on liver blood-sugar content, which appeared in *Chemical & Pharmaceutical Bulletin* (24:3202–3204, 1976). When ginseng-supplemented rats were given increasing increments of fat (2 to 10 percent) or protein (10, 25, or 70 percent), there was a marked *decrease* in their liver glycogen content. But when ginseng was administered either by itself or without fat or protein in the diet, then rat livers showed very high glycogen content. The scientists drew the following conclusion from all this: "Thus, it may be considered that the stimulating action of ginseng saponin is influenced by the nutritional status of rats."

What human inference this may have is simply that if you take a ginseng product near or with a meal containing *any* fat or protein whatsoever, you will *not* get the benefits you expect from it. It's just that plain!

In a second study appearing in a different volume of the same scientific publication three years later (27:419–423, 1979), another group of Japanese researchers from Toyama Medical and Pharmaceutical University noted that when there is "an excess of carbohydrates" in the diet, there is going to be "a significant decrease in enzyme levels" within the liver. So, be sure and take your ginseng between meals or away from those containing any type of carbohydrate foods, if you want to feel its maximum effects. Another report in the same volume (27:2494–97, 1979) suggests that when ginseng is taken during a mild food fast, there is a dramatic increase in liver enzymes. (None of these data, by the way, are found in any currently published herb book or those devoted exclusively to ginseng.)

The Medicinal Properties of *Panax*

In traditional Chinese medicine (TCM), ginseng root has become the "ultimate panacea" for what ails a person. Several pages would be required to list the numerous conditions for which it has been used in the past several thousand years. The majority have only anecdotal evidence backing them, but a small number actually have medical or scientific proof to justify ginseng being used for them. The following list has no particular arrangement to it, but does briefly mention each use and cites the appropriate reference for it as well.

> *Ginseng Properties*
>
> A. DNA/RNA stimulation and liver synthesis of protein
>   (*Chemical & Pharmaceutical Bulletin* 27:2130–36, 1979)
>
> B. Prevents intoxication by alcoholic beverages
>   (*Lloydia* 32:46–51, March 1969)
>
> C. Prevents or reduces cardiac problems
>   (*Chung Hua Hsin Hsueh Kuan Ping Tsa Chih* 10:147–50, 1982)
>
> D. Prevents and reduces malignant tumors
>   (*Arzneimittel-Forschung* 11:288–95, 1961)
>
> E. Reduces hypertension
>   (*Yao Hseuh Hseuh Pao* 16:860–63, 1981)
>
> F. Antioxidant protection against free radical activities
>   (*American Journal of Chinese Medicine* 9:112–18, 1981)
>
> G. Reduces psychosis and neurosis
>   (*Korean Journal of Pharmacology* 2:23–28, 1971)
>
> H. Overcomes liver dysfunctions
>   (*Yakhak Hoeji* 17:1–8, 1973)
>
> I. Boosts immune system defenses located within the lymph nodes, the spleen, bone marrow, and the fibroblastic reticular cells of hematopoietic tissues
>   (*Endocrinologica Japonica* 26:661–65, 1979)
>
> J. Adjusts body blood-sugar levels to avoid medical extremes between diabetes and hypoglycemia
>   (See reference in F)

K. Protects against bacterial-induced stomach ulcers by strengthening immune functions
   (*Chemical & Pharmaceutical Bulletin* 23:3095–3100, 1975)

L. Tranquilizes an excited central nervous system
   (See reference in B)

M. Prevents fatigue and lethargy
   (*Japanese Journal of Pharmacology* 24:119–27, 1974)

N. Reduces fevers
   (See reference in B)

O. Reduces elevated cholesterol and triglyceride levels
   (*Atherosclerosis* 48:81–94, 1983)

P. Manifests estrogenic hormonal activity in women
   (*Proceedings of the 11th Pacific Scientific Congress* 8:11, 1966)

Q. Removes male sterility
   (See reference in P)

R. Improves mental acuity and I.Q.
   (*Japanese Journal of Pharmacology* 27:509–16, 1977)

S. Protects against radiation and heavy metal toxins
   (*Japanese Journal of Pharmacology* 22:245–59, 1972)

Chemical Constituents

The Chinese probably know more about ginseng and have for a lot longer period of time (at least several millennia) than we do. But beginning in the early 1960s, Russian and Japanese researchers began serious investigative work to identify specific saponins within ginseng that account for many of its remarkable properties; they dubbed these ginscnosides (after ginseng) or panaxosides (after panax). Believe it or not, *Panax ginseng* has an amount of only 1.6 to 4.4 percent total steroid saponin content, whereas *Panax japonica* has a total yield approaching almost 10 percent (actually an average of 9.34 percent).

Other constituents include fiber—59,000 to 245,000 parts per million; simple sugars (about 5 percent), consisting of fructose, rhamnose, sucrose, and D-glucose; and lipids, in a range of 1.5 to 1.9 percent.

Ginseng root contains measurable amounts of vitamins A, B-complex, C, and E, but has a greater concentration of niacin than any other of the B-complex group. According to *Korean Journal of Pharmacognosy* (8:163–66, 1977), *Hanguk Sikp'um Kwahakhoe Chi* (15:133–35, 1983), and *Baichiun Yike Daxue Xuebao* (9:58–59, 1983), ginseng root contains the following arrangement of trace element minerals: calcium, average of 5,500 ppm (parts per million); copper (average of 11.5 ppm); germanium (5–6 parts per *billion*); iron (average of 203 ppm); magnesium (973 ppm); manganese (average 80 ppm); molybdenum (0.2 ppm); phosphorus (average of 3,100 ppm); potassium (6,415 ppm); sodium (can be as low as 40 ppm or as high as 6,000 ppm); and zinc (average of 40 ppm).

Making Your Own Ginseng Remedies at Home

Tea. *Never* cook ginseng root in a metal pot because the metal can destroy some of its properties. Always use enamel or glassware instead. Because true ginseng root is quite expensive, it is best to make a "double decoction" of the same. This is done by adding two level tablespoons of dried, sliced *red Korean* ginseng (the most stimulating) to one quart of boiling water. Cover with a lid and simmer on low heat for 50 minutes. Strain, add more fresh water, and then simmer it again for another 30 minutes. Strain and combine the liquids from both decoctions. Before refrigerating, add 1 level teaspoon of liquid ConcenTrace mineral supplement from Trace Minerals of Ogden, Utah; this greatly enhances the nutritional content of the root decoction (see the Product Appendix for contact and purchase information). Store no longer than three days; drink cups early morning and late afternoon, or late morning and early evening. Vary the times every few days.

Tincture. Tinctures keep longer than teas do and don't require the refrigeration. Also, the alcohol transports the ginsenosides into the system more quickly. Grind 1 handful of cleaned and chopped ginseng roots in a Vita-Mix whole food processor or equivalent machine, making sure you use the container blade that is intended for grinding wheat into flour or making nuts into butter. Along with the roots, add about 1-1/2 cups of vodka. Run the machine for 2-1/2 minutes. Be sure there are at least two inches of clear vodka over the herb when done to keep the soaking herb from coming in contact with any air; this prevents fermentation from happening.

Pour the mixture into a quart jar and screw the lid on tightly. Set in a cool, dry place away from light for two weeks. Shake vigorously every day for about 30 seconds. Strain twice through a fine wire-mesh strainer and layered cheesecloth. Then filter a third time through a clean coffee filter to clarify the liquid. This needs to be done so that tiny debris solids don't clog up the fine dropper tip of the dark-amber bottles you store it in. An average of 15 drops once or twice daily beneath the tongue is recommended.

Capsules. Although you can purchase ginseng root powder and stuff gelatin capsules yourself, I strongly recommend that you buy them already prepared this way from reliable manufacturers. It's so much more convenient and certainly requires a lot less time and effort. The average intake of single ginseng or ginseng-combination capsules should be somewhere between 2 and 4 a day; no more than 6 at a time should be taken within a 36-hour period, however. Capsules are handier and can be taken with you just about anywhere, as the tincture can be. If traveling to hot and humid climates, however, then the alcoholic extract may prove more suitable under the circumstances.

Tonic. For recuperating from a serious illness or medical problem, cook 1 cup of chopped ginseng root and 2 cups of rice in 6 cups of water for 3-1/2 hours; add the rice only in the last 20 minutes, however. Sweeten with pure maple syrup and administer in one-half-cup amounts every few hours until recovery is imminent.

Joanna Zhao has been the clinical director of the Santa Cruz, California, clinic belonging to the College of Traditional Chinese Medicine for a few years. Her own clinical experience has taught her that ginseng is helpful in expediting the labor of pregnant mothers. She boils 2 slices of Korean red ginseng root in 1 pint of distilled water for 35 minutes. This liquid is strained, more water is added, and the same roots are cooked some more for another

20 minutes. A second straining follows, with both brewed liquids being combined and given *warm* in one-cup amounts every few hours prior to the expected delivery.

Chew. Back in the early 1980s, a young acupuncturist and doctor of Traditional Chinese Medicine by the name of Francis Kiczkowski had a thriving Vermont alternative-medicine practice. He started using ginseng root in treating some of his patients' health problems that acupuncture alone couldn't help. But he turned to American ginseng (*Panax quinquefolius*) instead of regular *Panax ginseng,* believing that it had more active compounds in it than the other did. In doing so, he became the first alternative healer in America to pioneer the use of American native ginseng.

The more he worked with American ginseng, the more he came to respect this wonderful medicinal agent. In time, he developed a healthy alternative to regular smokeless tobacco, or what is called in some parts of the country "dip." His Root 100 Ginseng Chew was named after the old U.S. Route 100 that his company's headquarters, Vermont Ginseng Products, is located on. His chew comes in six different flavors: original, peppermint, ginger, cinnamon, wintergreen, and tangerine. All of them contain ginseng root, glycerine, and natural flavoring (except for the original). In the natural-foods market, peppermint seems to be the favorite. Several major league baseball teams really like the taste of the wintergreen; and in the sports-nutrition market, among those into bicycling, tangerine is preferred the most for some reason. The price per tin varies from $5.95 to $6.50.

"We developed this chew," Francis told me by telephone in a conversation we had on Friday, October 4, 1996, "so that there would be a greater and quicker delivery of ginsenosides into the body. We carefully monitor the ginsenoside contents of our products. We guarantee that there will always be anywhere between 850 to 1,000 milligrams of ginsenosides in our ginseng chew. The texture of the chew is comparable to finely ground nuts. You can take a pinch of it and place it inside next to your cheek and salivate on it for awhile. Or a pinch can just be put in the mouth, chewed a little, and then swallowed the same way you would regular food. If people can get past the concept of how we package it (in tins) and not associate the product with smokeless tobacco, then they will discover just how healthy and beneficial this can be to their bodies." For more information, write or call: Tom Herzig, Sales Manager, Vermont Ginseng Products, Pilgrim Park, P.O. Box 6, Waterbury, VT 05676 (1-800-270-0007).

> Ginseng,
> medicinal treasure—
> In thee
> I take great pleasure.
>
> Life
> as we know it now,
> Extended
> forever somehow.
>
> Mystery
> herb of ages past,
> Understood
> by us at last!
>
> —John Heinerman, Ph.D., author and writer of poetry

Chapter Five

Wheat Grass
The Food of Kings
and Common People

What Is It?

I asked my friend Ronald L. Seibold a while back how he might define wheat grass. I figured if anybody could give it the proper definition, then it would have to be this man. Ron, you see, is owner of Pines International of Lawrence, Kansas, which happens to be the *sole* provider of the only nutritionally rich and exceptionally high-quality cereal grasses that are organically grown in America's heartland. From Singapore to Sweden and Canada to Chile, Ron's wheat and barley grasses provide health and well-being to hundreds of thousands of people worldwide.

This self-styled rural sociologist rubbed his chin and thought a moment. "The o-n-l-y reliable wheat grass that I know of," he said, picking his words with great care, "is planted as seed in the late fall, remains dormant over the winter, and then slowly appears as short blades of grass when the ground begins to thaw. But it only remains *true* wheat grass for a very short period of time in its growth cycle. This is during what farmers call the 'jointing stage,' when the internodal tissue in the wheat grass leaf begins to elongate, eventually forming a stem. If harvested right at this specific phase of growth, when the cereal plant is at its peak of vegetative development and nutritional goodness, then it stays as *genuine* wheat grass until finally consumed."

When I casually inquired about the indoor, tray-grown variety that many health food enthusiasts pass off as wheat grass, my friend just laughed and said, "That may be a quick, cheap imitation that passes for it, but it *doesn't* meet the criteria for the real thing. Oh sure, it may look nice and green and taste very sweet, but it is poor in nutrients and hasn't had sufficient time for its sugar complexes to fully develop. It is only a child in terms of nutritional value when compared with the fully *matured* adult wheat grass!"

And that's how "the man from Kansas" with more than a quarter of a century agricultural experience behind him *correctly* defined the wheat grass to be discussed in this chapter.

Wheat Grass in Ancient Times

Wheat has been with humanity almost since the beginning of biblical time. We find the first mention made of it in Genesis 30:14 of the Old Testament. In fact, so important a food crop was it that certain times of the year were reckoned by it: "And Reuben went in the days of wheat harvest . . ." (Genesis 30:14) or "So she kept fast by the maidens of Boaz to glean unto the end of . . . wheat harvest . . ." (Ruth 2:23).

The wheat of biblical times was ordinary summer or winter wheat (*Triticum aestivum*) or the bearded wheat (*T. compositum*), which has several ears on one stalk. There was also an Egyptian variety (*T. tungidum*), a one-grained wheat (*T. monoccum*), and a species of wild wheat (*T. dicoccoides*). All these still grow at present round about the Middle East.

Wheat is specifically mentioned some 52 times in the Bible, most frequently as *hittâ* (the true Hebrew word is actually *hitputâ*). When the Children of Israel settled in old Palestine, they became terrific farmers and produced enormous quantities of wheat, most of which they exported to other places. Much of it went by ship to Tyre (Amos 8:5) and to other parts of the Mediterranean. Some biblical scholars are of the opinion, however, that in Jotham's time (between 747–732 B.C.; see 2 Chronicles 27:5) the farmers had all become lazy, because he demanded as payment from the Ammonites 100,000 bushels of wheat.

The wheat harvest in ancient times was actually the commencement of Israel's first month of the year, called Abib or Nisan (equivalent to our month of April). The harvest usually lasted until about the second week of the third month of Sivan (or June for us). The length of harvest time could vary, however, depending on the soil, situation, and time of sowing.

As a rule, the threshing was done with a long, flexible stick known as a flail (see Isaiah 41:16). It could be trodden out by oxen walking round and round over the cut wheat (Deuteronomy 25:4). Also, there was always the crushing or bruising of the wheat ears by means of a wheel from a cart running over it. This method is described for bread corn in Isaiah 28:28. The terms "corn" and "wheat" were used synonymously in those days. The passage in Luke 6:1 that refers to Christ's disciples "plucking the ears of corn" and "rubbing them in their hands" before eating them has reference exclusively to wheat. Even today, this custom is still kept alive by some Arab groups in the Middle East, who like to eat this *ferik* (the name they give it) in the same manner, about a month or so before actual harvest begins.

Some great biblical events have been associated with wheat. Gideon was threshing wheat at the time of his call (Judges 6:11); Ornan was also threshing the same grain (1 Chronicles 21:20) when he saw an angel of the Lord; Christ speaks about the end of the world when the wheat will be gathered before the burning begins (Luke 3:17).

The sowing of wheat was usually done in the winter time in the Holy Land. The common procedure was to broadcast or toss the seed out in front of the sower with a sweeping gesture of the right hand. Afterwards, it would be lightly plowed in. Jesus Christ took this sowing method and incorporated it into one of His most important parables, that dealing with the sower of good seed, some of which fell among and grew up with the weeds later on (Matthew 13:18–30).

And his reference to wheat bringing forth 100 grains (verse 23) was *no* exaggeration in the case of Egyptian wheat (see Genesis 41:22 for additional evidence of this). Wheat is believed to have been of Asiatic origin, coming from ancient Persia first and then later being passed on to the Egyptians, from whom the Israelites eventually obtained it for their own use after leaving that land under the guidance of Moses.

It can be said with certainty that much of the culture in those times was wrapped around wheat to some extent. To them it symbolized life and vitality.

The Greatest of the Babylonian Kings

One of the greatest military figures and ruling monarchs of the ancient world was King Nebuchadnezzar. He ruled for 43 years (605–562 B.C.), which is considered something of an accomplishment in those precarious times. This genius of warfare and mighty ruler managed to subsist on wheat grass and a number of other cereal grasses for a brief period in his life. They sustained and nourished him while he was, shall we say, temporarily suffering from something akin to Alzheimer's and morbid delusion (but more about this later).

The king's lengthy reign was marked by numerous ambitious public-works projects. More than 50 temple projects (both restoration as well as new construction) were organized throughout southern Mesopotamia. No fewer than five walls were built to enclose Babylon itself; he also surrounded it with a deep moat and filled it with hungry crocodiles. He spent enormous sums out of his treasury to build lavish palaces, dig costly canals and reservoirs for irrigation purposes, and erect great seaport harbors. But out of all these things, he is probably best remembered for creating one of the great "Seven Wonders of the Ancient World," this being the fabulous "Hanging Gardens" of Babylon, which he had put up for his Median wife, Nitocris.

Nebuchadnezzar was a devout and religious man, worshipping both his own Chaldean gods as well as the true and living God of Daniel and many other enslaved Israelites. It is interesting to note in passing that of all the Chaldean monarchs, only this man's name has survived through the millennia in folk myth and superstition. "I have examined," wrote Sir H. Rawlinson, a famous British explorer-archaeologist of the nineteenth century, "the bricks *in situ,* belonging perhaps to a hundred different towns and cities in the neighborhood of Baghdad. And I have never found any other legend than that of Nebuchadnezzar, son of Nabopolassar, king of Babylon" (from his *Commentary on the Inscriptions of Assyria and Babylonia,* pp. 76–77). Truly, his renown has lived longer in history than that of most other ancient monarchs.

Chomping Wheat Grass Like an Ox

Now comes the splendid tale of how one of earth's mightiest and wealthiest kings was reduced down to that of a lowly beast of burden and made to crop wheat grass in the fields like cattle. What took him from his palaces of pleasure to the smelly stables of working oxen was nothing less than his great pride and extreme vanity. His ego simply got the best of him, and he became lifted up in the vain imaginations of his heart. Put another way, he started believing too much in his own press clippings. He simply forgot, as we all are apt to do from time to time, that the "God of gods" whom Daniel worshipped had been entirely responsible for all his successes.

The fourth chapter of the Book of Daniel richly details out this grand event of suffering. Nebuchadnezzar was given ample

warning at least a year in advance in a very troubling dream that agitated his soul to no end. Daniel was called in and gave the correct interpretation, which foretold what events would happen if the king weren't more careful about his pride. But, in the end, as Nebuchadnezzar was strutting about in one of his many palaces within the city one morning, he spoke without thinking and bragged aloud to himself: "Is not this great Babylon, which I have built for the house of the kingdom by the might of *my* power and for the honor of *my* majesty?"

Whereupon a distinct voice from Heaven clearly told him, "The kingdom is departed from thee" this very moment! And in that "same hour was the thing fulfilled upon Nebuchadnezzar: and he was driven from men, and *did eat grass* as oxen, and his body was wet with the dew of heaven, till his hairs were grown like eagles' feathers, and his nails like birds' claws" (Daniel 4:33).

The Greeks called the condition of madness that overcame him lycanthropy (*lykos,* meaning wolf, and *anthropos,* signifying man). This rare but morbid delusion leads the sufferer to imagine that he or she is a wolf; it quite possibly is a mental atavism of the werewolf superstition. By his own admission in inscriptions he later had chiseled into some of his mighty monuments, Nebuchadnezzar gave an oblique reference to this temporary eclipse of his greatness and glory. "For four years, I was not found in the seat of my kingdom, which thing did not rejoice my heart. In the worship of . . . my lord, the joy of my heart . . . I did not sing his praises as I should have . . ."

What is all the more remarkable about this dark period of the king's life is that he managed to survive on nothing more than ordinary wheat grass and other common cereal grasses growing in the fields of Mesopotamia. The several different accounts from which this data have been extracted all report that he ate *nothing else.* In other words, he ate *no* meat, *no* bread, *no* orchard fruit or garden vegetables, and drank *no* wine, but only water. And while his overall physical appearance at the conclusion of his suffering made him filthy, dirty, wild-looking, and an object of loathing by some, yet nowhere does it say that he was emaciated or reduced to a starving skeleton. Granted that he probably lost some of his royal corpulency in the process and became more trim, but he certainly remained in good physical health from the wonderful nutrients in the wheat grass that he regularly chomped every day.

His sense and reasoning again returned to him one day just as suddenly as it had been taken away. The first thing the man did was to give "praise and honor" to the God of Heaven and earth. The second thing he did was to acknowledge the absolute *nothingness* of man and the total *everythingness* that belongs to God. His final admission before returning to his former pomp and greatness was this: "Those that walk in pride the King of Heaven is able to abase!" He never forgot this valuable lesson learned in the depths of humility.

Though the records are silent with regard to what he ate, it is tempting to think what the good king might have said regarding the cereal grasses he chewed on for so long. The taste may not have been all that great, but at least they saved his life.

He Takes Wheat Grass to Calm His Nerves

On Wednesday, October 2, 1996, I drove up to the famous mining town and ski-resort area called Park City (in Utah). A surprising number of famous and wealthy people have spacious homes and spectacular lodges here as their own private getaways that they can escape to any time they wish. Among the more noted are

Johnny Carson (the former host of NBC's *The Tonight Show*) and Robert Urich (TV actor in such programs as *Spencer for Hire* and *Vegaß*).

A friend of mine who wanted only his first name used is a helicopter pilot and invited me along for the "ride of my life." But Tom isn't just any ordinary chopper pilot; the big bird he flies is an enormous Sikorsky sky-crane helicopter that resembles a gigantic mosquito or praying mantis.

He explained to me prior to takeoff that this huge machine is powered by two turboshaft jet engines producing 9,000 horsepower and is capable of lifting 20,000 pounds at sea level, but only 12,000 pounds at the 9,400-foot elevation at which we were then situated.

I climbed aboard with him as he took this "Incredible Hulk" aloft. Renting at $100 *per minute,* this flying workhorse would snatch up one of 17 very tall towers, each weighing about 10,000 pounds, from the parking lot below us and delicately place it on a base at the Park City Ski Resort, where it would then be bolted into place.

A new tower was moved about every 5-1/2 minutes, and the entire chairlift was set in just under 2 hours. I was astonished at how calm Tom remained under such intense pressure. I knew that he was one of the best helicopter pilots in the business, but marveled at the fact that he didn't even so much as break a bead of sweat while attending to this very risky piece of dangerous business.

After we landed, I had a chance to put these questions to him. He laughed and said, "Well, John, I've just been following the advice given in one of your books." (He was referring, of course, to *Heinerman's Encyclopedia of Healing Juices.*) "In there, you mention that wheat grass is good to take for energy and mental alertness. Well, I drink a full 8-ounce glass of the stuff every morning just like you advise. And I'll tell you this, not only has it sharpened my focus for work this important, but it also has given me steadier nerves. Touch-and-go situations like what we went through this morning don't bother me anymore like they used to. I'm solid as rock and go about each task with a collective coolness that, quite frankly, even amazes me sometimes. Since I never used to be this way before, I have to attribute it to the wheat grass I've been drinking regularly now for nearly a year."

Screen Legend Retains Youthful Beauty Well into Her Eighties

In 1984, in New York City, the Film Society of Lincoln Center presented screen and stage legend Claudette Colbert with a lifetime achievement award for her work in the cinema and live theater. A reporter who met with her at that presentation later marveled in his article just "how impossibly young this [then] 81-year-old actress looked." How could this be? The reporter surreptitiously circled the legend looking for clues.

"If you're looking to see if I've had any work done, dear, no," sang Colbert cheerfully, already intuiting the writer's mission. The actress obligingly lifted the russet locks on the nape of her neck and behind her ears, revealing an absence of surgery scars, much to the other's amazement.

Well then, just how on earth did she manage to keep herself looking decades younger than what she really was? Was there some kind of secret potion she sipped or miracle skin cream that she slathered on morning and night? "No, dearie," she answered with her trademark throaty and bell-like laugh.

Sensing her interviewer was about to reach the end of his wits, she broke off the suspense by letting him in on her little "secret." "It's quite simple, dearie," she told him. "Every morning I prepare myself a big glass of green drink and have that with my breakfast. I've been doing that for over 50 years or better."

And just what went into that "green drink," the reporter wondered aloud. Well, "half of it is a fruit juice like pineapple, papaya, mango, or grape," she said. "Sometimes I will vary that with a vegetable juice like tomato or carrot, but generally I'll stay with the fruit juices. The other part is wheat grass that I grow myself in a special tray. I make quite a batch of it ahead of time and clip enough to fill a cup. This I put into a blender with my fruit juice and mix together. The drink is quite delicious and gives me a lot of vitality and energy."

"Oh, and it also keeps me looking young and radiant," she added as an afterthought.

Claudette Colbert was born in Paris in 1904; she passed away from the lingering effects of a recent stroke at her home in Barbados in midsummer 1996. Her most obvious assets were cheekbones that arched to heaven, a valentine face that was always fringed with demure auburn bangs, and of course, that one-of-the-guys voice that enchanted stuffed shirts and working stiffs alike.

Though she raised eyebrows as the scantily clad Poppaea in *The Sign of the Cross* (1932) and as Cleopatra (1934), Colbert established herself as one of Hollywood's most deft comic performers in *It Happened One Night,* which won her a 1934 Oscar.

She was born Lily Claudette Chauchoin. But since Chauchoin was hard to pronounce and spell, she selected the name Colbert at the suggestion of her mother, who remembered that a man by that name was finance minister to Louis XV. It must have brought luck: For 16 years, her daughter would be one of the highest-paid actresses in Hollywood.

The aspiring actress won her first featured part in the 1925 play *A Kiss in a Taxi.* When the stock-market crash decimated the theater audience in 1930, Colbert found herself Hollywood-bound.

She was sought after by the studios because of her melodic voice. When she played the saucy Poppaea in *The Sign of the Cross,* she sounded like a kitten that had just lapped up a saucer of milk. As the investigative reporter in *I Cover the Waterfront* (1933), she spoke with a rye-soaked voice. As the spoiled heiress of *It Happened One Night* (1934), she bubbled like champagne.

"One of the things that kept my voice strong and gave me a range of different tone variations," she told the reporter at the Film Society awards program in 1984, "was my fruit juice-wheat grass combination drinks. The few times that I missed drinking a glass of them every day, my voice would become weak and raspy."

It wasn't until pairing with Clark Cable in *It Happened One Night,* the surprise hit of 1934 and one of few pictures ever to sweep all the major Oscars, that Colbert revealed her flair for comedy. Thus established, she turned around and immediately agreed to make the melodrama *Imitation of Life* (1934), one of the best films of its time about interracial relations.

Colbert excelled in drama and melodrama. The women-at-war weeper *So Proudly We Hail* (1943) and the women-at-home tearjerker *Since You Went Away* (1944) are among her finest performances, declare film critics and fans alike.

Colbert's last great screen performance was in *Three Came Home* (1950), a wartime drama about Americans held prisoner by the Japanese on Borneo. That same year, she was scheduled to play a character named Margo Channing in a script Joe Mankiewicz wrote for her called *All About Eve.* Unfortunately, she slipped a disc, and Bette Davis got the plum role of a lifetime. After playing Troy Donahue's mom in *Parrish* (1961), she quit films for good.

She embraced television and live theater for at least three decades. In her 1985 stage performance, *Aren't We All?* she looked at least *40 years younger* than her actual age of 81—all due to wheat grass juice!

Las Vegas Comedian Always Energetic

Sometime during the summer of 1996, I went to Las Vegas, Nevada on some business. While there, I took in a comedy-dinner show at one of the lesser-known hotel casinos. A young comedian, aged 27, gave a very spirited 45-minute performance that was animated, to say the least. In fact, to many of us in the audience his boundless energy seemed virtually nonstop.

He was gracious enough to see me in his dressing room later on for a few minutes. After formal introductions, I explained what I did for a living and my purpose for being there. "I know from personal experience that talking takes a lot of energy," I began. "And you seem to have an incredible amount of it, because you never showed any fatigue the whole time you were cracking all those jokes out front on stage. How do you manage to keep your stamina strong for such energy-demanding performances as these?"

My host said he was willing to give me the information I desired, but asked that he remain anonymous. I agreed to honor his request.

He told me that he used a commercial brand of wheat grass juice powder twice a day in a special protein drink mix he made up in his blender at home, some of which he also brought with him to the casino for his evening performances. "Without the wheat grass, I know I would be hitting bottom pretty fast," he confessed. He said that his protein powder was whey- and soybean-based. He used two heaping tablespoons of the stuff to one pint of water, adding one whole sliced banana, one teaspoon of almonds or pecans, and three tablespoons of the wheat grass powder. "Sometimes I'll add half a cup of canned milk," he interjected, "but not that often."

"Wheat grass is my insurance for a quality performance every night," he concluded with certainty. "And that, my friend, is *no* joke!"

My Own Experience: It Keeps Me Regular

I've been using cereal grass and beet juice powders from Pines International of Lawrence, Kansas, for a couple of years. And like the comedian whom I interviewed in Las Vegas, I can say that these things do indeed produce significant vigor and vitality in the body. In fact, one glass of their Mighty Green vegetable drink mix—1 or 2 tablespoons of powder in 8 ounces of carrot, tomato, or pineapple juice—will keep a person going for up to 12 hours when intense physical activity may be needed.

Some months ago I decided to switch to Pines wheat grass tablets in the morning and late evening, though I still use their Mighty Greens periodically for lunch. Upon rising, I generally will take a small handful of the tablets—this amount can range from 10 to 16 tablets at a time. I repeat the same procedure just before retiring at night.

Ever since I've been doing this, I've enjoyed really good health in my colon. My stools are soft and consistent all the time; each bowel movement is easy and not at all difficult. And I no longer have an occasional flatulence problem that used to be somewhat of a public embarrassment whenever I ate in a hurry or did improper food combining. The only noticeable characteristic in my faithful use of wheat grass twice a day is the color of my stool—it is invariably a dark green.

For those suffering from constipation or mild diarrhea, I would strongly suggest you investigate the use of wheat grass as I have done. You can't go wrong by doing this.

Vegetable Chlorophyll, an Unbeatable Cancer Cure

In 1986, on my way back from Indonesia, I decided to take the *long* way home by crossing the subcontinent of India and stopping for a few days in the Netherlands. There, I drove to the village of

Vlaardingen, where I visited with Cornelius Moerman, M.D. This distinguished physician was then in his ninety-third year (he died comfortably in his sleep two years later, in August).

Despite his advanced age, weak eyesight, and slow movements, his mind was still sharp and his voice strong. I had come to inquire about his revolutionary nutritional program for fighting cancer. It would be only a few months later (actually on January 10, 1987) that the Ministry of Health at Der Hague (the equivalent of our own Food and Drug Administration) would make a public announcement finally recognizing the Moerman Therapy as an effective and reliable cancer treatment.

Although there are many parts to this doctor's remarkable anticancer program, a summary of some of the key elements can be made here.

> WHOLE FOODS are an *absolute* must! Dr. Moerman was a staunch defender of a diet that consisted of unprocessed or little-cooked foods. He believed that only through *whole foods* could you get the necessary enzymes the body requires for restoration of normal metabolic functions, whereas the processing and cooking of foods tend to destroy these *live* enzymes.

> NUTRITIONAL VIGOR, the good doctor insisted, was the only way the immune system could rebound and fight off cancer cells. His *favorite food* for promoting this was *vegetable chlorophyll*. I asked him to better define what he meant by this. He responded that it could be any dark, leafy greens *or* cereal grasses such as wheat grass, barley grass, rye grass, or young millet. These vegetable greens or leafy grasses could be eaten raw in salad form, drunk as refreshing juices (2 glasses a day), or taken as tablets or capsules (15 to 30 a day).

> EIGHT VITAL SUBSTANCES were always prescribed to promote energy and cellular regeneration. These supplements were given in the following average daily doses:

> | | |
> |---|---|
> | Vitamin A | 75,000 I.U. |
> | B-Complex (High-potency) | 4 tablets |
> | Vitamin C | 3,500 mg. |
> | Vitamin E | 600–800 I.U. |
> | Citric Acid | 5 tablespoons in solution form |

Iodine	8–10 kelp tablets
Iron	4 teaspoons in solution form
Sulfur	750–1200 mg.

Dr. Moerman reminded me that although his program gave considerable leeway to the dietary aspects, there was virtually no allowance for flexibility within the supplement phase of it. Patients needed to strictly adhere to it *every day* in order for the entire therapy to prove itself effective.

EAT CAREFULLY so that you always get the maximum nutritional benefits from your food. Eat slowly and masticate thoroughly so that every bit of food gets saturated with plenty of saliva before it is swallowed. This *predigestion* in the mouth is essential for regular digestion within the gut. The saliva is rich in enzymes, which imbeds the food with plenty of enzymatic action. So, if you are already consuming raw, whole foods that haven't been cooked or processed to death, you have a meal rich in enzymes. Then, once it is well chewed, it is getting additional enzymes put in everything that is ground up by the teeth and moved around in the mouth with the tongue. So once everything reaches the stomach, there are more than enough enzymes to help break things down faster and expedite the assimilation of food nutrients throughout the body.

JUICING formed the last part of his anticancer therapy. He told me what some of his favorite juice combinations were with his many different patients:

alfalfa sprout, beet root, and carrot
lettuce, parsley, and pineapple
green pepper, cucumber, and apple
spinach, celery, and grape
cabbage, kale, and pear

It will be noticed here that he generally put two or more chlorophyll items with *only one* kind of fruit; wheat grass was automatically included with each of the preceding juice formulas.

(*Note:* Pines International manufactures and distributes wheat grass, barley grass, a 27-mixed greens drink, and beet-root juice powder, all of which are ideal for adding to any of Dr.

Moerman's different juicing arrangements. See the Product Appendix for further details.)

For at least two decades, tens of thousands of Americans who have suffered from many forms of cancer went over the border to Tijuana, Mexico, to one of a dozen or more cancer clinics in desperate hope of finding cures for their diseases. About 60 percent came away satisfied with the treatments they received, with the remaining 40 percent unable to realize their fondest expectations.

I visited a number of these alternative medical clinics over the years and studied their different therapies. Those with the highest success rates usually incorporated some kind of vegetable chlorophylls into their programs. At least seven of these clinics utilized wheat or barley grass in their various green drinks. I've synthesized these different drinks down into one basic recipe that can be used with safety and efficacy to either prevent or treat existing malignancies. Of course, in such extreme medical situations, it's always a good idea to consult with a doctor before taking health matters this serious into your own hands.

Anti-Cancer Green Drink

1 small apple

1 medium pear

1/2 green pepper (including seeds)

1 tblsp. wheat-grass juice powder

1 tblsp. barley-grass juice powder

1 tsp. beet root juice powder

2 small leaves red cabbage

2 small leaves green cabbage

1/2 bunch parsley

2 leaves escarole

2 leaves romaine lettuce

2 leaves spinach

1-1/2 cups distilled or spring water

Put everything into a Vita-Mix whole food machine or equivalent blender, secure the container lid, and run the machine on medium for 2 minutes. Always make fresh; never refrigerate.

Nutrient Contents of Ordinary Wheat Grass

The following table suggests the nutrient contents of 100 grams dry weight of wheat grass:

Protein	32 grams
Total Dietary Fiber	37 grams
Carbohydrates	37 grams
Vitamin A	23,136 I.U.
Chlorophyll	543 mg.
Iron	34 mg.
Calcium	277 mg.
Vitamin C	51 mg.
Folic Acid	100 mcg.
Niacin	6.1 mg.
Riboflavin	2.03 mg.

(Courtesy of Ronald L. Seibold's *Cereal Grass, Nature's Greatest Health Gift* (New Canaan, CT: Keats Publishing, Inc., 1991, p. 8.)

The full potential of wheat grass hasn't yet been fully explored by the American populace. And it also remains to be "discovered" by most of the medical profession as an effective therapeutic agent in the treatment of diseases ranging from allergies and diabetes to infections and wounds. It is truly "the food of kings and common people" alike.

Chapter Six

Golden Turmeric
The Wonder Spice
and Healing Drug From India

Haridra (Sanskrit) in Ayurvedic Medicine

Curcuma longa (better known as turmeric) has been around for at least four millennia that we know of in the folk medicinal literature of India. *Haridra* (as turmeric goes by in the ancient Sanskrit) figured prominently in the earliest system of Indian medicine, dating back to about 1500 B.C. It was then recommended to decrease swellings and pain, being especially noted for its remarkable anti-inflammatory effect when it came to stomach problems and skin diseases. In fact, haridra was one of the centerpieces of Ayurvedic healing in those times.

But there can be no discussion of this spice without understanding something about the ancient culture of India. Sanskrit was once the classical standard language of ancient India, just as Latin was for Europe many centuries ago. It is believed that Sanskrit may have evolved from the language and writings of the Hittites (an ancient people of Asia Minor and Syria with Indo-European connections, who flourished from 1600 to 1200 B.C.). The oldest known stage of Sanskrit is Vedic or Vedic Sanskrit, so-called because it was the language of the Veda, the most ancient scriptures extant of Hinduism. This Vedic form of Sanskrit generally prevailed from 1500 to 200 B.C.

In the first edition of his classical work, *Chopra's Indigenous Drugs of India* (Calcutta: 1933), the author, Colonel Sir Ram Nath Chopra, M.D. (a specialist in tropical medicine and plant drug research) gave a brief history of Ayurveda (*Ayu:* life and *Veda:* knowledge), which is generally translated to mean "the science of life." It covers more than just medicine and is really a comprehensive knowledge of healthy living. In fact, it can probably be said with certain veracity that Ayurveda is the world's *first* true holistic approach to living. It is still widely practiced throughout the Indian subcontinent and caters to the needs of nearly 75 percent of the entire population.

Dr. Chopra recounted the antiquity of the medical aspect of Ayurveda (called Ayurvedic medicine) in this manner. "The earliest mention of the medicinal use of plants is to be found in the Rigveda, which is one of the oldest, if not the oldest repositories of human knowledge. . . . In the Atharvaveda, which is a later production, the use of [botanical] drugs is more varied although it

201

takes the form, in many instances, of charms, amulets, etc. It is in the Ayurveda, which is considered as an Upaveda (or supplementary hymns designed for the more detailed instruction of mankind), that definite properties of drugs and their uses have been given in some detail. Ayurveda, in fact, *is* the very foundation stone of the ancient medical science of India. . . . The age of Ayurveda is fixed by various Western scholars somewhere about 2500 to 600 B.C."

The two principal works written in ancient times about Ayurveda were the Susruta (which dealt in detail with numerous surgical procedures) and the Charaka (which covered more about medicine in general and included "a remarkable description of materia medica as it was known to the ancient Hindus). Both works were written in the Vedic Sanskrit (previously described). Because the language itself in which both texts were written was considered to be holy (due to the influence of Hindu scriptures also written in the same tongue), it stood to reason that the things mentioned therein were themselves also somewhat holy.

In the event the reader feels himself or herself wandering about in a bit of maze at this point, let me come to the rescue by getting right to the point. Haridra, the Vedic Sanskrit name for turmeric, wasn't just an ordinary name given to some plant, but rather a special *holy* name. And whatever else was mentioned about its uses or properties in the *sacred* Vedic Sanskrit had to imply a measure of holiness to it also. (In fact, the word Sanskrit means "perfected by the gods." Therefore, according to Hindu belief, whatever their many gods spoke or revealed to men was holy or "pure and perfect.") So any medical knowledge being transmitted to human sages from the Hindu gods and written in the "perfect" language of Vedic Sanskrit was viewed as nothing less than *sacred*. It can be assumed, then, to a large extent that haridra (turmeric) was one of many sacred remedies contained in these ancient medical scriptures (the Susruta and Charaka).

Turmeric as Vital Therapy for the Liver

Ayurveda is a holistic science and lays strong emphasis on preserving and promoting the fitness of healthy people, besides giving methods for the treatment of diseases. Hence, Ayurvedic medicine can be properly defined as "the system by which sound health of the *sharira* (body), *manas* (mind), and *atma* (the soul) are promoted and preserved." But this is achieved through different modalities, based on principles within its own conceptual framework. Ayurvedic medicine isn't just a health-care system dealing only with natural drugs. It is also a "way of life" and encourages methods for the promotion, prolongation, and maintenance of positive well-being *all around.* It emphasizes the importance of a specific daily routine *dinacharya* and seasonal regimen *ritucharya* along with diet, herbs, physical exercise, and good personal hygiene to achieve physical and mental health.

Without going into the complexities of trying to explain the conceptual framework behind Ayurveda in general, let me just say that it is based on certain essential doctrines known as the *Darshana.* In Darshana, the body's fundamental functional units are made up of three *dosha* (humours), seven *dhatu* (tissues), and *mala* (metabolic end products). When a state of health is present, then all of these are in equilibrium with one another. But when illness prevails, then there is an imbalance between some of these functional units. The goal of Ayurvedic medicine, therefore, is to maintain constant equilibrium between all the units or to restore such where any imbalances might occur.

According to ancient Vedic Sanskrit medical texts, the Hindu gods inspired the holy sages with the idea that *the liver* was one of the primary centers for the maintenance of health balance. So it wasn't unusual for Ayurvedic healers in the distant past to emphasize foods and drugs that would be good for the care of this vital body unit or organ.

It should come as no surprise that the liver was viewed in this manner. The Susruta spoke of *vaju* (air), *kapheh* (mucus), and *pittam* (bile) as those main elements continually moving through the liver. If one or more of them was out of proportion, then an unbalanced character would occur, often resulting in a disease process later on. For instance, the Susruta suggested that "too much bile caused anger or depression," whereas "too little produced timidity or cowardice."

Other ancient civilizations also held the liver in a similar high regard. Ancient Babylonians, upon seeing the liver's rich supply of blood in sacrificial rites, proclaimed that organ "the seat of the human soul." In a sense it is. The liver is one of the body's most vital organs, processing nearly every nutrient that comes from the intestines. The Etruscans (circa 750 B.C.) apparently used the liver for divination purposes much as the Babylonians did; both believed that the gods spoke through the liver. In China's oldest medical text, *The Yellow Emperor's Classic of Internal Medicine* (believed to have been written sometime around 2100 B.C.), the gallbladder was hailed as an "upright official" and the seat of courage, whereas the liver is the seat of anger and forms tears.

The involvement of the liver in strong emotions can be found in many Indo-European languages, be they modern, medieval, or ancient. In Akkadian texts, there is this phrase: "May your angry heart quiet down, may your liver relax"; and another, "May your heart be pleased, may your liver be happy." In a Hittite text appears, similarly, "Let them soften your heart and let them pacify your liver." Numerous other examples can be cited from African and Semitic languages, but this evidence should suffice to show that there once existed a nearly universal belief in the ancient world that *the liver is the seat of all our emotions.*

Haridra (turmeric) was regarded in ancient Ayurvedic medicine as the *chief* agent for promoting and preserving the health and well-being of the liver. In the beginning, so suggests the Susruta, it was ordained by the inspired sages to be consumed as a food. It was discovered at some point in time that this root usually went better with *other* spices than when used alone. Lengthy and considerable experimentation with a number of different herbs eventually produced a small group of distinct spices that ultimately paved the way for what came to be known later as curry powder. And turmeric, along with black pepper, cayenne pepper, coriander, cumin, fenugreek, and a few others became the central ingredient in several different curry combinations. Time and effort proved, however, that it be used more judiciously, since an excess of the root could leave a curry powder with a raw and earthy flavor somewhat reminiscent of an old and abandoned spice.

The Indian Veda, Hinduism's oldest and most sacred scriptures, taught that the gods gave turmeric its unique golden color to suggest its use for maintaining and giving life and health to the liver and gallbladder. Its intense yellow-orange hue was intended to be a reminder of the sun, where all of these Hindu deities were believed to reside. Turmeric represented so much of the essence of life produced by the sun that it was conceived to initiate a similar renewal response within those two organs. Ironically, turmeric is very sensitive to sunlight and should, like curry powder, be stored in darkness. So what the gods in their dwellings of light gave to Indians in ancient times for the benefit of the liver had to be hidden from the glory of the sun or else lose all of its nutritive and medicinal virtues.

In the seventh chapter of the Charaka is repeatedly mentioned the pairing of *Adrakam* (ginger) with Haridra. The reason given is simple: Ginger increases blood circulation, which in turn can expedite the delivery of turmeric to the liver. The two were always used in conjunction with each other in the older version of Ayuverdic medicine. Today, both still occupy an importance in the traditional (folk) medical system of India, but it seems they have fallen out of favor to some extent as the ideal pair for removing distress from liver and gallbladder and in its place substituting a restoration of health.

If we were to translate such ancient recommendations into prescriptions for ourselves, a revised dosage might read something like this:

I. For normal maintenance of the liver, take 1 capsule/tablet of powdered ginger root with 2 capsules/tablets of turmeric extract daily with one meal (usually lunch or dinner).
II. For treating imbalances of liver function, take 2 capsules/tablets of Adrakam together with 3 capsules/tablets of Haridra once or twice daily on an empty stomach.

If for some reason or another your system is unable to process either of these herbs individually or together, then you may safely rely on another equally effective alternative. This would be the combination of ginkgo biloba extract (2 capsules) and dandelion root (2–4 capsules). You can also add milk-thistle seed extract (1–2 capsules) as well if you feel your liver needs extra fortification or stepped-up treatment with natural substances.

Drug and alcohol addictions are nothing new to us. Written evidence from the past suggests that they've been with us for a very long time. Although not mentioning either specifically, the

Charaka pointed out that both Haridra and Adrakam were especially useful in removing the poisons of both substances that slowly accumulated within the liver. Regular supplementation with these herbs for several months could conceivably restore the integrity of this organ as well as surrounding ones such as the gallbladder, kidneys, spleen, and pancreas.

Another great combination that I've periodically used in treating various liver disorders is turmeric and goldenseal. Both roots are golden colored and exert magnificent healing influence upon the liver that is beyond the scope of this section to further elaborate on. I generally advise taking 2 capsules of each for problems such as hepatitis and cirrhosis.

Folk Applications

Owing to its brilliant golden color, turmeric root has been most closely identified with true saffron throughout the centuries. In medieval times it was often referred to as Indian saffron (*Crocus indicus*). Besides its pretty obvious use as an important culinary article for the flavoring and coloring of food, turmeric has long been a valued dyestuff. The root is probably the "sweet calamus," along with sweet cinnamon and myrrh described as "the principal spices" that the ancient Israelites carried with them in their famous exodus from Egypt.

Sun worshippers, speaking an Aryan tongue, made of Indian saffron (*C. indicus*) a sacred flower, and its yellow became a holy color. The demand for it was so great that eventually alternative sources for it had to be found. Hence, turmeric came into more prominent use for ceremonial functions, too. Hindu brides, for instance, are still painted with it, and married women in regions of India rinse their hands in turmeric water and rub it lightly over their cheeks when they wish to look their best. Lending a golden glow to the skin, it is used as a general cosmetic in many parts of Asia.

I became intrigued with the fact some years ago while over in that part of the world that virtually none of the teenaged girls there had any acne or complexion problems to speak of. The closer I investigated turmeric root, the more I realized that it actually helped to *prevent* many of the skin blemishes that are so common to girls and young women in the West.

In many parts of India and the Orient, turmeric is regarded very much as a prized charm. A bit of the root is frequently suspended around the neck of a newborn baby. Or else some turmeric water is dabbed on the child's head daily, until it is old enough to learn how to walk. In the Bengal region of India, should anyone become possessed by a tree demon, an exorcist is promptly summoned. He proceeds to wave a piece of burning turmeric root slowly and almost hypnotically in front of the victim's face. This, it is claimed, causes the evil entity to depart at once—for the disembodied cannot tolerate at all the smell of charred turmeric.

The taste of turmeric is related in some ways to mustard, since a number of prepared mustards have been blended with small amounts of this ground root. This provides a clue to the use of this venerable spice in modern foods. It goes well with chicken, fish, pork, rice dishes, creamed eggs, and spiced butters for cooked corn, snap beans, and steamed green cabbage. If you are tired of fixing baked or mashed potatoes the old familiar way, then try dressing them up with a pinch of turmeric mixed in with two tablespoons of melted butter, one teaspoon of chopped chives, and a tiny pinch of cayenne. You will be surprised at just how good the flavor is and how much of an improvement has been made in the same old spuds. Turmeric gives them a life all their own and actually seems to make them more tantalizing to the human palate. Try it for yourself and you'll see what I mean.

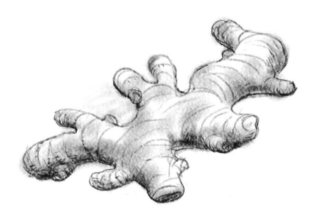

Since ancient times, this spice has been used by Ayurvedic practitioners throughout India as an agent that strengthens the stomach, invigorates vital body organs, and purifies the blood (by stimulating the action of the liver and kidneys). Turmeric also counteracts periodic disease (such as malaria) and produces gradual beneficial change within the system, usually by improving nutrition but without having any marked specific effect to speak of.

One-quarter teaspoon of the finely grated root is simmered in 1-1/2 cups hot milk for 10 minutes and then strained. It is allowed to cool down a little and then sipped when lukewarm for getting rid of a cold; this is a common household remedy throughout India. The root may also be pressed to withdraw its juice or else some (three tablespoons coarsely chopped) put in a Vita-Mix or equivalent blender with a small amount of water (1/2 cup) and processed for two minutes. This liquefied matter can then be blended with one glass of tomato or carrot juice to improve taste. It can be taken internally to neutralize the venom inflicted upon the body by bites from a poisonous snake or spider. A smooth paste made from some of this same liquid (by adding enough flour to thicken it) or made by adding sufficient water to powdered turmeric and then placed over the area of the bite will help to draw out toxins close to the surface. The paste can also be applied topically in cases of severe itching, inflammation, or eruption. In India, this paste is popular to treat leprosy. The liquefied root, when mixed with warm milk or suitable fruit or vegetable juices, will help relieve the vomiting sensation accompanying morning sickness suffered by pregnant women as well as taking care of liver problems and diarrhea.

Lord Robert Stephenson Smyth Baden-Powell inaugurated the Boy Scouts in 1908 and with his sister Agnes the Girl Guides (later Girl Scouts) in 1910. He was a military hero of the Boer Wars in South Africa and achieved the rank of lieutenant general. He authored different works on army tactics and scouting. During combat, he found turmeric root to be effective in treating intermittent fevers and edema due to bad water, inadequate food, and poor sanitation. By boiling the root for about 15 minutes, he not only obtained a strong tea but also killed whatever harmful microorganisms might have been lurking in the water he used for this purpose. Furthermore, he discovered that the skin could be washed with a strong solution of this tea to remove parasites that may have crawled beneath the surface.

One of the more common treatments with this remedy that I witnessed myself occurred during one of my visits to India some years ago. Leishmaniasis is a chronic and widespread skin infection common to parts of Asia Minor, northern Africa, and India; it is induced by the bite of an infected sandfly. A small, circumscribed, solid elevation develops on the epidermis; this soon enlarges to a nodule and then breaks down into an open ulcer (another nickname for it is "Oriental sore").

Ayurvedic doctors have a novel way of treating this condition. They mix together the equivalent of one tablespoon of powdered turmeric root and just a *pinch* (no more than 1/8 teaspoon) of *caustic* lime with enough water to form a smooth paste. Sometimes a few drops of sesame-seed oil (or some other kind of vegetable-seed oil) will be added to help retain moisture longer in the paste. Another thing that many Ayurvedic practitioners do is to drool some of their own *saliva* in with these other ingredients. The reason for this isn't quite clear, but I've been told that the rich enzyme content of human saliva increases the surface healing action of the turmeric. (Certain body fluids such as saliva and urine hold therapeutic importance in Ayurvedic medicine.) The paste is then smeared onto the suppurating ulcer and over inflamed joints. The application is very soothing and relieves any pain that may be present. Repeated treatments (twice daily) for up to a week or longer are known to clear up the worst case of leishmaniasis.

I asked a colleague of mine at the UCLA School of Medicine, who is a skilled dermatologist, if such a remedy might be of use in stubborn cases of flesh-eating bacteria, which defy all forms of conventional antibiotic therapy. He is open to alternative medicine such as this and didn't see how it could hurt. "At least it's something *different* that our medical system hasn't tried yet," he said. "It would be worth checking out." To the above Indian paste I would add a pinch of goldenseal root and 1/4 teaspoon echinacea fluid extract if treating something like flesh-eating bacteria.

A common practice still widely employed throughout India involves soaking a piece of cloth in some turmeric-root tea and then wiping away eye discharges in cases of acute conjunctivitis and ophthalmia. And where there are discharges from the ear canal, a tiny amount of finely powdered turmeric root and alum mixture is placed just inside the ear, but *not*—repeat *not*—inserted within the canal itself.

Poisonous scorpions and centipedes are pervasive in India. Ayurvedic doctors will sprinkle powdered turmeric over glowing pieces of charcoal held in a metal pan and have the injured parties inhale the fumes arising therefrom. This is said to greatly relieve the excruciating pain that such injuries produce. The patients are also given turmeric tea to drink, and root paste is smeared over the afflicted areas, too.

In experiments conducted many years ago by Dr. Chopra, he noticed that turmeric oil or tea promoted the flow of saliva and "gave a feeling of warmth and a sense of comfort in the stomach." He concluded that "it . . . seems to act as an appetizer, stomachic and tonic." And when turmeric capsules or tea were taken immediately after a meal, there "followed a marked diminution of secretion of the acids in the stomach." This tells us that turmeric is quite useful for heartburn and inflammation of the gallbladder (also known as gallbladder or bile attack). And when turmeric extract was injected into cats, it produced a fall in their blood pressures; this suggests it is of value in treating human hypertension.

Scientific experiments have helped to verify some of the folk applications for which turmeric has been used. Dr. Chopra was a leading pioneer in this kind of research. Others of his countrymen followed up with additional work years later. The book *Selected Medicinal Plants of India* by Bharatiya Vidya Bhavan (Bombay: Chemexcil, 1992, p. 123) summarized some of this. Application of turmeric powder over septic as well as aseptic wounds in rats and rabbits accelerated the process of healing to the extent of 23–24 percent in both cases. No side effects were observed with curcumin in a dose of 1200 mg/day for two weeks in 18 patients with rheumatoid arthritis. No significant change in blood pressure, hemoglobin, hepatic-functions tests, and renal-function tests were observed in these patients. Mild dryness of the mouth and throat was complained of by a few patients with bronchial asthma and treated with turmeric powder in a dose of 12 grams per day. This symptom was controlled with a reduction in the dose. Curcumin (a principal antioxidant constituent of turmeric) in a dose of 1800 milligrams per day for 90 days in rats and 800 milligrams per day for a similar period in monkeys was found to be quite safe. No evidence of skeletal or visceral malformations was observed in mice with 1600 milligrams and in rabbits with 600 milligrams on days 6 through 15 following copulation.

The foregoing data suggest that not only can some of turmeric's healing actions be verified scientifically, but also that even in larger doses it appears to be quite safe.

The Curcuminoids: Their Antioxidant Properties and Bioprotectant Powers

A trio of coloring principles responsible for the yellow pigmentation in turmeric root are called curcuminoids (named after the first part of its Latin binomial, *Curcuma longa*). These three phenolic compounds that were isolated from turmeric awhile back are curcumin (the main one), demethoxycurcumin, and bis-demethoxycurcumin.

This spice and its three curcuminoids are beginning to be recognized everywhere as effective plant antioxidants. Explaining the role of antioxidants usually takes a long and drawn-out process by those writing on the subject. But I'm going to take an approach so simple that even an elementary-school child can understand the explanation given here.

Antioxidants are naturally occurring substances that can be likened to strong fishing nets that capture and effectively inactivate scavenger molecules known as free radicals. Think of them as slightly crazed molecular sharks that zip around in your cellular sea, taking frequent nips and bites out of body tissues. But when antioxidant substances such as the curcuminoids are put into the circulating blood plasma, they exert a netlike force over these free radicals by restraining their activities and then rendering them inert so they can no longer cause harm in the system.

Free radical damage can lead to accelerated aging and weakened immune defenses, thereby exposing the body to a number of different diseases. But antioxidants such as these turmeric curcuminoids can reverse aging to some extent and halt the spread of illness, as well as reduce or totally eliminate the sensation of pain that usually accompanies such events. In one study with animal models, curcumin manifested *eight times greater* strength against free radical activity than did vitamin E (another potent antioxidant).

The two leading causes of death in America today, coronary artery disease and cancer, and one of the most painful diseases around, rheumatoid arthritis, are known to be caused by free radical damage to the body. But in repeated experiments with the curcuminoids, there were noticeable improvements and reductions of pain in each of these serious conditions. This isn't to say that turmeric compounds are necessarily cures for such problems, but they certainly can assist the body in better coping with such dire diseases. Not to mention also that these antioxidants help to *prevent* them from ever forming in the first place. This speaks well of their bioprotective abilities, wherein a person might want to take supplements that will keep him or her well for a long time.

The Sabinsa Corporation of Piscataway, New Jersey, is a world leader in curcuminoid research. The company was founded and is currently owned by Muhammed Majeed, Ph.D., who holds a doctorate (1986) in industrial pharmacy from St. John's University in New York City. He spent 15 years of his life in pharmaceutical research for drug giants such as Pfizer, Inc., before turning his attention to some of those herbal medicines used in the Ayurvedic medicine of his native land.

Turmeric was one of the first Ayurvedic botanicals that he chose for doing intensive research on. He hired the best scientists that money could buy and outfitted a laboratory with the latest state-of-the-art technology in order to make the research as thorough and complete as possible. What eventually emerged from all the funds and efforts put into this worthy endeavor was a unique product bearing the trademarked name of C^3 Complex.

It is sold in bulk form to the giant nutrition supplement and pharmaceutical industries, but distributed to consumers through a subsidiary, America's Finest, Inc. One medical doctor, who asked not to be identified by name or location in this book, was persuaded to prescribe it to some of his older patients suffering from thrombosis. He reported back that after putting them on it for several months he noticed significant decreases in their platelet aggregations, which generally obstruct blood flow. He also believed it greatly reduced their risks of stroke as well.

I have been using this wonderful antioxidant formula (2 tablets daily), along with dandelion root (3 capsules daily) and milk-thistle seed extract (1 capsule daily) for strengthening a mildly weak liver. In six weeks, I had some tests conducted on me by both alternative and regular medical doctors to determine the state of my liver's health. The various pronouncements ranged from "good" and "great" to "nice" and "outstanding." I discontinued the therapy for awhile, but resume it about every four months for the same length of time. One thing I've noticed is that my energy levels are up considerably, now that my liver is back to its normal functions again.

This C^3 Complex contains 250 milligram of curcuminoids, along with 5 milligrams of Bioperine (a black pepper extract), 100 micrograms of selenomethionine (calculated elemental selenium), 8000 I.U. of beta-carotene (vegetable-derived vitamin A), and 200 I.U. of vitamin E. Sabinsa scientists determined that these other augmenting nutrients work in harmony with the curcuminoids, and the extract of black pepper provides quicker absorption and assimilation of everything into the body. (For more information on C^3 Complex, consult the Product Appendix under the Sabinsa Corporation.)

Botanical Description

Turmeric, a native of South and Southeast Asia, is believed to have originated in the slopes of hills in the tropical forests of the west coast of South India. It is one of the plants that have been propagated as a vegetable for thousands of years. *Curcuma*, a genus in the family Zingiberaceae, consists of many hundreds of species of rhizomatous herbs distributed in India, China, Indonesia, Thailand, the Malayasian Archipelago, and Northern Australia. As in the case of ginger, which belongs to the same family, turmeric can be grown in diverse tropical conditions. It thrives best in loose, friable, loamy or alluvial soil, suitable for liberal irrigation and good drainage. Along with ginger, turmeric is thought to have been taken from Southeast Asia to China, and thence from there by transoceanic migration to Central and South

America. From the Americas, turmeric spread to the West Indies and subsequently to Africa.

Turmeric is typical of the herbaceous plant, with thick and fleshy rhizomes and leaves in sheaths that characterize the family Zingiberaceae. The plants reach a height of up to 3-1/2 feet. The leaves are alternate, obliquely erect or subsessile, and oblong—lanceolate and dark green, surmounting leaf sheaths tapering near the leaf and broadening near the base, enveloping the succeeding shoot. Inflorescence is terminal on leafy spurious stems appearing between the sheaths. Flowers, which are seen occasionally on cylindric spikes bearing numerous greenish white bracts, are narrow and yellowish white. Most cultivated varieties are sterile triploids, but stray inconspicuous fruits are known.

The underground rhizome, which is processed into the spice, consists of two distinct parts: the egg-shaped primary or mother rhizome, being an extension of the stem, and several long cylindrical multibranched secondary rhizomes growing downward from the primary rhizome. Both forms have transverse rings of leaf scars and dents of root scars. Based on their shape, the two forms used to be differentiated in the Western trade, the bulbs as *C. rotunda* and the fingerlike, cylindrical forms as *C. longa,* though both are from the same plant.

The varieties of turmeric under cultivation have probably evolved by unconscious selection. There are currently about three dozen named varieties mentioned as being grown in India, besides varieties grown since ancient times in China and Indonesia. There are also varieties that have been adapted for cultivation in recent times in countries such as Jamaica, Haiti, Peru, and other tropical and subtropical countries. They vary in gross morphological characters, yield, composition, and susceptibility to microbial and insect attack. Some of the variations may be inherent, and others due to agricultural methods and climates. These varieties are known by local names or the name of the region/area where the seed material originated or has been in continuous cultivation for a long time.

A somewhat distinctive feature regarding one of the root's medicinal applications is just how widespread the paste mixed with a little lime is for the relief of sprains, contusions, inflammatory joints, and bruises. This practice isn't just confined to India alone, but occurs with great frequency in most other tropical zones of the world, where different varieties of turmeric are cultivated. Also, its use for disorders of the liver and gastrointestinal complaints stretches from northern Australia and Indonesia all the way up to India and China. Whether these applications were transmitted orally through migration or developed independently by the local natives isn't known for sure. But at least it shows people in totally different cultures can recognize the same healing properties in this wonderful plant without having to contact one another in order to learn them.

Some Turmeric Recipes

Here is a short collection of some recipes calling for turmeric. Some of them are strictly medicinal, while others are for culinary enjoyment.

Albert Y. Leung, a retired biochemist, cited one simple recipe in his book *Chinese Herbal Remedies* (New York: Universe Books, 1984, p. 165). "For treating pain and itching resulting from sores or ringworm," he wrote, "turmeric is mashed in water and the mash is applied directly to the affected areas."

Encephalomyelitis is an acute inflammation of the brain and spinal cord that usually occurs in animals and not too often in man (where it can prove fatal). A recipe mentioned in *Acta Pharmaceutica Sinica* (17:695, Sept. 1982) describes giving a "hot water infusion of Yu-Jin" (*Curcuma aromatica*) to guinea pigs, which decreased their experimentally induced encephalomyelitis "by one half."

Researcher Richard Anderson, Ph.D., of the U.S. Department of Agriculture's Nutrition Research Center in Beltsville, Maryland, shared with me a simple spice mixture that he thinks can control, and even prevent, diabetes. "Take a pinch of cinnamon, a couple of cloves, half a bay leaf, and a teaspoon of turmeric," he said, "and make them into a tea by simmering them in 1-1/2 pints of boiling water, covered, for 15 minutes on low heat. Strain, sweeten with honey or vanilla extract, if necessary, and sip with a meal twice daily." Or else the powdered forms of these spices can be mixed together and put into gelatin capsules; take 1 per meal three times daily.

Making Your Own Curry Powder

1 tbsp. ground coriander seeds
1/2 tsp. ground mustard seeds
1/2 tsp. ground cumin seeds
1/2 tsp. ground turmeric
1/4 tsp. ground ginger
1/4 tsp. ground, dried, hot red chiles

Combine all these ingredients in a bowl and mix thoroughly. Transfer to an airtight jar and store in a cool place. Use this in any recipes calling for curry powder. Some of this can also be made into a simple paste and applied externally to the skin to draw out poison or help heal sores.

Curried Chicken Salad

1/2 cup light cream
1/2 cup yogurt
1/2 cup mayonnaise
2 tsps. homemade curry powder
1 cup apples, peeled, cored, chopped
2 medium stalks celery, chopped
2 tsp. chopped onion
1/2 cup toasted slivered almonds
one 3–4 lb. chicken, cooked

In a large bowl combine the cream, yogurt, and mayonnaise. Then stir in the curry. Next add the remaining ingredients. Finally break up the chicken into bite-size pieces with your fingers and fold into the dressing. Serve lightly chilled. Yield: six servings.

Anyone who's ever been fortunate enough to come under the taste magic of turmeric or been charmed by its warming pungency will know for a certainty that this "wonder food spice and healing drug from India" promotes appetite as well as good health in all who use it frequently.

Chapter Seven

The Power
of the Antioxidant Vitamins
A, C, and E

The Antioxidant Vitamins

The human species is unique among all of God's wonderful creations: we are the *only* creatures concerned with *staying young* as long as possible. Other forms of life—animals, birds, fishes, reptiles, and insects—accept their inevitable fates of growing old with a certain grace or factual understanding. But not us—no, many of our kind go to great lengths and extreme measures to hide the all-too-obvious, the fact we're growing old.

In the public's fetish for retaining its youth as long as possible, there has come to the forefront a plethora of ideas, plans, products, foods, and activities to help many of us try to turn back the clock of time so that we might look, feel, and think ourselves as being a little younger, perhaps. Among these numerous *antiaging* offers, which are usually short on miracles but long on hope, are something called *antioxidants.*

Two leading medical dictionaries define the word this way. *Stedman's Medical Dictionary,* 25th Ed. (Baltimore: Williams & Wilkins, 1990, p. 99) describes antioxidant as "an agent that inhibits oxidation and thus *prevents* rancidity of oils or fats or *the deterioration* of other materials through oxidative processes" (italics added for emphasis). *Dorland's Illustrated Medical Dictionary,* 28th Ed. (Philadelphia: W. B. Saunders Co., 1994, p. 98) gives its own expanded version of this definition: "One of many widely used synthetic or natural substances added to a product to prevent or *delay its deterioration* by action of oxygen in the air; rubber, paints, vegetable oils, and prepared foods commonly contain antioxidants" (italics added for emphasis).

By now the reader should have observed my own emphasis on the key words *prevents* or *delay* DETERIORATION. As we age, we slowly *deteriorate;* consequently, we need something to *decelerate* this process a bit. This is where an antioxidant agent comes in—to *not* make this happen so quickly. Spices such as garlic and turmeric, and herbs such as ginseng (all covered in previous chapters) are excellent antioxidants. So, too, are some of the things that bees manufacture (royal jelly) or gather in (bee pollen), which are outlined at the beginning of this book.

This chapter concludes with emphasis on a trio of important nutrients with significant antioxidant properties to them, namely vitamins A, C, and E. For years, they were recognized for facilitating other bodily functions with little attention given to their antiaging capabilities. The accompanying table summarizes information about each of them that was pretty standard some 20 years ago. In fact, aging wasn't even on the list. It has been only within the last several years that scientific research has given serious focus to their age-retardant power.

But antioxidants such as these wouldn't mean much if it weren't for a group of highly reactive compounds called *free radicals*. These have been briefly discussed in some of the previous chapters. Free radicals are formed by radiation; excessive ozone; smog and air pollution; cigarette smoke; meat that is fried, charbroiled, or barbecued; other food that is deep-fried; and by the normal breakdown of proteins within our bodies. The most abundant free radicals appear to be the peroxides and superoxides, which are merely fragments of oxygen.

Free radicals have an "extra" electrical charge that causes them to seek out other substances in the system in order to neutralize themselves. This initial reaction neutralizes the free radical, but in the process another one is formed. A chain reaction is thus initiated, and thousands of free radical reactions can occur within just a few seconds of the first reaction unless the extra free radical is immediately deactivated.

I liked the way that Elizabeth Somer, a registered dietitian, explained how free radicals work inside each of us in her book *The Essential Guide to Vitamins and Minerals* (p. 126). "The fatty membranes that surround cells are the prime targets for free radical attack. The shape and function of the fats in membranes are changed when a free radical attacks them. The damaged membrane is no longer able to transport nutrients, oxygen, and water into the cell or regulate the removal of waste products. Extensive free radical damage can cause the membrane to rupture and release its cellular components. These cellular components can further damage the surrounding tissues. Free radicals also attack nucleic acids that comprise the genetic code within each cell. Nucleic acids regulate normal cell formation and the growth and repair of damaged or aging tissues. The damage caused by free radicals has been linked to premature aging. Although why a body ages is only partially understood, all theories agree that at some

Vitamin Information Chart

(Courtesy of Vita Chart, Inc., Bronx, NY, Carolyn Hellerwest, editor)

Vitamin	Daily Dosage	Bodily Function Facilitated	Therapeutic Applications
A Fat Soluble	10,000–25,000 IU	Body tissue reparation and maintenance (resist infection), RNA synthesis, visual purple production (necessary for night vision)	Acne, alcoholism, allergies, arthritis, asthma, bronchitis, cholesterol (high), colds, conjunctivitis, cystitis, diabetes, eczema, glaucoma, heart diseases, hepatitis, infections and communicable diseases, migraine headaches, nephritis, psoriasis, sinusitis, tinnitus (ear ringing), tooth and gum disorders
C Ascorbic acid Water Soluble	500–5000 mg	Collagen production, digestion, fine bone and tooth formation, iodine conservation, healing (burns and wounds), red blood cell formation (hemorrhaging prevention), shock and infection resistance (colds), vitamin protection (oxidation)	Alcoholism, allergies, atherosclerosis, arthritis, baldness, cholesterol (high), colds, cystitis, drug addiction, hypoglycemia, heart disease, hepatitis, insect bites, prickly heat, sinusitis, stress, tooth decay
E Tocopherol Fat Soluble	400–800 IU	Calcium and phosphorus metabolism (bone formation), heart action, nervous system maintenance, normal blood clotting, skin respiration	Allergies, arthritis, atherosclerosis, baldness, cholesterol (high), crossed eyes, cystitis, diabetes, heart disease, menstrual problems, menopause, migraine headaches, myopia, phlebitis, thrombosis, varicose veins *External:* burns, scars, warts, wrinkles, wounds

221

point the body's cells have become unable to replenish their components and as one cell dies, other cells dependent on the dying cell also are lost. The accumulation of cellular debris within a cell also is associated with aging. Finally, the cells' inability to correctly replenish necessary proteins because of damage to the genetic code is common in aging. Free radicals contribute to all of these processes."

Besides hastening the aging process, free radicals are also blamed for initiating other health problems, some of which are compiled below.

- Arteriosclerosis/atherosclerosis
- Cancer
- Drug-induced damage to organs
- Enhanced susceptibility to disease processes
- Greater susceptibility to infection
- Heart disease
- Immune suppression
- Inadequate wound healing
- Increasing symptoms of joint, muscle, and nerve disorders (arthritis, muscular dystrophy, and Parkinson's disease)

Even though our existences depend upon oxygen for sustained life, oxygen has its "nasty side" as well. But "the body has developed a complex antioxidant system to defend itself from . . . free radicals," Ms. Somer notes in her book. "This antioxidant system is comprised of enzymes, minerals," *and vitamins*! The "antioxidants act as scavengers and prevent the formation of free radicals or bind to and neutralize these reactive substances before they damage tissues." In citing such antioxidant nutrients as copper, manganese, selenium, and zinc, she correctly points out that "they work in conjunction with an antioxidant enzyme and are [therefore] necessary for the enzyme to function properly."

But if the diet is nutritionally poor to begin with, then such antioxidant enzymes may not be produced or may prove ineffective with their corresponding antioxidant minerals. *Only* vitamins A, C, and E, according to her, "function as antioxidants *independent* of an enzyme." It may be worth noting here, in passing, that

Wakunaga of America is the only supplement manufacturer that makes a garlic-vitamin-mineral antioxidant product (called Kyolic Formula 105) comprised of Japanese aged-garlic extract, vitamins A, C, and E, and selenium. (See Product Appendix for more information on this fine antioxidant combination.)

The remainder of this chapter will examine each of these important vitamins in terms of how they relate to free radical control and inactivation. *True* stories will be presented to show how individuals from vastly different walks of life have used these wonderful antioxidant vitamins to their own excellent advantages, either obtaining them from whole foods or else through nutritional supplementation.

There is a *real power* behind this trio of nutrients. They are unlike any other vitamins in that the body depends upon them for a large number of functions, including putting free radicals into an inert or inactive state where they can't do the system any further harm. And although their effects are quite subtle, to say the least, their overall achievements eventually become evident in *how* we look, the *way* we think, and the *manner* in which we feel emotionally, spiritually, and above all, *physically.*

The Role of Vitamin A in Staying Well

"How We Keep Our 18 Kids Healthy"

Meet Scott Hancock Clark, 50 years old and a successful banking lawyer partner with Ray, Quinney & Nebeker, Utah's third largest law firm (90 lawyers and 120 nonlegal staff). He was appointed by the governor in 1994 to serve four years as chairman of the board of Child and Family Services of Utah. His wife, MaryBeth, who is also 50, is an English and language specialist in the state Office of Education. They reside in the posh and trendy upper-eastside Sandy community of Willow Creek in a four-story, approximately 6,000-square-foot house, which has 11 bedrooms, 7 bathrooms, and a 5-car garage.

Many other upper-income people, like the Clarks, live in similarly spacious digs. But what separates *this* wealthy Utah couple from the rest of America's rich elite is the *size* of their family. The Clarks, you see, have a total of *eighteen kids*—all of them adopted. As I sat and watched Scott list off the number of different nationalities represented in their brood, I began to get a sense of appreciation for his and his wife's *international* humanitarianism. The ethnic backgrounds of their 11 boys and 7 girls are as follows: one each of Vietnamese, Colombian, Chinese, and Iranian descent; two apiece of Korean, East Indian, Filipino, and African descent; four Bolivians; and two Americans (California and Utah).

They range in age from 6 months to 24 years. The lawyer father gave some more careful thought while enumerating the ages of each: an infant 6 months old; two 3-year-olds; two 7-year-olds; one each who is 9, 10, and 12 years of age; two 14-year-olds; three teenagers who are 15, 17, and 18; and five adults whose ages span from 20 to 24.

The adoption costs for all 18 kids exceeded $171,000. Since a number of the children have various physical problems requiring special needs or medications, the medical costs (covered mostly by health insurance) have easily run over $100,000. "School lunches alone cost us around $250 a month," Scott observed. Monthly food expenditures exceed this figure by four to five times.

"We seldom ever have any sickness around our house," Scott said. "We try to keep ourselves quite healthy, as a matter of fact." I asked if he and his wife took any vitamin-mineral supplements or gave the same to any of their children. "When they were very young, our family pediatrician may have prescribed some children's vitamins for awhile," he recalled, "but that's all they've ever had of this type of thing. We don't go to health-food stores or believe in nutritional supplements like you or the people who read your [self-care health] books may do. We follow what our doctors tell us to do the *few* times we've been ill.

"But we *do* believe in eating right," he continued. "We are strong advocates of *good* food and subscribe to the theory that you can get all of the nutrients your body needs through correct diet. We try not to be extreme in anything we do. For us, eating foods that promote good health in the body just makes good nutritional sense. You *don't* need food supplements just to stay healthy."

For vitamin A, the Clarks see to it that their family gets fish: "We probably have it baked or steamed several times a week; I tend to also have it for lunch about as many times during the week when I eat out (which is quite often)." The family also consumes a great deal of vegetables. "Both my wife and I eat quite a few sal-

ads when we work. At night our housekeeper will usually fix *two* different kinds of vegetables with whatever main course we're having. We're big fans of carrots, corn, spinach, and some types of squash." All of these items are rich in beta-carotene (the vegetable form of vitamin A).

There are a number of sources that the family turns to for their *daily* vitamin C requirements. "Oranges are *really* B-I-G at our house!" Scott said with an emphasized chuckle. "I'll buy a whole case of them for the kids to snack on when they get home from school. And I'll always bring a bag of them with me to work and put in the refrigerator that we have in our employees' dining room. I also buy lots of bananas and apples—I prefer the Granny Smith [green] and Delicious [red] varieties. I take sacks of them to work as well, and the kids will munch on them whenever they're hungry. We're also big juice drinkers at home; our kids like the hot kind of V-8, apple juice, orange juice, and grape juice. The only thing that has never gone big around home is grapefruit and grapefruit juice. For some reason, no one seems to like it very much. Pears are also a great snack treat—I usually buy a bushel of them when they're in season and sackfuls other times of the year when they're not available from local growers." The Clarks also obtain additional vitamin C from vegetables such as green beans, peas, lettuce, spinach, escarole, mustard greens, watercress, and parsley. He thinks that the many salads they consume on a fairly regular basis give them adequate ascorbic acid. Sometimes their housekeeper will make a big pot of chicken soup or stew that's loaded with vegetables that are rich in vitamin C. "I don't think we've ever suffered from too little of it," he said with a casual smile.

Those frequent salads and cooked vegetables that contain dark-green items give the family about one quarter of their vitamin E intake, he estimated. An additional amount comes from the safflower, sunflower, and corn oils they or their housekeeper cooks with. They are fond of cooked brown rice as are many of their adopted kids, who hail from those parts of the world where this grain is a major staple in the diet. And while no one in the family eats very much red meat (preferring chicken or fish instead) or eggs anymore, which are sources for vitamin E, they do consume other things that have small amounts of this antioxidant nutrient: peas, whole-wheat bread, fresh tomatoes, chicken breast, fresh apple and banana, cornflakes, and fresh carrots. Some of the kids eat nuts or nut butters, which are fairly high in vitamin E, too.

When I asked Scott if he knew what free radicals or antioxidants were, he spread his hands apart with palms turned upwards in a mimed confession as if implying, I don't know; you tell me. Following a brief explanation of these things, he shifted his weight in the chair he was sitting on and smiled knowingly. "We don't think about things like that. Nor do we worry about how old we're getting. Look at me—do I look healthy or not?"

I had to admit that he did, in fact, look pretty good for a man who was under a lot of job-related stress and had numerous responsibilities to his community, church, and family. He got up, walked over behind his desk, lifted off a large framed picture, and brought it over to me to look at. "This is a recent picture of our family," he said with obvious pride. "Do any of them *look* sick?" He made his point in a nice way.

Obviously, not everyone may agree with this lawyer's particular point of view, especially those who are health-food and supplement enthusiasts. They will beg to differ with some of these things, such as being entirely medically oriented when it comes to illness treatment, instead of considering safer, more natural alternatives such as herbs or vitamins and minerals. But the man's basic philosophy of getting most, if not all, of your necessary nutrients from the foods you eat certainly has to be respected.

Because, besides being essentially correct, it also squares very well with my own philosophy. Foods should *always* be our *first* source for vitamins and minerals, with nutritional supplements a close second. This way you're getting the nutrient as nature intended for it to be, instead of in an isolated form separated from everything else around it, as is the case with dietary supplements. The inclusion of fiber, amino acids, enzymes, alkaloids, oils, pectins, and other natural constituents *with* vitamins and minerals is absolutely essential to their *total* assimilation in the body. Otherwise, without such surrounding supports, they will not be fully utilized, but will have a portion of themselves lost through the eliminative processes of the body.

"We Feel Years Younger"

On Thursday and Friday, July 18–19, 1996, I flew to New York City to be on the TV Food Network (a national cable show with an estimated seven million viewers) program entitled, "In Food Today." The show hosts were Donna Hanover Giuliani (wife of New York's current mayor) and David Rosengarten. The live broadcast took place between 6:30 and 7:00 P.M. EST and lasted no more than four minutes.

The next morning, I did another show for Alternative Medical Television, hosted by my friend Robert Crayhon, to help promote my book *Heinerman's Encyclopedia of Juices, Teas & Tonics.* Afterwards, I took a taxicab from the Sheraton Towers in midtown Manhattan (where I stayed) to Kennedy Airport. My driver was Henry Charles from Queens (Rosedale), New York. He was from the Martinique Islands and used to be an accountant for six years before turning to cab driving. His wife is a licensed practical nurse at a major hospital, and the couple have two teenaged daughters.

As soon as we discovered how nice and friendly each of us was, a lively conversation ensued between both parties. Upon learning who I was, what I did for a living, and my reason for being in the Big Apple, Henry turned the discussion to one of my favorite subjects—anti-aging. He said that in his homeland,

"People don't show their age as much as they do here" (meaning New York City, of course). He attributed much of this to the diet: "Over there, people eat a lot of fish, root vegetables, and fresh fruit such as bananas, coconuts, guavas, mangos, and papayas.

"We didn't feel my age as much then, as we did upon coming to America," he continued. "We hadn't been here no more than two years than we both began to *feel* 'old.' " When I asked specifically what he meant by that, he replied, "Oh, we seemed to be more tired and worn out; we certainly slept a lot more than we did in Martinique." He also said their normally black hair started showing signs of premature grayness. "We figured it was the pollution and decided to do something about it."

What they did was to find inexpensive fish sources for vitamin A. "We started eating more canned sardines, herring, mackerel, and salmon. My wife found a place that sold guava, mango, and papaya juices, and we started drinking these instead of soda pop. We also ate more nuts and seeds." And since a Korean market was close by where they lived, his wife started buying more fresh, leafy greens and green vegetables. "We eat more salads and cooked vegetables than we did when we first got here," he admitted.

The upshot of all this dietary revision was a *noticeable* increase in the energy levels of Henry and his wife. "Our kids didn't need any more energy . . . they've got enough as it is," he laughed. "But we started feeling better already after the first week on our new diet." One of their daughters commented to the mother, "Mom, what's happening to your hair—all of your gray hairs are disappearing." Henry said when his wife heard that she first hugged her daughter and then took a mirror to check it out for herself. "She was quite happy at making that discovery," he added with a laugh.

Vitamin C, Nature's Free Radical Fighter

Regaining Health in Women's Prison

In the late 1970s, Frances Berenice Schreuder lived a rather fashionable New York City lifestyle on Manhattan's upper-scale eastside. Unfortunately for her, she became the central focus in a high-profile crime occurring in Utah that gained national and regional attention; in turn, this spawned an unflattering book and two scandalous made-for-television movies. Frances and her son Mark, who murdered his wealthy grandfather at his mother's request, went to prison for the crime of which they were accused. Both served 13-year stretches before being released in 1995 and 1996.

When Frances went to prison she was 45 years of age, a heavy smoker, a couch potato, a junk-food addict, and (to use her own words), "hopelessly overweight and out of shape." But when I got the "lucky break" that other journalists had been hoping for and interviewed her in the summer of 1993, she was then a svelte, nonsmoking, near-vegetarian exercise enthusiast who had just celebrated her fifty-fifth birthday. "Look at me now," I can recall her saying in a teasing way, as she flexed her muscles in a mock body-builder's pose, fully clothed, of course, in prison denim.

What landed me the prize "news catch" of the year was the fact that I wanted to focus on the woman's current accomplishments and future ambitions, instead of dredging up all of her horrible past as the other news reporters wanted to do. I was then editor of *Utah Prime Times,* the Beehive State's largest seniors newspaper. Under these conditions and terms, Frances agreed to several interviews and was fully cooperative, including letting herself be photographed for the first time since her incarceration.

The award-winning story that I did on her appeared on the front cover of the August 1993 issue under the triumphant banner: "Finding Life and Hope in Women's Prison!" I focused on her changed behavior as a model prisoner (which earned her the early release, by the way), her educational efforts, in which she earned two psychology degrees from Utah State University under an inmate-education program, and her new health lifestyle.

One of the things she discovered early on in prison was that her own smoking addiction, combined with lack of exercise and lousy prison food, contributed to a season of poor health, during which time she experienced frequents bouts of common cold and flu, not to mention many sniffles and sneezes along the way. "I knew that if I didn't do something in a hurry," she told me, "my body didn't stand much of a chance of holding up for very long where I was." She had this eerie premonition of dying of malnutrition or an invasive infection of some kind. But her anxieties in this regard actually worked for the better, and she made some decisive moves that started her on the road back to good health within a short time.

"I stopped smoking, for one thing," she continued. For another, she began a series of daily exercises that involved "a lot of bending, stretching, squatting, sitting, jumping, clapping, and walking." She also swore off coffee and switched to water and juices (when available) instead.

The diet change was a little more challenging. "The first several prisons I was in," she related with some obvious pain in her expression, "were terrible, to say the least." Not that she expected prison to be a country club by any means, but terrible in the sense "of the bad food they served us every day" and "in the bad attitudes of the other female inmates."

When she eventually got transferred to the Women's Correctional Facility in Draper, Utah, however, she found a much more ideal environment that was conducive to change and improvements in her diet and mental health. "Because the [female] inmate population here is much smaller than other places I've been and they have a bigger budget for food allotment," she noted, "we had access to more fresh fruits and vegetables" than anywhere else she had been. "I started eating more citrus fruits, like grapefruits and oranges, and drinking orange juice every chance I got [when they served it in the prison dining room]."

Another excellent source for additional vitamin C came from numerous vegetables and tossed green salads served fairly regularly. During both times that I interviewed her, I made sure to come around noontime when the inmates ate lunch so that I could eat with her and judge for myself the quality of the food being served. I had to admit to her that "the food here is probably better than it is in some of the restaurants I frequently dine at." She laughed and replied, "Well, it's your tax dollars that are giving us such good meals here."

With her assistance, we managed to compile, over a 15-day period, the approximate amounts of the food items she consumed and their vitamin C contents. This was done by her keeping a simple food diary of what she ate and about how much, and then comparing that information with the data provided by the federal government publication, *Nutritive Value of American Foods in Common Units* (Washington, DC: U.S. Dept. of Agriculture Handbook No. 456, 1975). Following is the list I drew up of what was consumed and its equivalent vitamin C content.

Food	Size of Serving	Vitamin C (mg)
green pepper (raw)	2 pods	188
Brussels sprouts (cooked)	1 cup	126
strawberries (overripe and mushy)	1 cup	88
broccoli (cooked)	1 cup	106
oranges	4 medium	264
orange juice (frozen and reconstituted)	2 cups	240
cabbage (raw and shredded)	1 cup	84
kale (cooked)	1/2 cup	25
grapefruit juice (canned)	1 cup	84
beef liver (fried)	3 oz.	23
tomato (raw)	1/2 medium	14
potato (baked)	1/2 medium	16
cantaloupe	1/4 melon	45
grapefruit (raw)	1/2 medium	44
tomato juice (canned)	1/2 cup	20
peas, green (frozen and cooked)	1/2 cup	11
milk (whole)	1 cup	2
bread (white and enriched)	20 slices (over 15 days)	11

In a little over a two-week period, Frances consumed a total of 1,381 milligrams of vitamin C in the different foods she ate in the prison cafeteria. This averaged to be about 92 milligrams per day for the 15 days that we did our research. The Recommended Dietary Allowance (RDA) proposed by the National Academy of Sciences for a woman her age was around 65 milligrams per day. So, in reality, Frances enjoyed a greater daily intake of vitamin C than did many other American women out in regular society.

Fortunately for her, she had quit smoking a few years prior to this when first entering prison. She did this at the time because she wanted to lower her risks of getting lung or breast cancer. But in so doing, she also raised her blood plasma levels of vitamin C significantly. What must be kept in mind, though, was that this brief study was conducted during the summer months when an abundance of fresh fruits and vegetables was readily available.

(Some of the vegetables were grown in a prison garden by inmates themselves, while other produce was purchased fairly reasonably from some local supermarkets as old produce—not good enough to be sold to customers, but still edible and not worthy of discarding.)

Frances was ecstatic about her dietary reformation. "I can remember about a week after starting on the program, how much better I felt. I didn't have so many allergic symptoms, and the sniffles and sneezes seemed to clear up. And whenever another cold or flu passed around among the rest of the inmates, my body resistance was strong enough to keep me well." And, in case any reader is wondering why the woman didn't avail herself of a vitamin C supplement, the simple answer is that *none* was allowed to be had by any of the inmates (probably due to concerns about illicit drugs being smuggled in). All of which goes to show that a person can obtain the *majority* of his or her vitamin C intake from fruits, vegetables, and other foods instead of always having to rely on tablets or capsules for the same.

Supplements Make Sense in Certain Cases

There is an appropriate time to augment the diet with vitamin and mineral supplements. One would be when an unexpected illness strikes and the body requires additional units of certain nutrients in order to combat whatever infection may be lurking somewhere in the system. Another might be during the cold winter months and during public influenza epidemics. Also, many of us have demanding jobs that require a great deal of energy and effort on our parts and carry with them a lot of stress. As such, we often are not in a favorable position to eat the nutritious foods we should be, nor are we able to consume them in an unhurried environment. So we end up quite frequently on junk-food binges that are gulped down in haste. And let's not forget lifestyle choices such as smoking, drinking alcohol, or using drugs, which can rob the body of many vital nutrients within a short time.

All of these likely scenarios demand that we use food supplements occasionally or with greater frequency. Certainly, our highly processed and overcooked foods leave much to be desired in the way of giving us the nutrients we need. Where else then may we obtain them, if not from supplements? But it's not always as simple as finding out which ones your body is lacking and then taking adequate amounts of the same. No, in fact, you need to consider taking *other* nutrients besides just those you know your body requires. I'm referring, of course, to *augmenting* nutrients.

Now, in the case of vitamin C, it would be the bioflavonoids, such as rutin or hesperidin, along with calcium and magnesium, that are going to enhance the performance of this particular nutrient within your system. I was among many of those supplement users who would take just vitamin C whenever I felt my body needed it. But then I gradually discovered that by periodically adding 250 milligrams each of rutin and hesperidin or taking a good 500-milligram bioflavonoid tablet with both of these in it, I was *extending* the life cycle of the vitamin C in me. Later on, I came across two outstanding products from Trace Minerals of Ogden, Utah—they are ConcenTrace Mineral Drops and Complete (Vegetarian) Calcium & Magnesium. By adding 6–8 drops of the former to a glass of water, juice, or herb tea, I was getting about 70 percent of the government's RDA. And 4 tablets of the latter per day with a meal nicely rounded out my calcium needs (see Appendix for more information).

But, more important than this was the significant boost my vitamin C seemed to be getting. Whenever I take vitamin C, I usually ingest anywhere from 1000 to 3000 milligrams *per day*. I do this *periodically*—say every few weeks for about one week—before giving it another short rest. During each period of supplementation, I've noticed that the two products from Trace Minerals have been extremely effective in helping to *maximize* the full potential of my vitamin C intake. This maximizing of a specific nutrient by augmenting nutrients that contribute to its support may be found in every single vitamin or mineral that our bodies require. In nature, of course, everything is pretty much in balance when we eat foods in their whole, raw states. But when ingesting these nutrients in supplement form, we need to remember to take others that correspond with them and enhance their bioavailability within the system.

Vitamin C is a wonderful free radical fighter. It helps to hold in check the otherwise riotous behavior of such crazy molecules. It keeps them from influencing in a negative way the normal electrical charge of other, healthy molecules. When there is less of such molecular static within the body chemistry, then a person feels more vibrant and alive. There is a robustness to the physical constitution, a verve to the actions, and a quickening of the mental sensibilities. Indeed, it may be said that when our vitamin C levels are high, as well as levels of the other two antioxidants, vitamins A and E, then there is a *chemical animation* taking place in us that delivers a glow of health that isn't always easy to find the appropriate words to adequately describe.

How Vitamin E Can Guarantee Emotional Stability

Two Women's Experiences with Wheat Germ Oil

Wheat germ oil is obviously obtained from the grain kernel of the same name. Due to its very high level of vitamin E, it's far less likely than other oils to oxidize or become rancid. Wheat germ oil contains some alpha-linolenic acid (LNA) and is a rich source of a 28-carbon fatty alcohol (octacosanol), which protects heart function and may help nerve regeneration. There is no richer source of vitamin E than wheat germ oil.

On one weekend in mid-August 1996, I did two radio talk shows by phone from my home in Salt Lake City. The first was on Saturday, August 17, at 8:30 A.M. MST with WFLP-AM in Pittsburgh. The show was "Natural Health," hosted by Larry Ferrario. After a few minutes of formal introduction and general bantering between us, the phone lines were opened to callers.

One of the first was a woman who identified herself only as Ellen. Rather than having a question for the program guest, she related an experience with wheat germ oil that both of us found pretty amazing. Ellen said that a while back she accidentally burned her abdomen with some boiling water that splashed from a pot on the stove. Rather than go to the hospital emergency ward, she and her husband decided to treat the injury themselves.

Her clothes were promptly removed from that area of her body and a cold pack of crushed ice cubes wrapped in a clean hand towel was immediately applied to cool down the injury. Afterwards, her husband got some wheat germ oil from the refrigerator and applied a thin layer over the wound with some clean cotton balls. A light gauze covering was then placed over it to keep debris away and prevent the oil from staining clothing or bedding. The same procedure (minus the ice pack) was repeated again 12 hours later, the next morning.

This treatment continued twice a day (morning and evening) for the next five days, after which time it was discontinued. Ellen said that the skin tissue returned to normal and except for a slight discoloration of the immediate area, near-total healing was evident.

As any responsible talk show host would, Larry thanked her for her comments, but was quick to advise listeners that such serious injuries should receive prompt medical attention and should not be treated at home. I concurred completely in this, and we went on to the next call.

The next day, Sunday, I did another radio program (also from Pennsylvania). This time it was with station WHAT-AM in Philadelphia with Glen Ellis, host of the show "Health Talk." About midway through the hour-long session, an older woman phoned in to tell the large radio audience and us about her experience with vitamin E. She said that she had been taking care of her aged mother, who was bedridden. Her mom had a number of bedsores on her back, buttocks, and calves. The caller mentioned that she found a can of wheat germ oil in the cupboard, which her mom had had for awhile. She smelled and tasted it for any evidence of rancidity—there was none. So, she poured a little into a cup and then holding several cotton Q-tips together, dipped them into the oil and wiped off the excess on the lip before swabbing each of the sores with it.

This treatment lasted for several weeks, being done twice or three times a day. The woman, who never gave her name, stated with discernible excitement in her voice, "My momma's sores all cleared and went away. I suggest anyone out there listening to me to try this stuff for sores or other skin problems. My teenage daughter, Allysha, used some of it on her acne after seeing what it did for her grandma. Her complexion improved in a couple of weeks. I mean, this is *g-r-e-a-t* stuff—everybody ought to be using it for something." My host and I chuckled over her last remark before going to a commercial break.

In the two cases just cited, wheat germ oil had obvious physical benefits in what it did for different women's skin. But it also provided a certain peace of mind for those using it. In Ellen's case, no scarring remained, which might have been traumatic for her. Also, her pain quickly subsided, allowing her to rest more comfortably. Had it not abated, she might have had difficulty sleeping, which would have intensified her anxieties. The caller in Philadelphia reported that her elderly mother "felt better" and "had a much better attitude" after "her sores started healing up." And the caller's teenaged daughter experienced a rise in her own self-esteem once her acne started fading.

Vitamin E Renewal of Frayed Nerves

The biochemical impact of emotional stress upon the nervous system may be compared with an old electrical wire that has become frayed with time, age, moisture, heat, and cold. Emotional distress of any kind can generate an overproduction of body substances such as adrenalin, hormones, hydrocholoric acid, and others, which can have a negative influence on the health integrity of the nerves themselves. Such substances, in abnormal amounts, can make blood plasma more acidic than alkaline. This acidic blood, as it passes over and around nerve strands, gradually "eats away" at the fatty protein casing (called myelin sheathing) that surrounds each nerve fiber.

When "holes" become evident in this casing, then the nerve is susceptible to viral infection or other kinds of problems that may interfere with the electrical conductivity passing through it from the brain to a number of different points located elsewhere in the body. The emotional equivalent of such bioelectrical "static" may be translated into unhealthy moods that have no rational logic or explanation to them. But if these "tears" in the nerve casing fabric are "mended" with sufficient intake of vitamin E or wheat germ oil, then whatever unanticipated psychiatric distresses occurred will cease just as suddenly as they began.

Therefore, it is more correct to say that this important nutrient *renews* damaged nerve linings, rather than to suggest it "strengthens" the nerves. Vitamin E helps the system to produce the necessary fatty protein that goes to repair damaged nerve sheathing. And when the nerves are no longer "frayed" biochemically, then they are better able to serve our emotional and physical well-being with clear and uninterrupted transmission of electrical impulses between the brain, heart, liver, and other vital organs.

The best brand of wheat germ oil that you could ever hope to buy *won't* be found in any health-food store. It is available only through some veterinarians or by mail order. Rex Wheat Germ Oil is 100 percent pure and unrefined, and, curiously enough, carries the words "For Animal Use Only" on its can label. Printed instructions on the back tell how much to give to cattle, hogs, sheep, horses, pigs, goats, dogs, cats, and mink. But oddly enough, it is also very good for humans. The reason the manufacturer printed the caution is because this particular wheat germ oil is *so* potent; it has a dark amber color and strong nutlike flavor to it.

It comes in a quart-size metal container and will last an individual up to two months or more. I recommend an average intake of one tablespoon daily with a meal. Our family has been using the stuff for several decades now and wouldn't be without it. I've mentioned it in public lectures and in some of my health books to tens of thousands of people across the nation. Those who've used it report back that they feel better physically and that psychologically they have more of a dynamic outlook on life than they did before taking it. Rex Wheat Germ Oil also has a number of external applications as well, mostly relating to skin and scalp problems. (To order this, send $65 to Anthropological Research Center, P.O. Box 11471, Salt Lake City, UT 84147; if ordering from overseas, add another $15 for shipping and handling.) There are, of course, less expensive brands of wheat germ oil in health-food stores, but they are inferior in quality and turn rancid very quickly if not kept refrigerated at all times. But the Rex brand can be stored in a cupboard for a long time without turning bad.

How One Dentist Uses the Antioxidant Vitamins to Keep Himself Young

Jeff Broman, D.D.S., has been our family dentist for a number of years. He has been in practice with his father (who himself has been in dentistry some 40 years) since 1982 and has looked into the mouths of approximately 6,000 patients. Jeff graduated from the University of Pacific School of Dentistry in San Francisco in 1982 at the top of his class. From the start, he has commanded the loyalty and respect of hundreds of patients, who travel great distances at some expense from *out of state* to come see him at his busy Salt Lake City clinic, which opens at 6:45 A.M. and closes by 3:30 P.M.

When I went for a number of appointments recently to see him regarding my own dental needs, he gladly showed me some of the places a number of his patients come from: the wealthy socialite from New York City; the retired business executive from Boston; the real estate broker from San Diego; the retired couples from Phoenix; and the football enthusiast from Tampa Bay. There's also the multimillionaire from Saudi Arabia; the chemist from China; and the sheep rancher from Australia, who come to see him about every 1-1/2 years. Obviously, none of them makes the trip just for dental purposes alone, but also comes to Utah because of other business they have to transact while here in the Beehive State. However, "It's nice to know that they trust me enough to let me be their dentist," Jeff said with a toothsome smile. "My prices are right, my work is great, and word of mouth is always the best advertisement that anyone could ever hope for."

On that Monday afternoon of October 1, 1996, when he took some time off from his crowded schedule to chat with me, Dr. Broman lay back in one of his own dentist's chairs as I sat on a stool beside him with writing pad and pen in hand. Some of the staff who passed by in the hall and peeked in thought it was funny, if not ironic, to see their boss assuming a patient's position, while I (as the patient they had just finished with) sat next to him on the dentist's stool conducting the interview. We really hadn't planned it that way; it just sort of happened in the process as each of us got comfortable for the question-and-answer session.

Jeff told me he had been an advocate of alternative health for quite a while. Whenever he felt a cold or flu coming on, he would resort to lots of rest, a liquid diet, homeopathic preparations, and some herbs and nutritional supplements to help recover. He also took adequate amounts of the three antioxidant vitamins that comprise the theme of this final chapter. "My intake of vitamin A is 20,000 I.U. per day," he said, "along with 1000 milligrams of vitamin C, and 400 I.U. of vitamin E."

"I'm 39 but feel like I'm 29," Jeff stated with pride. "I also watch what I eat. For breakfast, I might have some whole-wheat toast or a bran muffin, an herbal tea of some sort, maybe a yogurt, or some kind of dried cereal like Grapenuts, Wheaties, or

Cheerios. I generally bring lunch with me, which can range from a ham sandwich on rye to fried brown rice. Dinner entrees vary considerably—tacos, cooked fish, pastas, lots of salads, soup, and quite a bit of stir-fry food. I feel that my diet and those three antioxidant vitamins have kept me in pretty good shape."

One of the hidden benefits has come from his remarkably good health whenever he travels to Third World nations such as Kenya, where he donated enough used equipment to help open up a dental clinic there that he calls "Smile Africa." And though he's had several formal state dinners with the country's longtime President Daniel Arap Moi, he spends much of his time in surroundings less posh, eating food prepared in unsanitary conditions and drinking water of sometimes questionable safety. But through it all, "I've never once contracted a serious disease, nor suffered any ill effects from what I ate or drank," he boasted. He attributes his incredible immunity to such potential bacterial infections to vitamins A, C, and E and a sensible diet.

One other thing that I found intriguing was his mention of the chewing sticks used by many tribal natives. It was not uncommon at all to see a number of them hanging around the marketplace with these objects in their mouths. The plants used are very carefully selected for such properties as foaminess, hardness, or bitterness, and certain species are more popular than others. The natives will fashion such sticks from roots, twigs, or wood, using either a machete or pocketknife for this purpose; the sticks are typically eight inches in length and about a finger in width.

The stick is first washed, then gnawed on the tip to macerate it so that the end is frayed and brushlike. The teeth are brushed very thoroughly, and care is taken to clean both the inside and the outside of the tooth surfaces. Usually this procedure takes from 5 to 15 minutes, and the stick is often sucked for several hours after brushing is completed. It is common to see individuals going about their chores with the remainder of a chewing stick in their mouths. Or else they'll just stand on one foot leisurely chewing on one of them, while their other foot is bent inward at an angle and comfortably resting against the other leg.

"I've examined the teeth of many such stick chewers," Dr. Broman told me, "and have found little or no remaining plaque and gums that are usually quite pink and firm. These chewing sticks seem to correlate well with high dental health. The fact remains that in countries like Kenya where such use is popular, caries rates are bound to be very low and teeth are retained for longer periods of time."

A further investigation into chewing sticks revealed that many of these plants, which are indigenous only to the African continent, are high in vitamin C, natural fluoride, and tannic acid. These things combine to help remove plaque and prevent the formation of cavities, dental plaque, and gingivitis.

The antioxidant vitamins are just as important to human health needs as the other six items previously covered in this book: bee products, cayenne pepper, garlic, ginseng, wheat grass, and turmeric. Each in its own way serves some useful purpose in the promotion of our happiness and well-being. They are things we shouldn't be without. They are a part of the natural pharmacy that God created and ordained for our daily use and wise application. They are, in fact, "Nature's Super Seven Medicines," to be utilized with thanksgiving and skill by anyone who desires putting only the best into his or her own body.

Product Appendix

Chapter One

Montana Naturals Int'l., Inc.
19994 Highway 93
Arlee, Montana 59821
(406) 726-3214

Distributors of nature's finest product from the beehive, liquid propolis, for the treatment of sore throats, tonsillitis, laryngitis, and nagging cough. This propolis tincture is available in a 65 percent strength, extra thick version. It can also be used externally with excellent results for bedsores, leg ulcers, and open wounds. This company also carries a fine line of bee pollen and royal jelly products.

Chapter Two

Old Southwest Trading Co.
P.O. Box 7545
Albuquerque, NM 87194
1-800-748-2861

If you're into *really hot*-flavored foods, then this mail-order firm has just about every kind of chile and cayenne imaginable for a genuine mouth-surfing experience.

Chile Institute
Box 3003
New Mexico State University
Las Cruces, NM 88003
(505) 646-3028

Write to this place for membership information.

Sabinsa Corporation
121 Ethel Road West, Unit 6
Piscataway, NJ 08854
1-908-777-1111

A leading manufacturer of capsaicinoids from *Capsicum annum,* which are common ingredients in many topically applied arthritis relief products.

Chapter Three

Wakunaga of America Co., Ltd.
23501 Madero
Mission Viejo, CA 92691-2744
1-800-421-2998

The world's premier and best-selling aged-garlic extract is available from these people in liquid and capsules. They also feature a number of different garlic formulas (numbers 100 through 106), which are good for the immune system (nos. 100–103), the nervous system (nos. 104 and 105), the circulatory system and heart (no. 106), and in fighting free radicals (no. 105). Other combinations include Kyo-Chrome for blood sugar management, Premium Kyolic-EPA for management of blood cholesterol and serum triglycerides; Ginkgo Biloba Extract for improved circulation, and Kyo-Ginseng for sexual vitality and reproductive health. *No one* does garlic products better than Wakunaga, except maybe Mother Nature!

If you would like to obtain the latest updated information on Nature's ultimate antibiotic herb, you may call a toll-free Garlic Info Hotline at Cornell University: 1-800-330-5922. It is jointly sponsored by Cornell University and Sloan-Kettering Cancer Institute with major funding provided by Wakunaga of America.

Chapter Four

Total Life Concepts International
P.O. Box 990
Monument, CO 80132
1-800-426-4852

Suppliers of quality domesticated American ginseng root from Wisconsin in formula strength. Available in their Complete Renewal (a body makeover product) and Proactivin (an antioxidant detoxifier).

Wakunaga of America Co., Ltd.
23501 Madero
Mission Viejo, CA 92691-2744
1-800-421-2998

Makers of Kyo-Ginseng, a combination of Korean ginseng and Japanese aged-garlic extract, the best-selling ginseng formula in the world.

Chapter Five

Pines International, Inc.
P.O. Box 1107
Lawrence, KS 66044
1-800-MY-PINES (697-4637)

Manufacturers of the world's best wheat grass, barley grass, vegetable greens, and red beet root products. These cereal grasses and vegetables are all organically grown and can be trusted for their purity and quality. The company makes these products available in bulk powders, tablets, and juice concentrates. They also have Green Energy (a barley grass concentrate) and Mighty Greens (a drink blend of 27 different natural "super" foods). Pines International is owned and operated by American farmers in "The Heartland of America" (the Midwest).

Vita-Mix Corporation
8615 Usher Road
Cleveland, OH 44138
1-800-848-2649

For those wishing to make up their own wheat-grass juice-drink blends, there is no finer unit to use for this than the Vita-Mix whole food machine. The Rodale Test Kitchens compared a number of leading juice machines and found that the Vita-Mix unit was the most reliable and easiest to clean of all of them, as well as being very affordable.

Chapter Six

Sabinsa Corporation
121 Ethel Road West, Unit 6
Piscataway, NJ 08854
1-800-248-7464

This company pioneered research into turmeric antioxidants resulting in its remarkable C-3 Complex (marketed through its consumer products subsidiary, America's Finest, Inc.) Sabinsa is widely known for its Citrin, which has become one of the leading ingredients in many weight-loss products. (Citrin or calcium salt of (-)hydroxycitric acid is derived from the fruit rinds of *Garcinia cambogia* or "Malabar Tamarind.") It is one of the industry leaders in capsaicinoids (obtained from cayenne pepper), common ingredients in topical arthritis-relief products.

Sabinsa is a major source for fine phytonutrients and nutraceuticals for many nutrition supplement and herb product companies. It combines the technology of modern science with the principles of India's ancient healing system known as Ayurveda.

Chapter Seven

Vitamins A, C, and E work best of all when combined together in a balanced form. The ultimate free radical terminator on the market today is a product called CCAP which has not only this trio of important nutrients, but also other nutrient antioxidants taken from grapeseed, citrus, fruits and rinds, green tea leaves and tumeric root. Furthermore, it is the only antioxidant product in the world which is packed in both glass and metal containers to keep it as fresh and potent as possible.

Naturally Vitamins
14851 North Scottsdale Road
Scottsdale, AZ 85254
1-800-899-4499/ Fax 602-991-0551

Trace Minerals
1990 West 3300 South
Ogden, UT 84401
1-800-624-7145

The supplement industry leader in quality antioxidant minerals (ionic) that nicely augment the antioxidant vitamins A, C, and E. The best source in nature for such ionic minerals is the Great Salt Lake, located west of Salt Lake City, Utah.

Anthropological Research Center
P.O. Box 11471
Salt Lake City, UT 84147
1-801-521-8824

Supplier of Rex Wheat Germ Oil (a rich source of vitamin E). Comes in a one-quart metal can and costs $65 (postage included).

Information Appendix

Double the Power of Your Immune System Package by noted medical anthropologist Dr. John Heinerman includes a 90-minute video lecture given in October 1996 at Westminster College in Salt Lake City, Utah, and a 340-page book. The information in each is completely different. The video explains step-by-step what to do to gain a strong immune system. The book, on the other hand, is a series of programs specifically tailored for a large number of immune and autoimmune disorders. Each program is very detailed on how to deal with a specific problem. The package retails for $65.00. Send check or money order in this amount made out to Dr. John Heinerman, specifying what you want and mail to:

John Heinerman, Ph.D.
P.O. Box 11471
Salt Lake City, UT 84147 USA
(801) 521-8824

Index

A

Acacia honey, 46
Acarapis woodli, 6
Adrakam, 205
Aging:
    and cayenne pepper, 82-83
    and garlic, 119
    and vitamin A, 227-228
    and wheat grass, 190-192
AIDS, and garlic, 120-121
Ajoene, 140
Alcoholism:
    and bee pollen, 17
    and cayenne pepper, 72
Alfalfa honey, 46
Allergies:
    and bee pollen, 17
    and cayenne pepper, 72-73
Allicin, 139-140
All-Purpose Honey Teriyaki
    Sauce, 45-46
Aloe vera, 54
Amagase, Harunobu, 139
Angina pectoris, and cayenne
    pepper, 73
Anthropological Research
    Center, 168, 237, 246
Anti-Cancer Green Drink, 196
Antioxidant vitamins, 217-240
    and aging, 237-240
    Vitamin A, 224-227
        and aging, 227-228
    Vitamin C, 228-234
        supplements, 232-234
        and women's health, 228-
            232
    Vitamin E, 234-237
        and nervous system, 236-
            237

and wheat germ oil, 234-
    236
Vitamin Information Chart,
    221
Antipathogenic Qi, 147
Arterioscleriosis, and cayenne
    pepper, 73
Arthritis:
    and cayenne pepper, 73-75
    and garlic, 119
Ashwagandha, 156
Athlete's foot, and honey, 18
Ayurveda, and bees, 7-8
Ayurvedic medicine, and
    turmeric, 201-211
Aztecs, and cayenne pepper,
    55-57

B

Babylonians, and bees, 8
Bacillus larvae, 6
Baden-Powell, Lord Robert
    Stephenson Smyth,
    208-209
Basswood honey, 46
Bedsores, and honey, 18
Bee pollen, 10-12
    and alcoholism, 17
    and allergies, 17
    and cancer, 22-23
    and the common cold, 23-24
    and crippled sexuality,
        25-26
    and endocrine problems,
        27-28
    and gray hair, 27-28
    and obesity, 29
    and wrinkles, 33-34